Coffee To Go

The ups and downs of two Scots travelling North America in a motor-home

Coffee To Go

The ups and downs of two Scots travelling North America in a motor-home

Margaret Carrie

The Pentland Press Limited
Edinburgh • Cambridge • Durham • USA

First published in 2000 by
The Pentland Press Ltd.
1 Hutton Close
South Church
Bishop Auckland
Durham

British Library Cataloguing in Publication Data.
A Catalogue record for this book is available
from the British Library.

ISBN 1 85821 776 8

Typeset by CBS, Martlesham Heath, Ipswich, Suffolk
Printed and bound by Antony Rowe Ltd., Chippenham

This tale is dedicated to Ed, Dolly and Geo without whom our travels would not have been possible.
It is also dedicated to our children who thought we were mad to attempt this journey – which made us realise how right we were to do it!

Acknowledgements

Margaret acknowledges that her dream trip required a calm and competent partner, which she surely had in Martin. Both travellers thank family and friends at home and in North America for making their holiday possible. A special thank you to the good folks met along the way who made the journey so memorable and *Coffee to Go* such a joy to write.

A big thanks to Bill Oddie for agreeing to write the Foreword and for making birding on both sides of the Atlantic more pleasurable.

Many thanks also . . .
to MaryCarol Hunter for her outstanding drawings of the **pelicans** and the bald eagle.
to Jack and Lorry Denniston for their photograph of Santa Fe.
to Claire May for her photograph of the Sacred Heart Catholic Church in Grand Gulf Military State Park.
to Alan Mayes for his delightful cover illustrations and moose drawing.

Grateful thanks to our friendly and attentive editor Meg Ross along with all at The Pentland Press who were enthusiastic about the book and who have shown great courtesy to a senior fledgling author.

Foreword
by Bill Oddie

Back in the mid 1960s I travelled all over the United States with a touring version of the almost legendary TV show 'That Was the Week That Was'. Over a period of a couple of months we criss crossed the country, mainly in a coach and occasionally by air. It was an adventure of sometimes bizarre extremes. One day we would be basking in Florida sunshine, the next stuck in a snowstorm outside Chicago. One night we'd be performing for an audience of less than a hundred at a mining College in the mid west, the next for several thousand in a Texas astrodome. We rarely stayed more than a day in any one place, but wherever we did pause a while I would rush out and do some local birdwatching (or 'birding' as they call it over there). The result is that my American list is still longer than my British.

The other outcome of that trip was that I realized how utterly ridiculous it is when people in this country (Britain, I mean) say that they 'can't stand America', or Americans, or all things American. Frankly, it is as daft as saying that you 'don't like Europe', or indeed the world! Americans may share a common language – although even that is barely true, since it is a truly cosmopolitan country – but within that vast land there is an inexhaustible, complex and truly fascinating variety: of culture, people, landscape and wildlife. What's more, an awful lot of it is extremely enjoyable.

Since that first tour, I have revisited the States many many times – working, birding and on family holidays. I'll admit I love going to America. So I confess I'm prejudiced, but then my attitude is based on the fact that I have almost always had a wonderful time there. What's more, I'm pretty much addicted to many of America's unique cultural achievements: jazz, blues, bluegrass and country music, soul and gospel, Broadway shows, Hollywood films, Loony Toons, Walt Disney and – yes – Disney World, where I and my family had what we all agreed was the best fortnight's holiday ever. (And the Florida birding was pretty good too!) If I tried to analyse what it is about Americana that appeals to me, words – qualities – such as 'energy', 'unpretentiousness', 'positivity', would spring to mind. Or how about 'fun'?!

But of course I have obviously been brainwashed, haven't I? I am clearly an incurable yank-o-phile (see, I even make up ghastly transatlantic type words!). I do realize that the same elements that I love may be the ones other people can't stand. The music I find uplifting others may find a cacophony. The shows I adore may bore others. But one thing surely isn't a 'matter of taste'. American wild places and wildlife are undeniably fantastic.

But don't take my word for any of this. Read Margaret's words. Travel across the States with her and Martin, and you might just want to do it for yourself. Whatever else, you will surely come to agree that generalizations about America really are pretty meaningless.

As they say over there: enjoy!

Bill Oddie, April 2000

Contents

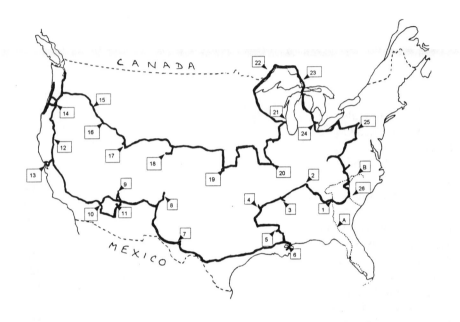

A	Trip to Florida	Dec 28—Jan 2	13	Dixon, San Francisco	Mar 18—Mar 22
B	Trip to Carolinas	Jan 12—Jan 21	14	Corvallis, Oregon Coast	Mar 24,25 &Apr 2-5
1	Athens	Leave Jan 24	15	Farewell Bend	Apr 6,7
2	Nashville	Jan 26, 27	16	Glenns Ferry	Apr 8,9
3	Gracelands	Jan 29	17	Salt Lake City	Apr 11
4	Lake Ouachita	Jan 30—Feb 4	18	Rocky Mountains	Apr 13
5	Grand Gulf, Port Gibson	Feb 6—Feb 8	19	Lake Kanopolis	Apr 16—Apr 20
6	Lake Pontchartrain	Feb 9,10	20	St Louis	Apr 24
7	Balmorhea	Feb 19—Feb 22	21	Waukesha	Apr 20—May 2
8	Santa Fe	Feb 25—Feb 27	22	Thunder Bay	May 7—May 10
9	Grand Canyon	March 2,3	23	Pancake Bay	May 11
10	Buckskin Mountain	Mar 4—Mar 7	24	Northville, Detroit	May 13—May 16
11	Cottonwood	Mar 8—Mar 10	25	State College	May 18—May 21
12	Corning	Mar 15—Mar 17	26	Columbia	May 28—June 1

Route Map

Introduction

The USA travel diary of two Scottish seniors . . . one aged 62¾ and the other aged 59½ . . . (when they started out, that is!)

Most of this diary was written by *her,* the senior senior, with helpful comments of the grammatical, spelling, mechanical and historical variety from *him* with bold red pen in hand. This at times (most of them) quite reasonably incensed *her.*

Most of the appendices and footnotes were written by *him,* the junior senior, with extremely helpful comments of the emotional and esoteric variety from *her,* without recourse to red pen, the caustic comment approach being preferred. This at times (one or two) unreasonably incensed *him.*

We will certainly not be the first couple who are getting on in years to set off across some of America's States in a Recreational Vehicle (RV from hereon) for four months and we will certainly not be the last. Many American seniors (we do approve of this comfortable terminology) have sold their homes and now travel a while and settle a while in either new or well-loved places; others are charmingly called 'snowbirds' because they leave their colder northern homes and pack up the motor one to spend the winter months in warmer climes like Florida, California, Arizona and Texas. Of course, there are folks from Florida, California, Arizona and Texas who travel north in the summer six months to get away from their too warm climate. The roads and RV parks on these north-south routes can, therefore, be a bit congested during the migration season! We were more interested in the migratory habits of our feathered friends, being enthusiastic, but very amateur, bird-watchers.

What may make us a little more unusual than most of the other part-time travellers we met along the way, is that we hail from Scotland and were setting out to see as much of America as possible within the timescale we had managed to free up from our busy lives back home. Our proposed adventure had been in the planning pipeline for some time, in fact ever since we realised that our nine-year love affair with this marvellous country had intensified to the point when it became something we really had to do. On previous trips we thought we had travelled quite large distances and had seen big chunks of the US. However, when we looked at the map on our return home we were shocked to

1

discover how very tiny the area we covered had been, and how vast a continent is North America. At the beginning of this particular US sojourn we imagined we might clock up around 10,000 miles in a motor-home, doing a few hundred more in a little tow-car. We underestimated both our stamina and our rig's enthusiasm for eating up the miles. When we reckoned up the final mileage and drew the completed route on our map back home, we found, to our delight, that this time we really *had* travelled!! Our route took us through many cities and towns, and we spent a lot or a little time in them depending on their appeal and our agenda. In some States the city or town population was displayed on the welcome sign and, in order to give an idea of the sizes of the places we passed through, we have given approximate populations as a guide in the footnotes.

Although we would arrive in the USA on 20 December 1998, we reckoned that our first day on the road would be at least a month later as we had some fairly important travel purchases to make. Our flight home was scheduled for 17 June 1999 and what happened between the arrival and departure dates would depend on several factors: how quickly we could find a reasonable well-used motor home for the limited dollars we had; the rate at which we felt we could or even wanted to travel; and of course the weather! One learns of extreme American weather conditions via the media from the relaxed comfort of Scottish armchairs secure in the knowledge that, although the UK weather is regularly wet and cold, it is seldom too uncomfortable or too extreme. One watches some extreme American weather conditions on the compulsive-viewing American weather channel from the relative comfort of American arm-chairs in the uncomfortable knowledge that one could be viewing some of them from too-close-for-comfort motor-home driving seats during four months on the road. Would we cope should we be faced with some or even *any* of them? We would find out! We would also discover if we two were sociably compatible. For many years we had been working some pretty serious hours, sometimes with our separate work tasks and sometimes on joint projects. We generally worked well together; would we play well together? We would find out!

Work commitments had been the deciding factor in the time of year in which we would travel. *He* had managed to persuade the Engineering Faculty at Edinburgh University that he could do with a six-month break, the first he'd had in thirty-five years of teaching there. *She* had managed to persuade the agency who employed her that she needed some respite from *her* gainful employment of respite care, which entailed looking after children with special needs in her home. Our intention was to visit as many of the States as possible, especially the southern ones, but were realistic enough to accept that these Scottish seniors and the hot USA summer weather were likely to be incompatible south of Alaska. Therefore we were pleased to be starting our travels in the winter months and in the south. However, the winter months in southern USA, as we had discovered in Texas and Georgia two years previously, can be as cold as east coast Scotland, although only for a day or too at a time, unlike the long inclement winter weeks we are more used to. So, we would come to appreciate the central-heating system of our future motor-home on cold mornings when that heating system was augmented by hot morning tea and woolly robes. (As we tell this travel tale, our language and spelling may undergo subtle changes. Therefore, for any USA vocabulary-challenged readers, for robe – read dressing-gown!) We would also find it quite difficult at times to understand the local dialects as we journeyed from State to State, and on several occasions, to our British astonishment, we would have difficulty in making ourselves understood. More of that later! We would also experience difficulties, even with the acclaimed Rand McNally Atlas *one* of us read a great deal of the time, in identifying the location of the US roads, from the big Interstates to the US Highways and the smaller American roads called State Routes. Or, more alarmingly, we would have problems deciphering the directions indicated at the Interstate ('I') junctions, which sometimes appeared to give directions contrary to the way we felt we should be heading. But we (well . . . *one* of us!) would quite quickly realise that it was OK for the I-40 East to be heading north, or would that be south, and that frequently a road would be part of several different routes so the signs could, therefore, multiply in glorious multi-coloured confusion. So we (*one* of us) stopped panicking when the I-40 E, which we wanted to travel, appeared to also be the I-75 N and the I-85 S (see appendix 2). However that same *one* of us did occasionally fall out with *his* beloved atlas especially when roads which were indicated as existing . . . didn't! We did have one or two heated discussions about the non-appearance of minor roads at exactly the place they should have been. *One* of us did in fact become almost as accomplished a Rand McNally reader as the other, and was very pleased with *her*self indeed (when *she* got it right that is!).

We also ran the gamut of emotions from A-Z as we traversed the highways and by-ways. For example:- **A** – **A**nxiety (*her* – re closet accomodation*); **B** –

Breathlessness (*him* and *her* – usually when over 8,000ft *)* **C** – **C**old-feet (*him* – as he stoically paddled barefoot in Lake Superior). You may recognise our **D** through **Y** alphabetical hang-ups if you read on to the final one:- **Z** – **Z**ombie (*him* and *her* – at touchdown in Edinburgh on 18 June).

But, for now, we would appreciate it if you would please imagine an extremely youthful almost 63 year-old *her* and an even more youthful (*he* thinks) almost 60 year-old *him* about to begin the greatest adventure of their lifetime together. Someone we know recently described himself as being one of the more-money-than-sense brigade. By 24 January, as we finally prepared to hit the road, we definitely considered ourselves as in the no-money, no-sense brigade. But if we felt poor dollar-wise and were slightly anxious about our apparent lack of common sense, we felt rich indeed to have this adventure before us.

With the introduction over, we can now begin and the first part, as we spend time with family and friends during the start of our American Dream, is written in shortened diary form. As we hit the road on our own it becomes more of a journal. We hope you enjoy reading it as much as we enjoyed doing it.

Georgia and Florida

Sunday 20 December

Arrived Atlanta,[1] Georgia on time (3.05 pm) after looo-ooong ten hour flight; luggage arrived too – all of it! Worries about immigration (*him*) and customs (*her*), discussed and re-discussed during the looo-ooong flight, completely unfounded. This country is marvellous! Athens[2] and the home of Mark and MaryCarol, marvellous too. Just as we remembered it all, including the large soft welcoming bed in the guest room which we managed to ignore until 8.30 pm (USA time now, of course,) and were justifiably pleased with ourselves at staying awake (almost) for twenty-three hours. Not bad for two seniors!

Monday 21 December

Woke at: 3.00 am (*him*), 3.02 am (*her – his* fault), 4.45 am (*her*), 4.49 am (*him – his* fault) 9.45 am (*him* – with kettle in mind), 9.55 am (*her* by *him* – with large steaming mug in hand). Isn't tea in the *very* early morning just wonderful!! Spent most of the morning unpacking all four extra-large suitcases (3½–*hers*, ½–*his*) and sitting on deck (verandah) in temp of 65°F watching the local birds pop by to meet us. Reacquainted ourselves with chickadees, Carolina wrens, juncos, red cardinals, house-finches, and so on.

This colourful country is marvellous. It would be really *really* marvellous if the Georgian clocks believed in ticking British time, for the large soft bed was beckoning again by 3.00 pm. But so was Home Depot . . . the place where the Hunter/Carrie Christmas tree was waiting to be purchased – and did we pick a beauty!! Well the Hunters did; we Carries were half asleep at the time, and a greenish twig would have done us. However we survived until 8.45 pm on this lovely day and then slept and slept and snored (*one* of us – drat *him*) and slept. Marvellous bed; marvellous country.

[1] *Atlanta (population)–395,000*
[2] *Athens–45,000*

Tuesday 22 December

Time to have a look at an RV (recreational vehicle, if you need reminding one last time). We borrowed Mark's enormous Ford Grand Marquis (getting the hang of BIG vehicles) to visit with Mr Smith of Winterville just up the road from Mark and MaryCarol's place. We'd first met him on 31 December two years ago when we had set foot in an old RV for the first time. He was pleased to meet us again and – yes, he did have a 33ft Winnebago which might just suit us. We climbed aboard. It felt comfy but enormous – perhaps too enormous? So we also looked at an elderly trailer-caravan and wondered if towing with a large pick-up truck could be the way to go. We also looked at a new trailer. The modern newness didn't suit us. We are much more at home in old and comfortable, so we went for a drive in the BIG Winnebago. It went; it rattled; it didn't feel quite right. But at least we had some possibilities to think about, and could mull them over for the next ten days while we-all celebrated the Festive Season.

Going out for lunch. The diners get real busy in Florida at this time of year!

Wednesday 23 December through Sunday 3 January

Christmas preparations were followed by a Christmas Eve party with Mark and MaryCarol as hosts entertaining many of their friends. To any party-goers who were prepared to listen, or didn't move away from the drinks table quickly enough, we elaborated on our forthcoming big adventure. Neither of us even blushed when Mark and MaryCarol wondered, while clearing away the party debris, why some guests left earlier than expected. However two of our very favourite people, Dot and Dac, *did* stay and the evening ended with some communal singing aided by some communal imbibing. Boy, were we in good voice as we harmonised perfectly on songs that are common on both sides of the Big Pond. It is always great to get reacquainted with people we admire.

Our wonderfully happy Christmas Day together was followed by – more packing. But . . . '*only one suitcase this time please, Mother,*' said a certain son whose arms still ached from previous luggage-lugging. One shared between us would be quite enough for a six day holiday in Naples,[3] Florida, we were emphatically assured, and it was – even if it was the largest of the four! Well, even a senior senior has to look *her* best in the Sunshine State!

Actually the only really essential pieces of luggage, we soon realised, were binoculars, as we enthusiastic birders discovered the real meaning of *gobsmacked* when we were introduced to the bird-life of Florida. There were **pelicans,** blue herons, **pelicans,** little blue herons, **pelicans**, night-crested herons, **pelicans,** Louisiana green herons, **pelicans,** small egrets, **pelicans,** large egrets, **pelicans,** woodstorks, **pelicans**, roseate spoonbills, **pelicans**, ospreys, **pelicans**, skimmers, **pelicans,** aninghas, oh, and there were – ***pelicans.*** This country is marvellous! With pelicans sitting, pelicans standing, pelicans fishing, pelicans flying, pelicans preening, pelicans diving . . . wonderful, wonderful real-life ***pelicans!*** Apart from having this amazing variety of birds, (including **pelicans**), and having a marvellous temperature, we found Florida a bit flat for our liking, and full of fat cats. A lot of rich people visit and winter there and we felt (and looked like) the poor relations, although the beautiful condo we stayed in, courtesy of our daughter-in-law's brother, made us feel temporarily rich. We were very thankful to all for making this holiday a great experience which included a boat trip in the Everglades, where unbashful ospreys nest on the tops of navigation poles for all to see, followed

---

[3] *Naples–19,500*

7

by a drive along Alligator Alley. This road goes across from western Naples to eastern Miami and if we didn't make it all the way across, and didn't see any 'gators, we revelled in bowling along a Florida road with such a wild name. We ate dinner one night with MaryCarol's hospitable brother and his family in a place called Tin City, a disused boatyard on a little river running into the Gulf of Mexico. Nowadays it is filled with small exciting shops, board walks and an amazing fish restaurant on the edge of a marina where the water was jam-packed with cat fish all congregating close to the restaurant's edge hoping for some tasty morsels.

But two things are forever etched in our memories from our time in Florida. The first was the immature bald eagle (huge and brown, but no white head) sitting placidly on the roof of the next-door condo in no hurry to fly away. The second, and best, was bringing in 1999 in shorts and T shirts with Mark and MaryCarol, sipping long cold G&Ts outdoors, glancing up from our glasses to look at the stars shining so brightly in an enormous sky. All this to the accompaniment of intermittent brighter lights from the dazzling celebratory New Year's firework display. Quite something! This country is marvellous!

Typical Florida on 31 December . . .
a mite warmer than Hogmanay in Scotland!

8

Monday 4 January through Monday 11 January

This could be described as the busiest, most expensive and unreal week of our six-month trip (probably our lives!). *Monday* we hired a car to get us around RV and tow-car dealers. *Tuesday* we bought the 28 foot 1983 Eldorado RV that we would call home for four months. *Wednesday* we bought the little Geo-Metro car which would take us to the Carolinas and then would follow the RV and us across America hitched to a tow dolly. We purchased Dolly on *Friday. Thursday* we spent a lot of time and more money as we dealt with the complicated but necessary vehicle insurance policies. *Friday* we shopped as we started *loading* the RV. *Loading* was one of the many new words we unskilled RV-ers were to learn and simply meant spending lots more dollars on essential equipment like bedding, cutlery, crockery etc, etc, not forgetting the absolutely essential real coffee maker. Fortunately the January sales were on and we did very well for the few dollars we had left! On *Saturday* one of us worried how *her* clothes would get into the tiny RV closet (wardrobe) while the other watched 'the game'! By now we had both become quite excited about American football and THE SUPERBOWL owing to Mark's insistence and tutelage. But *one* of us was more excited about it than the other and quite unexcited about closet space – so *he* shouldn't complain if his clothes end up in a poly-bag! On *Sunday* we both worried and this time about the same thing – *money* and how little we had left to actually DO the trip! However a few of Mark's serious G&Ts along with the excitement of catching up on the latest Superbowl scores helped to calm us down . . . a little.

Another Monday came around and found us packing suitcases again and loading Geo with them. This time we were setting off to visit with friends in the Carolinas. America is marvellous!

The Carolinas

Tuesday 12 January through Thursday 21 January

We spent the first night of this part of our holiday in Murphy[4] in the Nantahala National Forest in North Carolina, after driving 220 miles through the beautiful North Georgian mountains in great weather. On the second day we had hoped (especially *one* of us) to drive along part of the Blue Ridge Parkway which follows the Appalachian Mountains for 470 miles between the Great Smoky Mountains National Park and the Shenandoah National Park. As luck would have it the gates were closed as parts of the Park were snowbound. *She* was not unduly upset about this, as parts of the Park were also quite narrow and high. *He* was duly upset about this, especially when he watched the film *Nell* during a *second-home*-sick moment back in Scotland. Chapel Hill,[5] North Carolina, the home of our friends, was our destination that evening. We had met Lorry and Jack in San Antonia, Texas, two years earlier and then again with their daughter Mackenzie when all three paid a visit to our Scottish Respite conference. They made us most welcome for the three days we spent there and showed us around their new-home State which they were finding to be very different to the quieter real-home State of Iowa from which they had moved a few months earlier. (We would agree with that in due course.)

Chapel Hill is a pretty university town with great Botanical Gardens featuring an area and article about Scots emigrating with their innovative skills in horticulture to the US several hundred years ago – when the English had got too much for them. Not a lot has changed! Naturally a lot of our conversations with our North Carolinian friends included respite care, the programme within care-in-the-community which we-all have in common, and which had brought us neatly together in the first place. Visiting new friends in their home environment is quite different to chatting at conferences and we got to know Lorry and Jack really well, appreciating their warmth, humour and friendliness. 'Come and stay with us in Scotland one day,' we urged, as

---

[4] *Murphy–1,600*
[5] *Chapel Hill–39,000*

11

we said our farewells; and they did – six months later! 'Go and stay with our folks in New Mexico,' they urged; and we did – six weeks later. American friends are marvellous.

Respite also loomed large when we visited Connie and Leon in Columbia,[6] South Carolina. We had also met them on two previous occasions concerned with respite conferencing. We had another smashing few days with these dear friends, even when the overseas seniors were persuaded to talk on Scottish Respite to Connie's colleagues and families and to Leon's sociology students. Great fun, and a learning experience for us all. (Well, we hope the students were paying attention.) To make up for having us work, Connie and Leon gave us a wonderful day in the historic city of Charleston[7] where the pretty east coast town is richly endowed with old houses, once the homes of the cotton barons, and which is still full of opulent southern grace. *He* had a really big thrill when Leon suggested that we go see the Best Friend of Charleston which turned out to be one of the first railway steam engines to plough the southern railroad. We women just admired the men admiring the engine and took pictures of our admirable guys in real close proximity to a best friend!

So, we left the Carolinas on Thursday 21 January, wondering if our journeying would take us back to these lovely States and to the good friends who lived there. We were a little anxious as we contemplated a family- and friend-less four months ahead of us: no one to guide us around new territory or to help us appreciate the finer things about their homeland. This was not to be the case for some parts of the journey, and we were in for some pleasant surprises! But, along with the anxiety, there was a growing excitement as we entered Georgia. For tomorrow – we collect Ed.

[6] *Columbia–98,000*
[7] *Charleston–80,000*

Ed, Geo and Dolly

Friday 22 January

We first met Ed the Eldorado, our *very* macho high-powered RV, on the morning of 5 January in an RV Dealership 65 miles north of Athens. We had to bid him a reluctant *au revoir* only two hours after making his acquaintance. We left him with Chris, our friendly salesman, with whom *she* had bargained for one looo-ooong hour of that time until it was agreed that *her* price was the right price. By the end of the journey *she* would have come to realise that Ed was worth thousands of dollars more than his actual bargained-for cost, and feel guilty that she had demeaned his stature by essential miserly haggling. Chris, bless his generous heart, assured us that Ed would be well looked after while we holidayed with Geo in the Carolinas (also male, we decided, and *very* cute).

It was wonderful to meet up with our RV again and to be introduced to his characteristics by Eric the Dealership's *Get-To-Know-Your-RV* Guide. *One* of us was more fascinated by the generator, the propane gas and water tanks, the heating/cooling systems and the wonderful outside cubby-holes all around Ed which would hold all manner of tools and things. The *other* one of us was more fascinated by the comfy armchairs, the shower, the micro-wave, the curtains, and the wonderful cubby-holes all round Ed's insides which would hold an amazing amount of clothing – and other essential *loaded* things. We eventually said goodbye to the nice, nice men and with heart in mouth *one* of us got into Ed's unfamiliar driving seat and with heart in mouth and fingers crossed the other *one* of us got into Geo's familiar driving seat, only uncrossing *her* fingers as *he* confidently drove Ed out of the gates and on to the highway. *She* and Geo followed closely behind (they knew their place). This convoy arrived back in Athens in one piece with both vehicles and owners in buoyant mood, which certainly showed in the step of a certain RV driver. *He* had already perfected *the RV strut* which we had previously noted was a style of gait required once one owned a motor-home. *She* wondered if he would also succumb to the full-beard, bib overalls covered with innumerable badges, matching cap and cigar, also sported by many male RV-ers. She thought the cap and overalls could be quite fetching on him and the latter need less laundering, but beard, badges and baccy – no way! *She* also intended to strut her stuff eventually – but behind *him* of course!

Geo had seemed quite admiring of Ed as he followed him home to Athens, but now came the crucial test! It was time to revisit our friend Gordon Smith, who had sold us a second-hand tow-dolly (see relevant and crucial appendix) in spite of the fact that we had rejected his Winnebago (now with more appreciative new owner). He would undertake the necessary work to hitch Ed to Dolly who would then be ready to partner Geo to the west coast and back again. Mr Gordon (the name his employees gave him) got his assistant, Alan, to do most of this work, and it would be hard to find a more charming quiet and respectful young gentleman anywhere in the world. Alan appeared to us to have stepped right out of the pages of the southern novel *Cold Sassy Tree*, and his skills did not end with motor maintenance; he was also a volunteer fireman and ambulance driver. We have made the acquaintance of so many great people like Alan and Mr Gordon in Georgia to say nothing of friends like Dot and Dac which makes it one of our very favourite places. So we would find it hard to leave it for some time . . . but that we must do . . . and soon.

Saturday 23 January

Today was a pretty busy one from dawn to dusk as we loaded Ed with all our essential bits and pieces. There were a few worrying moments, especially when it looked as if the amount of clothing was greater than the sum of the space of both closets, but it all fitted eventually and we were amazed at how much stuff we could cram into Ed's innards and outards. Exhausted and excited we took Mark and MaryCarol out for a *farewell-for-the-meantime* meal before climbing into the large comfy bed we had come to consider ours. The bedroom was only slightly smaller (albeit with different dimensions) than all of our soon-to-be four-month home. Ah well, to sleep, perchance to dream of smooth empty roads, large beautiful camp-grounds filled with wonderful bird-life, and – *tornados*? *NO*, no, just a playful strong wind outside, and too much late-night cheese inside!

Sunday 24 January through Monday 25 January

The day had eventually arrived and we could put it off no longer. Not that we wanted to, well – not reee-ally, although now that it was actually happening, *one* of us was not so convinced as to the sanity of this senior travelling couple. *She* was considering, following a rather sleepless night highlighted by tornado terrors, the possibility of hiring a bunch of videos showing (in glorious storm-proof Technicolor) the splendours of the US of A, which could all be viewed from Ed's swivel armchairs in the safety of our family's yard. Doing a virtual reality trip seemed like a more sensible plan. Somehow, the other three were not greatly enamoured of this idea and two of them opted instead (and quickly) to take departure photos. And so, at approximately 12 noon, replete with brunch, the male half of this stalwart insane twosome started Ed's engine and we prepared to take our leave of family and Athens. Ed seemed momentarily to agree with *her* about the sanity of taking this senior pair to the other end of the country and back, as he coughed a bit and spluttered a bit and took a few breath-holding minutes to decide *'what the heck'*, and allow his powerful macho Chevrolet 474 engine to burst magnificently into life. Within seconds

All ready to go, we think, and all dressed up for it!

15

we were on the highway and heading west – well, east and north first according to the signs at junctions.

We were certainly heading into – well, Georgia, actually, but a different county (for goodness sakes!). It did seem reasonable to be relatively near the relatives on our first night RV camping. *One* of us found the 101 mile journey to Allatoona Lake Park, 25 miles north of Atlanta, exciting and a great sense of achievement; the *other one* found the destination exciting and a great sense of relief. It had been one thing *she* discovered to follow her beloved as he drove solo in the big bus, quite another to be right up there in the front passenger seat with him as *he* (in her opinion) got far too close to everything on her side of the road. It was also not a little nerve-racking to be in the centre of five high speed lanes on the Atlanta loop (ring-route) especially when one really wanted, apparently, to be in one or other of the outside lanes looking for one's junction to the I-something-else heading north or is that east? Anywhere but here, *she* thought, and longed for the safety of the Athens home. But Allatoona Lake camp resort at 4.00 pm far from noisy Interstates was pretty, the reception warm, and the chosen site was almost on the lake and away from the few other campers. A cup of tea made for the first time with the new kettle and the world was wonderful. America is marvellous. Having settled in and placed lovingly around their home the new coffee machine, the new toaster, the new CD player etc etc, a walk around the peaceful lake was called for with stops for camera angles and shots. The tranquillity was suddenly and rudely interrupted as an earth-shattering bellowing noise erupted around them. 'A train. How very exciting,' *one* of them enthused. *He* then went on to say, 'I wondered when we went over the level crossing just outside the camp entrance if we would be lucky enough to see one.' See one; we saw or heard ten more in the next two hours and all VERY CLOSE by. This kind of luck, *he* should experience on his own!

By the morning we had discovered that large American goods trains do not sleep during the night either, preferring to make their presence felt as they crossed and recrossed the near-by level crossings making at least *one* of us a bit cross. The *other one* counted each crossing engine as, apparently, really LARGE goods trains need several engines to push or pull their loads, *and*, apparently, each engine has to hoot (BELLOW) as it crosses the level crossings. This-all was explained to a sleepy cross-eyed *her* by an animated wide-eyed *him* over breakfast. But there were other things about that place to make one feel truly lucky: the space, the birds (we saw our first USA brown tree-creepers

16

there) and the lake. So, we decided to stay another night and spent the time between breakfast and bed in exploring the small towns around Lake Allatoona and the high dam towering above the water. That night the trains were fewer, or had we just grown accustomed to their pace? We also grew, as we travelled across the USA, to have a healthy respect for the way America moves much of its heavy freight by rail. If only it didn't have to bellow so loudly as it does so, and if only we had not always been so *lucky* in our proximity to these loud frenetic freight-carriers.

Allatoona Lake with a wee bit of the high dam

Tennessee and Arkansas

Tuesday 26 January

We bade a fond farewell to Georgia, for the time being, and headed north for Tennessee and Chattanooga,[8] stopping for gas on the way. Now, *he* showed no sign of nervousness as he guided the full rig of Ed, Dolly and Geo skilfully in to the gas station and in between the busy gas pumps. This, perhaps, was in part due to *her* helpful comments of exactly how very *very* **very** close he got to *everything* as he manoeuvred Ed into position at pump number 12. Feeling in need of a little sustenance after this close gas encounter she went into the store alongside the station, making for the drinks counter and the coffee machines in particular. *Coffee to go* from gas station stores across America became a must for the heroes of this tale, and there are few that we did not try wherever we stopped to give Ed or Geo some sustenance of the petroleum variety. Sometimes we indulged in 20 oz cups for approximately 80 cents (50p) per go; sometimes we had only 16 oz or 10 oz cups depending on how many miles we were travelling that day which would require more frequent stops. It was often a great relief that we carried our very own loo from coast to coast and from coffee stop to coffee stop. The coffee was nearly always excellent, with some distinct flavouring added in some States. There is also usually a good variety of coffees to choose from including the more exotic ones like Irish cream and vanilla. *She* reckoned, when standing courageously on a weighing machine some weeks later, that her love of rich smooth creamy vanilla *coffee to go* might be the reason for the machine sighing loudly as it delivered a far from satisfactory verdict on her figure. Perhaps, too, having scrumptiously delicious American doughnuts, muffins and Danish supplied on racks right beside the coffee machines was a mistake for some calorifically-challenged travellers. But those scales were weeks away! For now, coffee to go with a few sample doughnuts, muffins and Danish were to be enjoyed. Enjoyment-wise *en route*, there is nothing to beat the thrill of that jump down from Ed followed by the dash into the gas station store to see which coffees

---

[8] *Chattanooga–152,500*

and cakes are on offer. Ed, bless him, had a rack in the space between us which took the largest of polystyrene coffee-to-go cups, thus enabling us to have enough coffee to go to float several battleships and keep the loo feeling flushed with success.

It felt so good to be entering another State and a town whose name was synonymous with old-time movies and songs. Neither of us needed our *shoes-shined* or had a *choo-choo* to catch, so we made for the Chattanooga visitor centre and this one would remain a favourite of the very many we would enter. It was just off the I-75 but in a lovely hilly location with picnic seats and tables placed to make the best of the views to another lake. The welcome was so friendly from the centre's advice staff who were intrigued at our planned trip and did not seem to think we Scots were too daft! From Chattanooga (what a memorable name to say again and again . . . Chattanooga) we continued north on the I-75 (from Chattanooga) to Nashville, another exciting name, and we were very excited about being part of its country-western culture. So with Ed's cassette player happily tuned to Johnny Cash singing about '*a boy named Sue*' and Tammy Wynette extolling the virtue of '*standing by your man*' Hmmm!, we arrived at our chosen RV park which was pleasant enough and fairly empty. We settled in, *one* of us doing the manly outdoor thing of hooking up to water, electricity and the less-mentionable sanitation, while the *other* made the requisite tea – slowly as *she* didn't want *him* to think she had it all that easy indoors.

The park was approximately 17 miles from the outskirts of Nashville[9] and the home of a dear friend from Scotland, Fiona, who has been in Tennessee for a while involved with a very important research programme at the private University of Vanderbilt. The three of us had a lovely evening together eating, chatting, reminiscing and then going into Nashville proper to the most awesome hotel we are ever likely to see. Called the Grand Ole Oprey Hotel, it spans over fifty acres with nine acres of indoor gardens and a flowing waterfall that creates a winding river on which boats take guests for trips alongside huge restaurants replicating the image of the old magnificent anti-bellum southern homes similar to the actual ones we had seen in Charleston, South Carolina. This awesome hotel has 2,883 guest rooms, 85 meeting rooms, 5 ballrooms, 10 lounges and 3 swimming pools, along with fountains trying to reach the

---

[9] *Nashville–490,000*

ornate high glass ceilings. Quite something, for the 7th largest hotel in the country!!

We said a sad goodbye to Fiona and promised to keep in touch as we had done for twenty years since she first came to visit us as a young schoolgirl. Our past and Fi's are forever linked – and we like that.

Wednesday 27 January

We returned to Nashville to see it in daylight and found ourselves at coffee time outside a café-bar from whence came the sound of our-kinda-music, real country-western stuff – the kind to make your heart miss a beat or two. We went in and were greeted enthusiastically by the bar-tender. The coffee was wonderful but was surpassed by the morning entertainment given by a country-western singer called Marty who sang like an angel and would perform 'any ole songs you-all would like to hear'. We sat there spellbound for an hour or so, the only folks in at that time of day, while the mugs of coffee were regularly replenished (on the house) and we absorbed the atmosphere of this fun place called Legend's Corner Bar. The walls were covered in LP sleeves of yesteryear and the previous evening's cigar smoke still filled the air as Marty sang our special favourite, 'King of the Road'. We had the best morning cuppa ever! Before we left, Marty, who came from Louisiana, advised us to go up into the hills of Arkansas, if we needed some beauty, peace and quiet. We said we'd certainly think about doing that. As we left, with the good wishes of the delightful bar-tender and the few other guests who had trickled in to hear the music, Marty played us out with the suitable *'On the road again'*!

After a late-ish lunch we had a quick look round the Ole Oprey itself, situated along the road from the hotel named after it, which had so delighted our senses the previous evening. But we could only admire this theatre from a distance as roadworks made its car park inaccessible and the nearest temporary one just too long a walk. It looked great from the outside and smaller than we had envisioned. As we returned to the RV we now called home, it was raining lightly. The first rain of our trip so far.

Thursday 28 January

Today we made Memphis,[10] still in Tennessee, and drove round it in torrential rain: part of a lingering storm which had hit both Tennessee and Arkansas badly the week-end we left Athens. We nearly saw the Mississippi River for the first time as we temporarily left Tennessee, hurtling across the bridge into Arkansas. This bridge joins the two States which Old Man River divides. Halfway across is a sign which announces to any travellers willing to glance up from their acutely concentrated gaze on the wet and fast I-40, that they are now entering the home State of President William Clinton. We were on our way to Arkansas for the bit of peace and quiet and beauty Marty had suggested were our due, and the camping ground was just across the bridge. The camp park we had planned to stay in, partly because it was called Tom Sawyer Park, had been flooded by the Mississippi. Even the Old Man could not take any more rain for the time being. They were hauling people off when we phoned to make our reservation. So we ended up in a place almost on the I-55 in the town of Marion[11] just across the border and the bridge. It was noisy (from the traffic) but friendly. It was also very very wet, if not also a little flooded. That day's driver (still *him*) was glad to bring Ed and the constant swishing of his large but efficient windscreen wipers to a stop as we parked in one of the less puddled areas. *She* had offered to drive Ed for the first time that day but *he* seemed less than enthusiastic – for some peculiar reason!

It seemed a good evening to tackle the growing pile of laundry as this was one RV park which did have a laundromat; not all do (which gives a great excuse for not doing any). Geo, released from his shackles and Dolly, was raring to do his bit in the rain and took us the fifty yards to the laundry-room. With both whites and coloureds (this for any laundering enthusiasts) safely through their respective machines and the gi-normous tumble dryer, we returned to Ed with dry laundry carried in the arms of rather wet people. The heavens were now well and truly open and even dashing from Geo to Ed had dampened our spirits and soaked our anoraks. Throughout the night it rained and rained and rained.

[10] *Memphis–610,000*
[11] *Marion–4,500*

Friday 29 January

. . . and it was still chucking it down at breakfast time. We naively thought
that it might have cleared up in Memphis and we should retrace our steps of
yesterday – even see the Old Man. Fat chance! And if driving on the interstate
in bad weather in Ed had seemed risky, then doing it in the little fellow (but
the one with a *big* heart) was a nightmare. It was hard to tell, as huge trucks
thundered past on lanes on either side of us, how hard it *was* actually raining
as the spray from their wheels almost submerged us anyway. Were we *in* the
Mississippi? . . . *one* of us wondered as the *other* clung for dear life to the
steering wheel and tried to see out of the windscreen – if only for a moment.
So we were experiencing one of the extreme weather conditions which had
seemed bad enough on TV screens. This torrential rain was similar to that of
the heaviest rain *she* had lived through in tropical West Africa many years
before and bears little resemblance to even our heaviest of Scottish downpours.
She had closed her eyes by now and completely missed the turn-off to West
Memphis . . . so had *he (*and *his* were open). Eventually we found our way to

Well, we really did it. This country and Elvis are marvellous

23

our destination – Graceland, the home of Elvis Presley. We had both unexpectedly found ourselves very keen to go there this after seeing the tour advertised, and had decided that we would visit it before spending time in the city of Memphis proper. We will always be pleased that we made this decision.

Graceland is a small charming mansion which visitors can enjoy without feeling hustled. The individual head-phone commentary as the guests tour the house and grounds is excellent. The views of the splendid, but small, rooms furnished in a very gentle but distinct Elvis style offer a close-up of the legend and his music, to say nothing (which he never did) of his charitable giving to his less fortunate fellow Americans. The basement of the house displays not only his clothes and awards; it also shows in one small corner a plaque of thanks from charities, grateful for his generosity. Our visit of house, grounds and remembrance garden which holds the family graves, lasted for almost two hours and we left feeling that we had spent time with someone very special. We recommend it to all who find themselves in Memphis, whatever the weather, and to both seniors and juniors! We had our photos taken wrapped in waterproofs against the background of the legendary musical gate to Graceland and will ever regard this souvenir of that incredible morning with great fondness.

If Graceland is charming, the strip in the small township as you near the house is not! In fact it seemed particularly squalid, given the home it introduced, and had presumably sprouted with its eateries and tacky souvenir establishments, many using the legend's name, after Elvis had left home. Such a shame. This country has some less-than-marvellous bits!

As the weather had not improved one bit we decided to forego the Memphis experience and head back to base, still unable to get a glimpse of the river as we re-crossed the bridge. That is the very wet afternoon this journal had its first words typed in. So you-all have the Arkansas weather to blame for being our readers.

Saturday 30 January

One full week under our belts and what are our feelings at this sodden stage in the trip? Well, one of them was wondering why Arkansas is pronounced Arkinsaw. We-all had not realised this fairly important fact when planning our tour of this great country and reckoning that a visit to Arkinsaw, home of newsworthy Bill Clinton, would be good. So we looked, back in Athens, for Arkinsaw in the pages of the revered Rand McNally, but to no avail, which slightly appeased the *one* of us who grumbled about some of its places being non-existent! Mark had seemed astonished when he had to explain to us that Arkansas and Arkinsaw were one and the same place. We assure you that Arkansas was Arkansas and not Arkinsaw when at least *one* of us was at school. But not, apparently, for most American school children. According to one tale we were told, there was a wee bit of argy-bargying about what to call it. The Indians wanted to keep their name Arkinsaw, while the white (northern) settlers preferred Arkansas. So to save any more arguing they had a pow-pow over a pipe and some apple pie with ice cream and came up with the sensible solution of spelling the State Arkansas, and calling it Arkinsaw. Pretty neat, huh? (and makes one wonder what the real winners here put in those peace-pipes). A good story, told us by a guy who kept a straight face. It's probably fictitious, as most good stories are!

We had come to a few other conclusions at this early point of the trip when the miles travelled so far had reached the amazing total of – *only* 783 from Athens. So, the first one was that we should aim to push on a little faster, trying to average more than 112 miles per day if we intended to make the planned trip before the millennium. Another was to try a little harder to find a weather channel on the radio and avoid very wet places if possible. Other conclusions ranged from checking that loo paper is regularly on the shopping list, to checking all of Ed's joints after any torrential rain-storms in order not to be *so* surprised when feet thrust into expected cold sheets turn out to be feet thrust into unexpectedly damp sheets. One determined drip of rain through a worn piece of sealant can make night-life a trifle uncomfortable! *One* of us concluded that it was not necessarily a relaxing thing to keep looking round and out of Ed's rear window as they travelled, even if *her* reason for doing this was to check that Geo was OK. She would eventually admit to her spouse that she felt weird at times to see the spunky little chap being hauled along with his radio aerial pointing heavenward. Didn't seem quite right, somehow, bless him!

We were also amazed at this point by the poor condition and structure of many major Interstate roads compared to the remarkably good surfaces on some of the minor roads. This caused us to wonder how the commercial drivers who travel great distances on these Interstates put up with the constant jarring vibration that bad road surfacing creates. At first, while *one* of us was coping with the sometimes sudden change in road condition (often from county to county it seemed), the *other* was in the living quarters separating the cooking utensils from the cleverly remembered loo rolls, and returning them to their respective cupboards whose locks were not completely wonderful. (Sorry Ed!) *He* learned to expect road conditions to change abruptly; *she* learned that towels were useful things for jamming recalcitrant belongings into their rightful travel space. Both were pleased at their improving route-finding skills and that it was all going surprisingly well – fingers crossed!

So we left very wet Marion, Arkinsaw (we're with the Indians) and took a route west and south to Mountain Pine[12] and Lake Ouachita (pronounced Wash-it-aw . . . isn't America marvellous?) a State Park still in Arkansas. Guess we should spell it correctly now that we know where it is! Only *two* nights at the most would be spent here, because we absolutely had to push on and get more miles under our belts.

[12] *Mountain Pine–850*

Geo, Ed and Dolly enjoy the sunshine at beautiful peaceful Lake Ouachita

26

Sunday 31 January

Our eighth day 'on the road' and we awakened at 7.00 am and thought we might have died and gone to heaven as we sleepily viewed the scene from our bedroom windows. We were on the edge of Lake Ouachita, in our first State Park, where the scenery was breath-taking and the peacefulness just wonderful. So we raised our morning tea mugs to Marty who told us we'd like it and was so right! No I-noise, no train-noise and joy of joy . . . no rain-noise. We dressed not wanting to miss any of this lovely day where the sun was trying so hard to shine for us too. We breakfasted with nature's own music as hundreds of birds including juncos, tree-creepers and that Carolina wren, who came everywhere with us, sang their songs for our delight. Cheeky squirrels jumped on Ed's wing-mirrors, trying to persuade us to part with some crumbs.

We opened the door to share the remains of our repast with them and a few curious and hungry crows who had also arrived to see what was on the menu and thus spotted a family of loons ducking and diving on the calm lake and a very large bird circling over trees on the other side of the water. Out came the binoculars and we knew we had something larger than a turkey vulture in our sights and *yes* it was, well, *perhaps* it was, a bald eagle. Was it too much to hope that he might come closer some time for us amateurs to be absolutely sure. This country is marvellous!

Our fellow campers agreed with us for, although it felt like our kingdom, we were sharing it with four young people camping under canvas and a couple of teachers and their adopted Korean daughter Heather who has special needs. Unlike the tenters and ourselves, this family were in a really serious fifth-wheeler (very large trailer towed on a pick-up truck: see Appendix for the Mechanically Minded). They also had another vehicle, a station wagon, with them, presumably to make journeys for their daughter more comfortable. The four young people were packing up their tents as we walked possessively around our little acre and were pleased to stop and visit with us for a while. They had travelled for ten hours on Friday from Lafayette in Louisiana just to spend two nights here and we could quite understand why. Before they set off in their cars we exchanged addresses and were warmly invited to look them up when we got to Louisiana. We promised to try, as there was to be a Mardi Gras Parade (this sounded a bit special) in Lafayette on 16 February and Jimmy, Angie, Carlton and Lisa would be pleased to have us as their guests. We expected to be well on our way through Texas by then, but who knows, at the rate we travel! Later that day we had this paradise to ourselves as all our new acquaintances had gone by noon, and no others had yet arrived. 'Pinch me,' he said to her and she did. His 'ouch' – without either 'it' or 'aw' was lost in the warbling of our happy wren.

The day continued to be wonderful; we played house for a wee while; we took some holiday snaps; we wandered by the lake to the near-by boating marina whose lights had glistened at us as we prepared for bed the previous evening; we watched the boats on the lake; we ate lunch on our patio by the lake; and we even enjoyed the essential food shopping which took us back down the hills with hair-raising hair-pin bends we'd climbed the day before. Now *one* of us feels *he* has to point out at this moment that the *other one*, who has not as yet driven Ed, was pretty round the bend *her*self as we came up the twisty inclines to Mountain Pine, muttering about how marvellous camping sites on Interstates were. A complete reversal of *her* view of only a few hours earlier! (thinks . . . 'must stop letting *him* read this').

As the day drew to a close and we were still the only happy campers on Lake Ouachita we reflected on this last day in January and remembered its goodnesses to us: the splendour of the scenery; the people who had been pleased to meet us; and, of course, the birds. Even if our alleged bald eagle did not return, we had seen our first common flicker, a very pretty woodpecker, who apart from doing his own thing up in the pine trees had also come close by at lunch-time as he hunted in the soft pine-needles for one of his favourite foods – ants. Ah well, we can't all like sausages and hash browns, which *he* is cooking for supper as *she* writes. 'Marvellous country,' she says, 'pinch me,' and he does. Her louder ouch, is not quite lost in the sound of the sizzling fat!

Monday 1 February

The crows woke us. We didn't mind. It was almost 7.45 am and *one* of us badly needed her morning nectar. The *other one* got up reluctantly to put the kettle on. Well *he* did choose the non-wall side of the bed! (*he* thinks!). As we sipped our hot tea to the gentle noise of the hot-air furnace we also warmed up. It was winter still in these here hills. During breakfast we considered our options for this first February day, also discussing our longer-term strategic plans (with the Rand McNally to aid us, of course). For the former it was agreed unanimously that a day around our home would be the preferred choice;

as to the latter, again agreement was swift and unanimous – we would stay around paradise for a few more days. We could catch up with the mileage later . . . *easy!* Decisions over, breakfast things cleared, and one major task awaited one of us . . . emptying the *'black water tank'* (see appropriate appendix).

Sewage disposal is a necessary evil when RV-ing; it has to be done every two or three days (and oftener if too much coffee-to-go has been consumed). Some sites have individual disposal units along with their more regular companions of mains water and electricity. Some don't and this one didn't! As *she* had taken care of bed-making and white-water dish-cleansing, it seemed only fair that *he* should take care of 'black water' chores. She left him to it as she sought out other company in the visitor centre. The ranger was only too happy to have her part with more rent once she had explained about extending their visit from two to six nights. The ranger informed her that the weather was to be warm and sunny and that yes, it probably had been a bald eagle yesterday and to look out for pied-billed grebes, belted kingfishers and hawks. She noted the snakes in a tank close by and discovered that of the six found in these parts, two were poisonous . . . *very!* She was delighted to discover that this was *mostly* their hibernation period. It is also the *acknowledged* hibernation period of the black bear found in these parts, she was informed. She hoped that the black bears also acknowledged this information. She wandered over to the gift part of the centre away from the unhibernating eyes in the snake tank and found much of interest including an amusing book written by two southern gentlemen attempting to make southern speak a 'mi-at mo' understandable. There were also many postcards of the region's wild life including red-tailed hawks, bald eagles, raccoons, red foxes, beavers, and bob cats. Having purchased the book and a few wild-life postcards to have as reminders of this delightful place, she walked slowly back to the lake to meet up with the guys and the hopefully emptied black-water tank. But they had not returned from 'the dump'.

As she approached their place a big bird flew close by and on to the branch of a tree, and yes, it was a red-tailed hawk. She didn't need binoculars for this birding exercise as this chap was only too happy to be observed. And no wonder – what a beauty. Ed and his driver returned too noisily for the red-tail and he flew off. She was sad that *he* had not seen this raptor and hoped another chance would occur. Morning coffee (to stay) was enjoyed at our outdoor table as the bright sun had warmed up the land. There was only us, the squirrels and a few (too few?) birds. There was a sudden noisy bird-call and *she* who had by now read about red-tailed hawks from the birding book, identified the sound as coming from one of them. We had learned to have the binoculars around our necks at all times during daylight hours, which was a wonderful idea if one wanted to see a bird instantly but could prove tricky for some things like cooking and black-water sports. There were actually three red-tails above all making their asthmatic – kee-ee-ee-rrr sound. They did not come near enough, however, for him to see them as close at hand as she had done earlier. We decided it was time to explore the surrounding woodlands and she went in to put on her boots. *He* called urgently and quietly for her to come back outside . . . ***now***. 'We have a bald eagle,' he said. She looked heavenward. 'No, on that tree over there,' he said, pointing 100 yards away across a tiny inlet of the lake. She couldn't see the eagle at first and became frustrated in her anxiety not to miss the big bird. His more precise directions did it, and there on the uppermost branches of a long-needle pine was the eagle. A big, *very* big, *very* handsome bald eagle indeed. Every detail of him was crystal clear, for the glasses brought him to almost touching sight. His

Flying in to have a look at these odd Scots. I do like Ed!

30

white feathered head was magnificent with yellow beak and yellow eyes surveying all beneath his perch; his brown luxuriant feathered body so perfectly groomed; his yellow claws, effortlessly gripping the tree, were long and strong. Absolutely magnificent. We decided that he was sitting there on the top of the pine overlooking the lake to catch a late breakfast. We later read that his staple diet is dead or dying fish floating near the water's surface as he can't dive for live ones, and that he and his peers are becoming rarer because of man's pollution of lakes and rivers. Water pollution is hard to take at any time but we found it even harder to cope with after meeting our kingly friend. He and we stayed like this for twenty-five minutes in contemplative silence before he suddenly preened himself, shook out his feathers and, swooping down from the tree, came very very close above our heads making his presence felt, and then he veered across the lake and out of sight. We had hoped, of course, that the king and his breakfast would have come together with outstretched wing and claw. This country is marvellous, where rare hawks and eagles come to visit with man, instead of man having to spend hours seeking them out in damp and cold. But we were now feeling a trifle chilly as we had stood or sat or leant against comforting tree trunks with glasses clutched in numbing fingers for quite some time to watch this splendid symbol of America.

We decided it was time to get our feet back on the ground and take our planned woodland stroll; each still in quiet mood, absorbed in our thoughts of the magnificence of mother nature and her kindly gestures. It seemed incredible to believe that less than an hour ago red-tails and bald eagles had been mere images on pretty postcards to buy and admire. Then the real things had swooped into our lives making them richer and giving us live images to keep, along with the paper ones. *She* hoped, however, that the bears and snakes would keep on hibernating on this sunny morning and not feel the need to bring their live images into our already full lives. We had heard that beavers were also in this neck of the woods and looked hopefully during our stroll, which took us along the banks of streams, for signs of beaver-dam – but none. Nothing for it, then, but to view the man-made one which has turned part of the Ouachita river into Lake Ouachita – a feat of engineering which impressed *one* of us rather more than the *other* especially as *she* found herself being driven up another twisty dam' hill!

Tuesday 2 February

It was good to know that today we did not have to pack up Ed and travel south to the next State. We had time to do what we chose, and we chose to visit Little Rock,[13] the hometown of William Clinton. Hot Springs,[14] our nearest smaller town, also claims some of this honour, so we visited them both and found them both pleasing in different ways. The larger, Little Rock, had its requisite city sky-scrapers, Governor's House, JFK and Roosevelt roads along with a super Cracker Barrel country store and restaurant which not only has an assortment of goods to die for, but also the best hash-brown casserole and fried cinnamon apples with bacon imaginable. It is also the store which, we had discovered earlier, has a great system of lending out talking books. They cost $3 per week and could be exchanged at any of the 372 other Cracker Barrel retail outlets throughout most of the USA. We had one to return which had kept us enthralled as we chugged along the I-s to get to Lake Ouachita, and which we also listened to some evenings as our very own book at bedtime.

American TV programmes did not enthrall us too much and we had decided not to purchase/borrow a TV for this trip. Many of the more regular travellers have amazingly large satellite dishes which they lug around with them and position with dedication, as they set up their space to enjoy country life! Oh dear, we sound a trifle smug here, but nothing like as smug as we felt that evening when some camping company arrived. The first van to appear was an 18 foot job even older than Ed (sorry old chap, more *senior* than Ed). The second was a camper van whose dimensions were not much bigger than Geo. So, we waited until they were settled in and then strutted in true 'we're bigger than you are' RV-speak, as we passed by our contemporaries *en route* to our evening woodland constitutional. Childish, of course, but this was the first time *we* were the ones with the serious motor-home. Ed visibly swelled with importance and Geo's bright blue body sparkled as he realised that he was the only tow-car on the block. Dolly, as most females do, just humbly preened a little. We all enjoyed our moment, as this was unlikely to occur again.

---

[13] *Little Rock–176,000*
[14] *Hot Springs–32,500*

Wednesday 3 February

Another crisp cold sunny morning and over breakfast we decided that this day would be spent entirely by our lakeland paradise, and entirely by ourselves, as our fellow campers had left after an earlier breakfast than we felt necessary for our relaxed life-style. We did, however, take a stroll up to the visitor centre; *one* of us hadn't seen the snakes and the *other one* thought *he* should, while *she* took the opportunity to admire again a sweat-shirt she didn't need but coveted as it had *that* eagle on the front. *He* wasn't impressed by either snakes or sweat-shirt, but did perk up when the junior Ranger announced that there was to be an afternoon boat trip on the lake. *She* bought the tickets as *he* was out of funds *again,* wondering how her hero could have missed *so* many bank cash dispensers during yesterday's city tours! For a man who could spot a bald eagle across an inlet *he* was amazingly unobservant when it came to spotting a bank machine.

The trip was outstanding; Jim, the ranger who acted as boat-driver and guide, gave an inspiring and amusing commentary as we sped along on a quite small raft sitting on white plastic patio chairs un-attached to the deck. It was cold on the lake and we were glad we had added a layer of clothing. The bald eagles we had been promised we would view were not sitting around on trees (as some of us were more used to) but playing around a mile up in the warm thermals. (*She* wished she'd worn hers.) Apparently all raptors like to stay high when the weather is sunny and descend only when the clouds and evening also descend. Never mind, we did see beaver houses but no inmates. Perhaps beavers only surface when the clouds are evident too. Lake Ouachita beavers don't have to build dams; man made this one to save them the effort. But they do build intricate large houses around the shores and go up into the woods to gnaw on trees to get the exact sized pieces which Mrs Beaver demands for her kitchen cabinets. But around these parts wood is plentiful, both soft and hard from pine to oaks and hickory, and all of it natural original woodland.

The trip was made even more pleasant for us because of our four boating companions. Rich and Jan Hardy live in California and were holidaying in Hot Springs with Rich's cousin Ron Schwingel and his wife Judy. They live not so far away in Wisconsin. We chatted above the engine noise on all manner of things ecological, Scottish, Californian, Wisconsian and Arkansian. By the time we disembarked we six sailors were very comfortable with each other and, after some camera action, our new friends followed us home to meet our travelling trio and to have some hot afternoon tea to compensate for lakeland chill. *One* of us was very glad that the soft brush and blue plastic shovel had been employed in the morning to clear up the pine needles, crumbs and other unidentifiable flotsam which had accumulated on Ed's beige carpets (wall to wall of course!). The *other one* quickly pulled the curtain across the shower cabinet which also doubled as the dirty laundry repository. Thankfully, the late afternoon sun was warm and, after Jan and Judy had been given a very brief guided tour of Ed's living quarters and Rich and Ron had glanced in male brevity through the doorway, we had tea on our patio. Our first-ever RV guests were served tea in our as yet unused cups and saucers, while we drank out of the well used mugs. Tea was accompanied by biscuits our guests had thoughtfully put in their car (must add cookies to the shopping list!). We promised our new friends a more dignified and sumptous repast should they ever come to Peaston, Scotland, and were not surprised when they-all said they wished to do this one day. Most of the Americans we had met so far expressed a desire to visit our homeland, especially when it was also the original homeland of their Scottish ancestors, as is the case with the Hardy clan. As the late afternoon shadows grew longer, all six of us found great pleasure in getting to know each other and our histories. Our guests proudly showed us a few photos of their families. We proudly showed them the many photos we had taken of Ed, Dolly and Geo.

By the time our guests departed, we found ourselves with both California and Wisconsin addresses and very warm invitiations to visit both establishments. Visiting Rich and Jan in Dixon, California, was a distinct possibility, but we might find it harder to get into Wisconsin as our current travel plans, which were getting beyond reasonable limits, did not include time-out in that State. But, who knows? We would dearly love to meet up with these good folk again – and even – again? Later, after our guests had departed, we found ourselves discussing the mad idea of hanging on to our travel companions so that we could come Stateside again – and again?? This was a good thought with which to end the day as we ventured up the road in the twilight and a little way into the woods to see if some of Lake Ouachita's nocturnal creatures would come out to visit too. We were rewarded with a few glimpses of a large, very red, red fox, a much larger and more colorful (note occasional change of spelling) canine than we are used to back home. The night grew darker and we prepared for bed and our talking book. This one was read by the author, Bill Bryson, who now lives in New England and who had walked a few hundred miles of the Appalachian Way with bears and snakes, as well as foxes, for company. Jim had told us on the boat that there were black bear in these parts, and that they didn't hibernate much here as it a warmish location.

. . . So *he* took a honey bun into the camp ground showers that evening, just in case! *She* conjured up a picture of a possible scenario – *him* passing the soap to a fellow camper in the communal shower room to have a big bear get mad when melon scented soap was the proffered food and not a juicy bun, or an even juicier steak. She quickly thought of other things, like tomorrow being the last full day at Camp Lake Ouachita. With some of the southern dialect in the recently purchased book ringing in her ears, she decided that 'that black-bar thang a mi-at mo pleasin' to contemplat rat na-ow'. He returned safely, somewhat bemused by her very warm bear-hug!

Thursday 4 February

She had planned to do some serious writing the day before to catch up with the story so far. It had been like that most days, but something better had always come along. How could one not prefer almost to *walk on water* while talking with delightful people. Yes this *was* a marvellous country and it was the people we met, along with the idyllic surroundings, which made it that way. So here we are, almost two weeks on the road, and so much to tell as *she* pulled the lap-top towards her. *He* was supposed to be writing postcards but was out with the binoculars (again) and persuaded her away from her writing to view two red-tails flying directly overhead showing off their wonderful striped under-garments. A pilleated woodpecker on a nearby tree was quite able to ignore the overhead aerobatics (he was too large at twenty inches for hawks to digest) and was much too busy knocking on wood looking for grubs. Did he find some? He didn't stay around long enough to ask, but moved on to a different site, much as the campers who arrived a few moments later did. What do they need to make a perfect camp-site, we wondered? Ah, but they've come back and are parking after all. Not on the lake-side with its magnificent views, but right next to the toilet and shower block! So that does it for them then! Or, as our good friend Connie would say, '*Whatever floats your boat!*' Perhaps Ed, Dolly and Geo had threatened the new van! We didn't mind; we had the lakeside to ourselves and the picnic lunch of toasted bagels and cream cheese tasted all the sweeter without other campers to observe the cheesy-butter dripping off our chins.

The last afternoon at Ouachita was mostly spent in dam photography (*one* of us more eager to do this than the *other*). *She* was, however, even less eager to find the necessary laundromat and food outlet! This wonderful site lacked these facilities, which was not a major drawback, until we ran out of clean knickers and cornflakes, that is. We hadn't run out of either quite yet, but it was much easier to do one of these chores before getting on the road again, as parking spaces are a little cramped at most laundromats for big rigs. Also, one could not be confident that facilities which were listed in the RV guide as being available, like the one we intended to stay at tomorrow, would actually be either open or in working order at this quiet time of year. So, with the camera loaded with film and Geo loaded with laundry, we made our way down the twisty twenty mile road to Hot Springs, leaving a smug-looking Ed basking in the sun. We had visited Hot Springs a few times by now and were not overly impressed with the driving skills of its residents as we *always* witnessed the recent results of a bump or two which called for the local law-enforcement officers to appear, no matter how insignificant the bump appeared. What this did was to lend an air of drama to even the most minor collision and often, especially when more than one officer arrived at the scene, held back all the passing traffic on either side for many moments and miles. Today was no exception, and the two we witnessed had the usual impressive entourage around the scene. But we were not kept back either time, presumably because little Geo could get round most anything. Bless his big heart!

With all the domestic stuff out of the way we drove up to the dam where *one* of us caught its majesty from every conceivable angle and the *other* watched a belted kingfisher have more luck with his cleverly crafted bill than the four men up to their waists in the lake water were having with all their fancy fang-dangled fishing gear. It was dusk when we arrived back 'home' and we looked out over the peaceful evening lake with the boats bobbing on it, for the last time. We needed something to cheer us up and considered cooking a southern supper of fried chicken, corn biscuits, white gravy and black-eyed beans followed by a local dessert described in the southern book as – 'cawfee ass-cream with pocawn pa'. But we lacked both the enthusiasm and the ingredients. Our evening repast ended up in simpler fashion with cheesy french toast and baked beans followed by yoghurt which we ate with lumps in our throats. As we prepared for our now accustomed bed-time of 9.00 pm, we wondered if we would find another paradise like this one somewhere along our trail. We doubted that it would be in tomorrow's private RV park located in north-west Louisiana and we were awesomely right about that!

Friday 5 February

We left Lake Ouachita around 9.45 am having dawdled our way through breakfast and then the preparation-for-take-off chores. We said our farewells to the Park staff, promising to do our best to return one day. None of us wanted to leave (and we include the trio in this) but cheerfully talked of pastures new as we drove away, tossing around names like Baton Rouge and San Antonio and Santa Fe and San Francisco, all of which lay excitingly before us. It was not that easy to be cheerful but neither was it that easy for *him* guiding the full rig down the twisty road to Hot Springs and the first Interstate of the day. So as *he* concentrated on this, *she* concentrated on clinging to the arms of her seat and not shrieking too loudly with fear as he negotiated the high tricky bends. It was a relief to reach Hot Springs and a greater relief to leave its busy-ness behind.

Our first stop of the day was close to Texarkana,[15] an aptly named border town with a bit of it in Arkansas and the rest of it in Texas. So we briefly put a toe in Texas round about 12.30 pm as we ate our sandwiches in the truck (lorry) parking area of the Texarkana visitor centre. Truck parks are indicated as the proper place for RVs to rest awhile, and this is not a problem until one finds that the only space available is between two enormous trucks with engines left running – presumably for some good reason! Smoked ham, tomato, mayo and diesel fumes is not one of our favourite sandwich combinations, so we ate quickly without thought for our digestive juices.

---

[15] *Texarkana–22,600 in Arkansas and 31,600 in Texas*

Louisiana and Mississippi

Friday 5 February (continued)

XXXXX Private Camp ground on the outskirts of Shreveport,[16] Louisiana was our destination for a one night stop *en route* to the State of Mississippi. As we got to within two miles of the place which had sounded pretty reasonable in the *Trailer Life Guide* which had awarded it many Brownie points (see Appendix 6) we realised that we could have been too trusting. You may recall that we have described some other private camping parks as being worryingly near either major roads or railway lines but having other pleasing features to compensate. This one had both serious road and rail transportation around its perimeters with the added bonus of being directly under the flight path of a major Airforce Base. As we arrived in our exceptionally quiet motorhome, jets were screaming overhead *en route* back to base after a day of Airforce Ops.– unless World War 3 had broken out and we were somehow unaware of this! Any pleasing features were absolutely non-existent at Camp XXXXX and we could not work out why it was crammed full to bursting with motor-homes of all ages, shapes and sizes. We had a quick decision to make here as we needed three things at this point in the late afternoon: propane gas (the tank was reading alarmingly low); a place for the night which was close to our route south-east; and, of the greatest importance, the driver needed a break. We had no choice but to succumb to the joys of XXXXX and grab one of two remaining spaces before they were taken by other fast-approaching RV-ers. Neither of us could quite believe that we were prepared to fight for a space in the RV-camp-from hell! We parked a disgruntled Trio with some difficulty in a space not much bigger than them, and put the kettle on, hoping that this would make us view our thankfully-very-temporary-home with less distaste. But that would be a negative! *He* took Ed to fill up with propane. *She* drank her cold tea disconsolately in Geo and he cosied himself around her, seeming to appreciate her anguish.

And then a mockingbird came close and she saw her first thrasher with his

---

[16] *Shreveport–198,500*

glowing chestnut back a few feet away on the ground, and thought – if they can live here all the time, we can manage for a night. When he returned he found her smiling with the sheer absurdity of it all. Last night the awesomely beautiful Lake Ouachita. Tonight, the awesomely awful XXXXX.

The next locomotive approached and, if we had thought the railroad at Lake Allatoona was too close for comfort, then this was so close we could have been on the darned thing! *He* had discovered, while chatting up the owner of this desirable residence, the reason for the business of the park. Tomorrow evening a mini Mardi-Gras would occur with parade and dancing and music and much fun in Shreveport. 'You will be staying over for it of course?' their host assumed. Another negative!

Saturday 6 February

We mentioned at the beginning of this tale that Ed had shown some reluctance to start as we left Athens. Well, to be honest (and talking very quietly from the bedroom in case he should hear) we can tell you that Ed had been a poor morning starter a few times and eventually one morning he wouldn't wake up

Camp XXXXX, Louisiana.
Note the close proximity of our neighbours and the 6.45 pm freight train to Shreveport

at all. His best friend Geo came to the rescue then, and on any other occasions when Ed was feeling that wee bit sluggish. All we had to do was to attach the two friends by their manmade umbilical cord (jump leads) purchased at a local auto parts store in rainy Marion. *He* eventually read the manual with closer attention round about mid-Texas, and worked out that *his* starting tactics would have to differ from the starting tactics suggested in the book. To be fair to *him* and the manual, the disparity on starting arrangements seemed to be in the differing opinions of the word cold! To *him* starting from cold meant coping with those dreech Scottish *cold* mornings mentioned earlier. The manual, on the other hand, was referring to the quite different USA *cold* mornings which could be seriously cold further north. When this was explained to *her* it sounded reasonable (especially if it meant less traumatic mornings). When this was explained to Ed he was very reasonable about it and began his day with true American/Scottish grit, albeit with a now clued-up Scottish/American driver turning the key. This morning, however, at the first touch of his starter button Ed roared into life. We reckoned he was as pleased as we were to be leaving XXXXX, Shreveport, La. But we had found one redeeming feature in this otherwise featureless place. There was a phone hook-up and we could send another batch of e-mails. There's always something to be grateful for in this life, *she* commiserated with the thrasher and the mockingbird as we left.

Before we met Marty, who had encouraged us to explore some of Arkansas, we had intended to head south from Memphis into Mississippi via the I-55, down through the highly recommended Natchez Trace Parkway scenic drive, stopping in the Park for a night or two before making our way into Louisiana for the first time round about New Orleans. Now, after our first decidedly unscenic stop-over in La, we were heading east into Mississippi and would enter the Natchez Trace Parkway lower down, staying, for one night only, at another State Park very close to Old Man River himself – if not practically in it! Then we would return to Louisiana near New Orleans, where we could absorb all the joys of a city associated with jazz, river boats and casinos. We reckoned we were due a peaceful night, preferably devoid of trains and planes, where we could unwind before the roulette wheels beckoned.

Thus it was that we arrived at Grand Gulf Military State Park, Port Gibson,[17] Miss Sippy, as many of the local worthies referred to her – it would seem that

---

[17] *Port Gibson–1800*

if the river is male then the State ought to be female. There we met the ranger, Brister, who advised us that we could either park our RV in the lower, quite pretty park, or negotiate the steep twisty narrow road up into the higher wooded part of his domain. For us there was no competition, and besides we could do twisty, steep and narrow by now couldn't we? Easy! So '*go easy*' *she* pleaded! It was a dawdle, and worth losing every one of *her* nails on the way up to our second quiet paradise of this trip. No lake up here, but lots of space, lots of birds and lots of magnificent trees through which we could glimpse the great river himself. And no other campers! There was only one problem which we both recognised instantly. This was no one-nighter. This was, well, maybe two? This country is marvellous!

We admired a family of tiny lizards who, fortunately for all of us, were living around the water inlet of the site next to the one we had chosen. In fact, we had every site to choose from and could leave these wee creatures living it up in their preferred habitat. The lizards seemed happy to be admired, multiplying as we watched and giving a superb acrobatic display as they ran up and down their water pipe. We also admired a dozen or so red-headed woodpeckers flying busily about. This was the first time we'd seen these small (ten-inch) peckers who could make just as much noise, knocking on wood, as their pileated cousins who were twice their size. This woodpecker is the only completely red-headed woodpecker; all of the others who have red in their head feathers have it either as distinct flashes or as red crests. This delightful family were not in the least put off by the sudden appearance of these pale-headed binocular-clutching species of the human race who had distinct flashes of silver in their head plumage. There were other birds around, we could see and hear them; but they could wait until tomorrow, unless they were owls, for so far we had not had the pleasure of making the acquaintance of *any* American owls and there were so *many* whom we desired to meet.

Sunday 7 February

. . . and it was tomorrow. We had completed two weeks and eleven hundred and ninety-four miles. Admittedly, and excitingly, there were several hundred more in front of us – but perhaps not today! The breakfast conversations were fairly suggestive. *She* suggested that he needed a day off from driving. He agreed. *He* suggested that it would be a great pity to come to this place full of history and not learn something about the American Civil War. *She* agreed. *He* and *she* agreed to have one more day at Grand Gulf Military Park.

It had seemed puzzling, at first, that a State Park used for recreational purposes should be sited round a military museum. But we found the two blended extremely well together. Many visitors come to the Military Park, which records the significant part this once busy port played during the Civil War. An old building housed a small museum where battle relics, including early and tattered Confederate flags borne by proud soldiers, were on display. Outside the story continued, courtesy of some of the original dwellings, where once lived some of the first settlers to arrive at Port Gibson. Bits of farm and domestic appliances were lying around to catch the eye, such as an early corn shredding machine and an even earlier plough. A charming small church, where both soldiers and civilians had worshipped a century and a half ago in the town of Port Gibson, had been brought to this historic site. It had been

Sacred Heart Catholic Church – Grand Gulf Military State Park, Port Gibson, Mississippi

43

reconstructed with every detail intact, and was now part of the museum where its continued preservation would be guaranteed. The Park also provided interesting walks through woodland, passing grassy sloping mounds which were once the dug-outs of Confederate soldiers during battles. The details of their battles with military gains or losses were inscribed on metal plaques at significant points along the trail. These mounds were now home to deer and other grazing wildlife. It seemed to us an excellent idea to combine both nature and history in this way, especially when we heard other visiting seniors explain to their grandchildren the historical facts about a war which took place long before any of them were born, and then to discuss with the young people the splendours of nature which had existed long before the Civil War and which will continue to exist, provided man remembers not to wage war against the world's most natural mother and her offspring.

Monday 8 February

. . . and another day dawned bright and full of southern promise. It seemed a pity, they unanimously agreed without a suggestion of guilt, not to visit Port Gibson itself. And surely one more night in this wooded bird-filled place wouldn't hurt. Owls had hooted and screeched, but nary an owl had visited Ed and Co. And, wouldn't it be a sin not to see the town which General Ulysses S. Grant said was 'too beautiful to burn', when he marched through in 1863 on his way to Vicksburg and a bigger battle. And then there is the river to see more clearly.

Port Gibson has a certain old-world charm mixed in with the apparent poverty of a town which once had been a place of industry and industrious people. The only obvious big industrial employer we could see was a rather run-down cottonseed mill which made oil for animal food. No wonder that so many of the younger generation of a predominantly black population idled outside shut-down stores and offices. A nuclear power station a few miles up-river would employ some people, but it was a far cry from the merchant port which had been full of industry and import-ance until the Mississippi river had changed its course many years ago. Port Gibson's houses were indicative of the lack of present day funds, whether tumble-down shacks or large old anti-bellum homes with porticos and verandas. The latter houses, which certainly must have been too beautiful to burn, still showed a shabby elegance of yesteryear. But no matter whether shack or mansion, *all* of the gardens were full of many different coloured camellias (the Mississippi State emblem) which were truly beautiful to see. In Scotland we pay a small fortune to purchase camellias and are very lucky if they bloom for us each year; more usually their blossoms are frosted before they open fully. Here they were everywhere. Other semi-tropical plants grew in profusion along the roadsides and in yards. Daffodils were also in abundance, making us momentarily a bit homesick, which was pretty stupid as our Scottish golden hosts would not be appearing until late March. We did not see any snowdrops which *would* be out in abundance in the garden back home.

Claire, a member of the Grand Gulf staff, suggested that we might like to pay a visit to the Quilt Gallery in town where we would find Essie Buck, who would easily be persuaded to show us around. Essie was a lovely friendly lady who laughed a lot as she took us round the quilt display room next to the workroom where many of the townspeople meet regularly to quilt together. The one *she* liked best was one of Essie's own. Called 'Two by Two', it depicted Noah's Ark and was quilted in tones of yellows and oranges, so cheerful, just like the creator of this beautiful work. Sadly, shortage of dollars and suitcase room stopped *her* making a purchase that would have made her day. After only a few days in what was to become one of our favourite States, we were not all surprised by the courtesy of the black population towards us wherever we went and Essie Buck was no exception. Most white Americans, whenever they learn where we hail from, claim Scottish ancestry – which is wonderful. Black Americans are just pleased to meet us and love our accents, which is equally wonderful. We were flattered when these good folks sometimes prolonged our conversations just to listen to us for a bit longer. Certainly we did likewise. We could not get enough of the southern drawl. So, although we may not have managed to take one of Essie's quilts away with us, we did take away lovely memories of her and her kinsfolk's warmth to strangers visiting their town. This country, with its diversity of peoples and cultures, is just marvellous!

Back at the camp we wrote a few e-mails as Claire had kindly offered to let us use their phone hook-up and in doing so we spoke at length with Bud, the director of Grand Gulf Military State Park. We extolled the virtues of his establishment, including our delight with the red-headed peckers, but wondered at the absence of owls in this heavily wooded park. Bud offered to show us the hole in a bit of sandy bank where a screech owl lived. He also took us to the best place in Grand Gulf to observe a great variety of woodpeckers, including a pair of pilleateds. When we told him of our pleasure in the Park and all that it offered visitors, he was pleased but honest, saying that its quaintness was its main attraction. This may be true, but it is also the dedication and welcome of the staff in the US State Parks which make them great places in which to spend quality time! We visited the woodpeckers' spot in the forest and saw not only the pilleateds, but also downies and red-bellied woodpeckers, all of whom shared the same lot of trees happily and noisily. The sound effects of this tree-boring community resembled a load of carpenters drilling for America! We visited the home of the screech owl twice without success, once in daylight and then again in the dark when the forest had taken on a new and unfamiliar black aura. No screech owl emerged but we saw our first raccoon who continued her supper before sliding into the blackness; a blackness which felt a little eerie, and which made us choose indoors and a decaff! Between the visits to the home of the shy screecher, too shy to pop his head out and say, 'Hi, and whooo-ooo are you?', we had gazed a little more at the Mississippi, first of all from the very high look-out near the top of the camp grounds, and then down on its banks at Fort Coburn adjacent to the camp. Both sightings were memorable, the latter especially so, as the trails there continued the Civil War story while getting us slightly closer to the river. We met a lady walking her dogs who lived at the edge of the river. She stopped to chat for a while and we learned that the river floods in this low marshy area quite frequently around March. Her house, like almost all of the houses in this small village, was built on a raised platform about ten feet above the ground. She kept a row-boat underneath her house to transport her to solid ground during the river's effusion.

One final memory of this remarkable place for *her* was meeting two wolf-like dogs on a mid-morning solo walk (*he* was engrossed with some male macho RV-thing). When she first saw the greyish German-shepherd sized animals in an opening between the trees halfway up a slight incline, she had been surprised, but unafraid at first, despite their sudden silent emergence. They disappeared almost as quickly and certainly as silently as they had come, without even breaking a twig. *She* had at first assumed that these canines had an owner somewhere around who was equally silent, and yet was not completely convinced by this assumption. So what were they? At the same moment as the word wolf entered her mind, a considerable quickness entered

46

her pace and she hurried back to base for much-needed coffee, with caffeine this time. Safely sipping the welcome beverage and trying to talk at the same time, she ruled out her wolf-identification theory as daft. Surely we were too far south for wolves. *He* agreed with haste. Probably just dogs then, out doing a bit of unsupervised hunting. Bud, on hearing *her* story, told with a few embellishments, *en route* to 'pecker-paradise next day, immediately identified them as coyotes and enquired if we had not heard their unmistakable night-time howls. Recognisable, coyote howls may be for Directors of State Parks; for Scottish travelling seniors they were obviously quite unrecognisable. The ascending *yip-yip-yip-yip* howling, which Bud skilfully demonstrated, would not have immediately made us think – *coyote!* Anyway, *she* felt justified in having hurried home more quickly than she had thought possible, given her years and doughnut circumference. There was also a wistful feeling of regret that the pair of coyotes and she had felt the need to part in such haste.

His favourite memory of train-free, plane free, truck-free Grand Gulf was a new noise: the deep throbbing from the diesel engines of the tugs pushing the barges a mile away on the Mississippi. He longed to see them at closer range, but had to wait a few thousand miles for that experience. For both of us, the memories of the majestic live oaks (even if owl-free) would be talked about for years to come. But then so much of this marvellous country would be and, as we spoke that evening in anticipation of the States to come, we little knew just how much!

Tuesday 9 January

Bud and Claire came out of their offices to wish us farewell as we reluctantly said goodbye to yet another place now firmly in our hearts. We will keep in touch, as they requested, by e-mail when we can (which we do), and *YES* we will try to return one day. Today we are heading back to Louisiana leaving the State of Mississippi, but not the river. Another State Park, called Saint Bernard, about twenty-five miles south-east of New Orleans on the bayous and swamps, would be our next and quite different setting.

Our feelings of regret quickly vanished and our mood became optimistic, which it always did once we were on the road again. The reason we came was to travel as many miles of this country as we possibly could, and to absorb all it had to offer. It would not all be as perfect as Ouachita and Grand Gulf, as we had already discovered. You might appreciate why we were a little apprehensive as we re-entered Louisiana. We went into the visitor centre, which most States have accessible just inside their boundaries, as we wanted some more information about Louisiana RV parks (un-private ones if possible). A free bag of goodies, full of info and ideas, was our prize: a much-appreciated welcoming gesture. We were told that we had picked a great first night to visit New Orleans as there was a Mardi Gras parade there that evening! Mmmm! Mardi Gras, we were discovering, is BIG in Louisiana, a State which always loves a party. To reach our destintation we would have to cross the great river again and circle right around the city. It was quite a way to go and we decided to check that there was room for us at the chosen site, just in case too many people were partying that night. By now we were used to State Parks, admittedly further north, being virtually empty. Louisiana State Parks during Mardi Gras, however, was a different ball of wax altogether. There was only one space left at St Bernard and the policy of many State Parks, as we knew, is not to take advance reservations. (see Good Sam's appendix!) It was only 1.30 pm and we would not reach this particular New Orleans park much before 3.30 pm. It was too risky. We commiserated with each other over lunch as it looked as if Louisiana's bayous and swamps would have to do without us. So we looked through the newly acquired bag of info, trying to find another State Park within spitting distance of New Orleans and preferrably on the north side of the city. Two State Parks caught our eyes, quite close to each other, but *not* close to the big city, we later discovered. We chose the smaller of the two which sounded picturesque, and hit the road, getting to number one choice at 3.15. By 3.15 and 20 seconds we had been told they were full up. The good news was that there were still spaces in the other State Park about twenty miles away. But we should hurry; did we know it was Mardi Gras? Well, *yes!* The twenty mile journey at twenty miles an hour went through two small towns whose strips (see appendix) went on forever. They both boasted fairly narrow streets which had an amazing number of junctions with traffic lights, all turning to red at our approach. It seemed like a long hot eternity (temperature in February in Louisiana averages 70-80°F) before we got to Fountainbleu State Park. A very cross young lady who kept being interrupted by almost constant phone-calls (to see if there was room at the inn by the sound of her consistent clipped responses) told us we were in luck. There were a few spaces left, she told us, then asked if we knew it was Mardi Gras? Well, *yes!* She produced tickets for two nights telling us to find one of the remaining spaces ourselves. We did, and have no idea why this one had been left till almost last. It was the largest and in a lovely shaded wooded area, with palmettos growing in between the trees which were filled with bird-song. We were indeed lucky.

Settled in, the question was – should we change out of sweaty garments (temperature now 78°F) and hit the town and the parade? Well, *yes.* Why not? Looking at the requisite page of Rand McNally explained why not. Our route through the towns to Fountainbleu had taken us even further away from the big city and, although New Orleans was about twenty-five miles away as the pelican (**pelican?**) might fly, it was at least fifty miles by wingless Geo. So for this reason we opted to stay home and party on our own with pelicans, *yes* – **pelicans.** Fountainbleu State Park is on Lake Pontchartrain (with French accent, please, we *are* close (well, quite) to New Orleans). This is a humungous natural lake whose other shores stretch way beyond the human eye. We sat by its edge on our own with only brown **pelicans** for company as they swam and dived on its glassy surface. We also gazed in dumbfounded awe at the twenty-five mile causeway (the longest bridge in the world) which disappeared into the distance as it crossed the lake to New Orleans and its Mardi Gras. It was so good to see **pelicans** again and to watch them catch their supper. Wonderful wonderful **pelicans.** The sun sank in the west, as it does wherever you are in the world, which for us on 9 February was Lake Ponchartrain, La. It was the most marvellous sight, that fairly fast sunset in a sky shaded in all manner of pinks and reds. At that moment, we realised what it is about this country that we, from a so-much-smaller place, most admire. It is the vastness of it all, whether lake or forest, and where even the setting sun seems larger and the dusk more beautiful. This country is marvellous. Well, apart from its bitey things, that is, which, as darkness fell, decided to bite us in every place they found and some we wished they hadn't!

Wednesday 10 February

We set off for New Orleans[18] with great enthusiasm, covering the fifty miles by mid-morning and interstate. The decision to take the slightly longer route by five-mile long bridge across a smaller portion of the lake was *hers.* The

[18] *New Orleans–500,000*

causeway was great to admire from a distance, *she* reckoned, but awfully close to the lake for an awfully long way. The *other one* was reasonably content with this as the shorter one was toll-free! Our first reaction to the city we had so much wanted to see, was of its sprawling size and its spaghetti-junction-type concreted multi-highway entrance. Like most large American cities it was well-endowed with skyscapers. We had supposed it would be different, distinctly French. The French Quarter was, when we eventually found it. It was also recovering from the previous evening's parade. One thing was immediately clear: we would never have found our way to this exotic part of New Orleans in the dark for the Mardi Gras parade, and we were relieved that we had not tried. We found a car park close to the river and decided to have an early lunch in one of the many restaurants in the area, and chose typical Louisiana dishes with names we had heard often in songs. So it was gumbo, jambalaya with red beans, rice and garlic bread; but no crawfish pie on offer today! Most of the meal was fine (not great) but gumbo will never be consumed by *either one* of us again. It was a shock to the system (much as haggis would be to a New Orleanian) from its muddy seaweed colour to its extraordinarily strong fishy flavour. Not so much fillet gumbo as foul gumbo! *One* of us managed only a very few spoonfuls even with large bites of garlic bread and helpings of rice. The *other* ate most of *his*. Food prices in New Orleans during Mardi Gras were more memorable than the food. The jambalaya, a chicken dish in a spicy tomato sauce, was pretty good but the red bean dish was too bland. Maybe we were unlucky in our choice of restaurant. Maybe we should have waited another day until New Orlean's restaurants had recovered from Mardi madness. Maybe gumbo always tastes this way. We were fed up because this was the first time we had been served an unpalatable meal in America, made all the more unpalatable by its high price. Eating out in America is extremely cheap compared to the UK and the food is of a high standard. This restaurant, we noted, charged higher prices for all dishes on their menu which included the more regular fare of burgers and fries. After lunch, and several mouth-enhancing Werthers to take the taste away, we went to the piers and saw the authentic paddle steamer, *Natchez*, go past. *One* of us paid the boat deep respect via photography and long admiring glances. The *other one* offered *him* a trip aboard the thing while *she* shopped. But we had missed the boat for that day. We decided to drive along the recommended tourist trail which took us past the French-styled houses with balconies garlanded in the purple, gold and green colours of Mardi Gras.

Very colourful. The human population, gathered in New Orleans to celebrate, were also decked out in hats, beads, garlands and vests in the above colours. Very colourful!

Our route, back in Geo, continued on through open parkland to the botanic gardens and the English quarter. Quite different, more stately, less colourful, more geometrically trim. Typically English – huh! There being no Scottish quarter (with colourful kilts of purple, gold and green) we made a left towards the interstate and Lake Ponchartrain and – got lost, hopelessly lost. This was due to road works with their obligatory detours. We found ourselves back in the botanics where we relaxed before attempting the detours again, listening to that Carolina wren, still following us around, and watching yellow-bellied sap suckers (more woodpeckers). Just a wee reminder that in the UK we have three resident species of woodpecker: the green, the lesser-spotted and the greater-spotted. Neither of us had ever seen the green variety in Scotland, and the spotted ones can be pretty hard to spot too.

Back in Fountainbleu Park at the lakeside, we communed with nature and the **pelicans** watching them fish as the sun sank. This time we wore insect repellent over our insect-bite-soothing-cream, socks over the bottoms of our

The Steamboat Natchez, *New Orleans*

51

trousers, and long-sleeved high buttoning shirts under sweatshirts, despite the temperature being in the high 70s. We still got bitten! The **pelicans** and the sunset were brilliant.

Thursday 11 February

We moved away from Lake Ponchartrain to Denham Springs[19] today, and a privately owned RV park which, although not as picturesque as the State Park we had left, was quiet and spacious. We had come here because there was no State Park in the area and hopefully to renew our faith in private camping grounds. This one proved helpful with that – at least on that first day. We found a pleasant site and some welcome shade under another large magnificent live oak tree. We should explain here for folks who are arboreally-challenged, that *live oak* is a species of oak, not an oak which considers itself to be more full of life than other members of its family. There are sixty species of oak in America and Canada, some deciduous, some evergreen. The live oak is an evergreen, naturally! We have only one species of these great trees in Scotland, while our son Mark has three in his acre yard back in Georgia.

This park got us within thirty miles of Baton Rouge which we would visit on the morrow. We sat under the comforting arms of the oak and had a very late lunch. Our intake of daily bread depended on the miles we had to travel to the proposed new destination. Our intake of 'coffee to go with snacks' depended on our gasolene stops, which depended on the miles we had to travel. The latter kept the wolf (or coyote) from the door and we were becoming used to breakfast, lunch and supper being movable feasts. Today lunch had moved to 3.30 pm. As we tucked into our filled rolls and 'coffee at home' a rather dishevelled figure came limping towards us from an even-more dishevelled camper-van, bearing a piece of paper in his outstretched hands. We are not proud of our first thoughts of this man with his sad outward appearance and slurred speech. Robert, as we came to know him, offered us the piece of paper. It was a computer printout of the weather forecast for the area, predicting a local thunderstorm that evening followed by much colder weather. Robert, as we later found out from the camp owner, had been seriouly injured when the naval rescue boat he commanded had been blown up. When

[19] *Denham Springs–8,400*

this occurred we do not know, because in the two days of our friendship with Robert he only mentioned his misfortune once. This was to Martin when the two were looking at all of Robert's computer equipment in his trailer home. He simply said that he 'had been to hell and back'. We think he was aged about thirty-five, but it was hard to tell.

This was the place where we saw our first cat-birds and pine siskins. We also tried to identify the many sparrows around, while the Carolina wren (now well travelled) sang her evensong. We gave up on the sparrows, for now, but would try again another day – with more success. Meantime, we regarded with some amusement the field of robins around us – dozens of them. American robins are quite different to the ones we are more used to, being bigger – blackbird size. They have black backs and heads, with brick-red breasts, white ringed eyes and white moustaches. We had seen them many times before but never so numerous in one small place and obviously enjoying their food-searching birdie-dance in unison. They ran a few paces then stopped with cocked heads before running a few more paces, and so on – synchronised worming.

The forecast which Robert had thoughtfully delivered to us was accurate, differing little from the one in the national newspaper, *USA Today*. Ever since the downpours of Tennessee, we had come to depend, as we travelled, on the clear and consistently correct forecasts across America depicted on its weather page with an easy-to-read weather map. *He* also enjoyed the bits *she* read out from this newspaper as he concentrated on his driving. It kept us up to date with things national and international, and took the place of our Scottish daily! A short mild thunderstorm with heavy rain arrived at about 9 pm – and . . .

Friday 12 February

. . . and it was 30 degrees colder this morning! WOW!! Instead of the more accustomed air-conditioning going on with the kettle, it was the warm-air (hotter, *please*, dear) central heating. So *she* wore her long wool coat scarf and gloves to Baton Rouge, while *he* sported his heavier anorak, denim cap and gloves. Those bites didn't itch quite so much today. Baton Rouge[20] also had busy tortuous highway lanes leading in to it. But the capital city of

---

[20] *Baton Rouge–220,000*

Louisiana had an oustanding State Capitol building, the tallest in the United States, which welcomed visitors including large parties of noisy school children. We (quite) like children, especially when they are in school, but this lot were a bit hard to take, constantly breaking free from their orderly crocodiles and harassed teachers, with ease. *One* of us *just* made the Ladies Restroom before thirty schoolgirls all tried to get through its doors at once. We decided not to go up in the overflowing child-filled lifts or by the thousands of stairs, to the top of the building to see the view around Baton Rouge. We felt old and cold when outside once more.

We took our sandwiches (no *way* were we eating local today!) to a small lake in the grounds of the attractive State University of Louisiana, hoping that no-one would move us on – and no-one did. We watched the loons and the moorhens on the water trying to swim against a breezy current and saw a pair of great egrets digging deep into the lake bottom and coming up with bills full of what could have been gumbo. Urgghhh! On the way back from Baton Rouge, a pair of wading Louisiana herons were observed feeding by *her* but not by *him,* who was adjusting his driving mirror at the time. It is always hard when *one* of us spots a really exciting thing to share, at a moment when the *other one* is having to concentrate on less exciting road manoeuvres. The roads in Louisiana all seemed busier than everywhere else we had been (except major cities like Memphis) and of course it was this Mardi Gras thing. The actual Fat Tuesday, speaking derivatively, is when folks eat as much as they can prior to Lent with its fasting demands, and was scheduled to be celebrated on 16 February this year. But early celebrations had been in evidence *everywhere* in Louisiana since we had declined taking part in the one in Shreveport a week ago. During a recent phone-call with Mark, he wondered why we had chosen to be in Louisiana at this particular time. We didn't actually *choose* to do this; Mardi Gras just happened to be impeding our carefully planned tour of the southern States. To be honest, had we stuck to our mileage intentions we would have been well through Texas before Louisiana began to eat its weight in celebratory food. To be even more honest, when we did find out about it, we had no idea just how *BIG* Fat Tuesday is. We decided we could not face another Mardi Gras town and Lafayette, home of the lovely people we met in Arkansas, would have to wait until another time. We senior Scots were all city-ed out.

On our last evening near Denham Springs (not a town which impressed us much) *he* visited Robert back at camp to collect our e-mails via his phone-hook-up while *she* dealt with laundry matters, and discovered that it does. It had been surprising how easily we came to accept that certain items of clothing *could* be worn at least a day or so longer than usual to save panic attacks on whether the next location would have a laundry facility or not. Our way of coping with this was to hang up used garments in closets and to take them out a few days later pretending they smelled of fabric conditioner rather than stale sweat. However as we had not become complete slobs, we did do laundry when the facility was too obvious to ignore. One small thing marred this last evening. Two families arrived; one of them upset that we were sitting in their space underneath their tree. They had camped here *once* before. They made their presence felt by moving noisily in to the slot next to ours despite there being many other empty ones. This was their right and we accepted it. What was harder to accept was that we were made to feel usurpers as our neighbours (and their friends) partied loudly commenting on immigrants from Georgia. (We decided to keep quiet about our real home – just in case!) However we did drown out the party noise by playing some of our favourite music courtesy of our favourite band – The Royal Scottish National Orchestra. One of the things we missed most away from home were our regular evenings in the company of these musicians and although it was not the same as being in the concert hall we felt uplifted as we listened to them. They would play for us across many miles of North America.

Saturday 13 February

Before we left Denham Springs, our sleeping neighbours, and Louisiana quite early and pretty noisily (Ed's engine can really rev-up when he has a mind to), we saw our first eastern bluebirds; a pair singing to each other and canoodling. We would meet their west-coast and mountain cousins a little later. The true sky-blueness of the back feathers of these perky little birds (well the male . . . she is a little less colourful . . . of course!) is wonderful to behold, especially for the first time. They didn't hang around long as a bully-boy robin saw them off his patch. We could sympathise with the bluebirds! It took a wee while to say *farewell* to Robert; he wouldn't have the too-final sounding – *goodbye*!

Our next stop was Texas, not a town called Dallas but a much smaller more southern one called Beaumont. I-10 was our route, by-passing Lafayette and more Mardi Gras preparations and crossing miles of swampland, where alligators frolicked – well, lay submerged in the mud. We were pleased to see the swamps and 'gators (from a distance) as we had missed them earlier on, around New Orleans. Two years before, we had seen an alligator family almost too close for comfort when Mark and MaryCarol took us to a conservation park near Savannah. Bi—ig brutes, always on the look-out for something to eat – raw!

Talking of raw food may make this a good time to mention vultures – the birds always flying around in most of North America. All vultures are large birds with a naked head and hooked bill – not wonderfully attractive. They feed almost entirely on carrion, occasionally attacking newborn or wounded living animals. Most hunt by sight, soaring and watching for other vultures descending to feed; some have a well-developed sense of smell. Of the two species we saw frequently one is the commoner red-headed turkey vulture (26-32 inches...wing-span 6 ft) with two-toned black and grey wings; it is distinguishable by the way it soars with wings in a shallow 'v'. The black vulture is grey-headed, is less prolific and smaller (23-27 inches) with a shorter tail which has a barely visible white patch. At dusk they leave their hunting high thermals and come down *en masse* to roost. We occasionally observed them sitting in a family group over a typical vulture meal of – anything dead. There is also a widespread family of birds we especially like called grackles; 12-13 inches of irridescent long tailed noisy gregarious members of the blackbird family. The tail accounts for almost five inches of the total length. So far this trip, we had seen (and heard) only the common grackle, strutting about uttering their cheering call, mostly a deep chuck-chuck sound. But we remembered from our visit to San Antonio, Texas, two years earlier that their cousins the long-tailed and boat-tailed grackles had a variety of calls including one that sounded like a jarring squeaky gate. We hoped to meet more of the cousins now that we were back in this immense State with its diversity of landscape.

Texas and New Mexico

Saturday 13 February (continued)

Scotland fits nine times into Texas which is approximately 267,000 square miles. We had to cross many hundred miles of it along the I-10 between the Louisiana and New Mexico borders. A road sign said Beaumont—28 miles, El Paso—863 miles as we crossed the border. (It seems common practice to give the mileages to the nearest and farthest towns along the interstate as you enter each new State.)

American readers will probably know that this State is the size of Ohio, Indiana, and all the New England and Middle Atlantic states combined, and will also appreciate that its vast area encompasses forests, mountains, deserts and dry plains, and a long, humid, subtropical coastal lowland. If the geography of the State is varied, real Texans are not, being immensely proud of their State, believing it *is* America with its single star flag dating from its years of independence giving it the nickname of the *Lone Star State*. The name Texas is derived from its original Spanish owners' word for friend or ally – *teyas*. We had seen a few folks wearing stetsons as we moved west but the serious stetsons worn by every Texan male from ten to ninety (and a few females) would have impressed the original designer of these broad-brimmed ten-gallon hats, namely John Batterson Stetson, an American hat manufacturer born in New Jersey in 1830. Wonder if he had the big friendly Texans in mind as he sat at the drawing board hundreds of miles away in a quite different culture? Wonder how many east coasters wear stetsons? One thing is for sure, *she* loved the way stetsons were doffed by any males getting between her and the coffee-to-go machines with '*Ma-am*' said in Texan drawl as they doffed! Texas is marvellous.

The owner of East Lucas RV park in Beaumont,[21] East Texas, was happy to announce to the binoculared Scots that there were indeed both long-tailed and boat-tailed grackles around and also ivory-billed woodpeckers. We were pretty surprised to learn that these particular 'peckers were here, as they were

---

[21] *Beaumont–114,000*

57

considered an extremely rare or even extinct species with the most recent unconfirmed sightings being in Mexico several years ago. With dusk arriving fast we left the settling-in process to gaze hopefully in the direction our host last saw the ivory bills, but no cousin of the pilleated woodpecker emerged to be recorded. We might, with a lot of luck, see one in the morning. Even a wee bit of luck would be good, we agreed as we prepared for bed that night, feeling somewhat anxious and kind of low. We had not found much to enjoy in Louisiana apart from Lake Ponchartrain, with its **pelicans,** other bird-life, and Robert. So we had been pretty happy earlier in the day to leave it behind especially as this State had dealt us a final blow which was the major cause of our depression and anxiety.

Although, as we established earlier, quite a lot of freight is moved by rail in the USA, most of it is transported by road in gi-normous trucks which shed their tires as they do in the UK (only we call them lorries with tyres). There is, consequently, a fairly constant stream of large and slightly less large pieces of hard black rubber along the interstates. As we were nearing the Louisiana/ Texas border, travelling happily along in the inside lane listening to the final chapter of our latest talking book, we came across one of the larger pieces, recently off-loaded. One of the gi-normous trucks was passing us at high speed in the middle lane so this tire flotsam could not easily be avoided. Despite the driver manfully braking hard and swerving as much as possible on to the hard shoulder, we struck rubber with Ed's front wheels. We-all really felt that blow but drove on slightly shaken, not overly-concerned until a few minutes later, when a car with three young men in it waved to us in passing indicating that we should pull over on to the hard shoulder. We did so and they followed suit to tell us that we were shedding quite a bit of water. On investigation we found that Ed's grey water tank was well and truly broken – in fact deceased. Obviously the tyre-some interaction had done the damage. First thoughts of annoyance and dismay were followed by second ones of relief that it had not been the black water tank for fairly obvious reasons! (Do refer to the correct appendix if you feel the need.) We drove on after thanking the young men for taking the time to stop, wondering what this would mean for our immediate travel plans which would include white water use and grey water disposal (Appendix 1 . . . the pleasanter bit). Crossing the border into Texas was memorable only for our worried silence which grew as we drove through quite unattractive Beaumont, stopping for culinary supplies and a phone in order to find a place to lay our heads. Which turned out to be the one *without* the ivory-billed woodpeckers and the one without much space to call our own. We hardly noticed our cramped life-style. Troublesome tanks were foremost in both minds as we toyed with macaroni cheese. Tomorrow was another day; we were in another State and things could only get better. Yes?

Sunday 14 February

Not immediately, that was for sure. Valentine's Day began for us at 4.30 am when some resident motor-home owners prepared to leave for work. They did this by rev-ing up their pick-ups, located in a parking place right beside chez Carrie, till they hit major decibels. The early morning risers were road construction workers, we later realised when they returned equally noisily bringing their equally noisy mates with them for their 6.30 am breakfast break. Sleep between 4.30 and 6.30 was impossible owing to the memory of yesterday's road and rubber incident. So we planned the careful language we would use to discuss with the park owners their reasons for allowing their advertised quiet country recreational facility to be home to early-rising construction workers. But at 7.45 am we left, when park owners were still asleep in their double-glazed house well away from the activities of their residents. It was no surprise to find many of the other non-residents doing the same thing. The alleged ivory-billed woodpeckers were also either asleep, still in Mexico or all deceased. We were on our way to San Antonio, a hopefully quiet new park with an RV repair centre nearby.

Over the sandwich lunch made in the wee small hours, we read in *USA Today* that USA tomorrow was President's Day and a national holiday. It was therefore unlikely that many RV maintenance centers would be open – even to Ed. But today was fast ending as we neared another privately-owned RV Park, descibed as in a quiet location on a river, in the small town of Seguin,[22] about thirty miles east of San Antonio. It was also seven miles from a large RV center which we had spotted as we left the I-10 for the park – and, who knows, maybe it didn't worry about National holidays – being in Texas. We decided to spend a night in this park, which was certainly on a river – the Guadaloupe river to be exact, but perhaps not its most eye-appealing stretch. The first thing that our eyes beheld was an amazing amount of debris hanging

[22] *Seguin–19,000*

59

from trees, mostly along the opposite river bank. We later discovered that this was due to floods and wind some weeks earlier. RV Park YYYY was busy, filled with large modern RVs belonging to an enthusiastic group rallying together to commemorate President's Day. This togetherness seemed to include outdoing each other by the size of the brightly illuminated decorations strung colourfully around their vans and on any available debris-free trees. There did not seem to be many birds around camp YYYY, apart from a few muscovy ducks. Not to worry, tomorrow we would move on towards New Mexico which we could reach in three days time and have Ed's bits sorted there, either in Albuquerque or even Santa Fe while staying there with Marjorie and Bryant (parents of Jack in North Carolina). Washing dishes and ourselves in a tablespoonful of water for a few more days till Ed had his new grey-water tank would, we concluded by 9.00 pm, be preferrable to another night of cable TV coming in loud unwelcome bursts from our highly lit-up and very close neighbours. If Shreveport's camp XXXXX was the Louisiana RV park from hell, then this just could be the Texan one – with lights on!

Muscovy ducks – the only good thing about camp YYYY

Monday 15 February – President's Day

. . . but it wasn't *so* bad, we agreed in the morning when TVs were silenced while the enthusiastic rallyers breakfasted together in the camp-ground meeting hall. There were no near-by trains and the minor road close by had little traffic. The view might not be the best and the birds were spending President's Day elsewhere. These more positive thoughts on this park were flagged up to make us feel better about spending a second night here after discovering that the local RV center was open for business. It did *not* have the requisite tank, *but* they could order one immediately; it would be there first thing tomorrow, and fitted by mid afternoon. *He* was all for it, being anxious that another such obliging salesman would be hard to find anywhere else soon, especially as the 750 miles between San Antonio and the New Mexico cities were 750 miles of pretty barren terrain. *She* wanted Ed to feel complete again but had a nasty gut feeling that we were doomed to spend more than another thirty hours in YYYY. Deciding to spend the rest of that day away from it in the city of San Antonio,[23] which we had happily visited two and a bit years ago, seemed a good plan. This was a mixed experience, as we had to find our own way into the city this time. Last time we were honoured guests, met at the airport and able to enjoy the visual festival atmosphere of San Antonio in December, as we were driven to the outstanding Hyatt Regency Hotel.

San Antonio is the size of Birmingham, only more attractive, so, not surprisingly, we got lost several times before arriving at the hotel for a late lunch instead of morning coffee. It was as splendid as we remembered with its glass lifts, restaurants and the San Antonio River running through the indoor hotel plaza before wending its way out again to the acclaimed River Walk (Paseo del Rio) which is bordered by many gift shops and eateries of all descriptions. The Hispano-Mexican culture is very obvious in San Antonio both population-wise and in its architecture, foods and festivals. There is also a wonderful assortment of goodies to buy. Halfway along the river-walk, which had been ablaze with lights and decorations in December 7, we came across a small glass factory with gift shop selling the most exquisite assortment of glassware from ornate boxes to exotic animals. We left it with a few well-chosen purchases and, being fairly close to the famous Alamo, we decided it was time for another history lesson which we feel should be shared with any British

[23] *San Antonio–936,000*

61

readers as ignorant as we were about this fascinating battle. Alamo, a former Franciscan mission, was erected about 1722. Later it was used as a fort, and it is now preserved as a state monument because it is the site of the most heroic episode of the Texan War of Independence against Mexico. On 6 March 1836, a Mexican force of more than 2,000 men beat the 187 Texan defenders of the fort, killing all the brave soldiers including the American frontiersmen Davy Crockett and James Bowie. A few civilians survived. However, the Texans had fought hard, and the Mexicans lost 600 men. At a subsequent battle in which the Mexicans were defeated, the battle cry of the Texans was *'Remember the Alamo!'*. We will remember the Alamo, not least because of a preserved letter written, just before the battle, by one of the defending Texans to his family. This poignant note made the outcome of the battle more real, and the change of Texan and American history more memorable, than did either the ancient fort or its modern commemorative plaque.

Getting out of San Antonio proved to be every bit as hard as entering it, and it was dusk when Rivershade hove into view. The colourful lights adorning the motor-homes gave a rather nice welcome and we began to think that we could be worse off – until the television news entered our lives. It wasn't the news itself that made the problem – it was the fact that we could hear every syllable of it. The close proximity of neighbours in most of the private parks would upset us just about every time we had to live in one. We went to bed with an extremely funny TV programme, judging from the shrieks of hilarity wafting in through the double-glazing. We were not amused!

Tuesday 16 February, the day after President's Day

. . . and the day we gave up hope of leaving Seguin for at least twenty-four more hours and the day before *she* had a disastrous hair-do.

'This is the first time the couriers have let us down,' said the big Texan owner of the RV center as he doffed his ten-gallon hat in *her* direction. 'But,' he continued, 'it will come on a later delivery for sure.' He raised his hat as he dashed our hopes on two further occasions that day; the last one at around 4.30. A quick veil is best drawn here over that fruitless day when we did nothing other than call in on our big Texan friend between eateries and returning with a despondent Ed and equally upset Dolly and Geo, to YYYY. We should have been able to accept this as a small set-back and laugh our way back to floodlit camp debris, or we should have searched for another more attractive place to stay in between calls to the repair center. We did neither, preferring to wallow in our misery and be snappish with each other. What a waste of valuable sight-seeing time. This country can be very annoying! Oh well there was always the nightly episode of the American version of *Coronation Street* on next-door's cable TV to look forward to. Surely tomorrow would see us well on our way to pastures new. Hmmmm!

Wednesday 17 February

We hooked Ed up to water and electricity at the RV repair center after another day in which promises were broken, tempers were frayed – and lost. *She* yelled a lot, *he* yelled a little, *she* had her hair cut and permed to quieten her down and pass the time, and yelled even louder when she saw the result! Eventually, with yet more timely promises unkept, the new grey water tank was fitted, but with the cautionary note that it should not be used for a day at least – just in case! *He* saw the good sense in that; *she* saw red! The RV center owner, sorry for letting us down and realising that it was now dark and a bit late to find a local RV park which would *not* be YYYY (we had optimistically and enthusiastically booked out) suggested we just stay put in his yard. It seemed a friendly sensible suggestion. There was electricity; there was water to put in the white tank (but not to send to the grey one – just in case). We parked between two large RVs whose owners had left them for repairs (we hoped for their sakes it was not for new water tanks). Our view from the bedroom was the garage wall; the view from the front windows was of the headlights of the busy truck-laden I-10. Not quite Lake Ouachita or Port Gibson. We settled to sleep around midnight, when the big trucks also seemed to turn in, as the interstate became much quieter. We did not miss our ex-neighbours and their TV.

Thursday 18 February

. . . until 4.00 am at which time the trucks were wide awake and back on the road beginning their early morning pilgrimage to whatever promised land lay ahead of them that day. We wondered where they had been between midnight and 4.00 am and why they couldn't have stayed wherever that was for a few hours longer. (Which might also have meant a few less tyre-shedding hours!)

We joined the trucks on the I-10 by 7.00 am, with early morning tea to go nestling in Ed's handy cup holders. With twenty miles of the San Antonio loop safely behind us and now travelling west on the US 90, we found a picnic spot to eat our blueberry morning cereal with toasted muffins and coffee. Scrumptious. Things were looking up. After washing the dishes, we decided to find out whether or not the new grey water tank would hold its liquid without letting it fall through on to the US 90. It did. This cheered us up inordinately and we began to feel the Carrie travel optimism return.

Today's destination was Seminole Canyon State Park in the foothills of west Texas. About fifty miles from San Antonio the terrain began to change subtly. The earth became more gritty, almost sandy; the trees were thinning and being replaced by scrubby bushes and the palmetto plants, which had graced the roadsides since Mississippi, gave way to yuccas, sagebrush and cacti. The few trees there were, however, had an amazing number of large hawks sitting on their almost bare branches and they were definitely *not* the same hawks all the time, although sporting obvious similarities. *She* became frustrated trying to identify them. *He* became even more frustrated listening to her gasps of 'Look at that brown one with cream or that grey one with cream or that light-headed one with grey *and* brown *and* cream,' unable to take his eyes off the road to see any particular hawk, never mind try to help identify the exact species. Hawks, it would seem, were as tricky as sparrows to identify; in Texas, at least, some of these vari-coloured birds just didn't exist according to the bird book being hastily perused by an exasperated *her*. She wished she'd never got interested in birding, however amateurishly, and had brought her knitting instead. *She* could knit a hawk more quickly than identify any of these. A professional birder, soon to make our acquaintance, told us that almost all of the hawks we would see around here were variations of the red-tail first seen in Arkansas. The only red-tail we were unlikely to find was the Texan red-tail which was rarely found in Texas. Complicated? You bet! It was almost a relief when the terrain continued to change so much that trees and hawks disappeared completely.

We passed through the small town of Del Rio[24] on the Rio Grande, which is the largest river in Texas flowing south-east-ward for about 1,300 miles,

[24] *Del Rio–30,700*

and which forms the border between Texas and Mexico. The Rio Grande (called Rio Bravo in Mexico) carries little water during most of the year, but floods occur after periods of heavy rain. In Del Rio we needed to make a right in the middle of town heading away from the border into the desert and mountains. However a stop for gas at a station in the town centre disoriented *one* of us and we went straight on. We did not realise our mistake and were full of admiration for the wonderful smooth four-lane highway which had suddenly replaced the uneven two-lane US 90. A wonderful sweeping curve in the road, bordered by unusual trees, led to a large square area with flags flying. One side of the square had toll booths; behind them a large bridge crossed the Rio Grande. We became aware of armed uniforms patrolling in front of the toll booths. *She* was full of respect for the way *he* and Ed did the fastest u-turn in the west taking us away from an unscheduled visit to Mexico. Foreigners getting lost was probably an everyday occurrence to the men patrolling the Texas/Mexican border as they didn't raise their firearms in our direction. How many foreigners got lost after coming out of a Del Rio gas station was probably unrecorded. The gas station in Del Rio was a welcome sight for the second time in half an hour and we made a more map-oriented turn this time.

All habitation was left behind as we climbed further into the foothills. By now the cacti were enormous and the large yuccas were flowering. There were no hawks or other wild-life visible and no people. No-one either travelling with us or in the opposite direction. High mountains and barren wastes were all we saw as we climbed ever upward. *One* of us wished there was someone else around. The someone else who materialised with only four miles to go before the town of Comstock and Seminole Canyon was an immigration officer at a road-block which *she* was convinced had been set up because of our spirited flight from an official border. The officer asked for our passports after agreeing that yes, it *was* very hot and that yes, the town of Comstock *was* only four miles away. He was pleasant but unsmiling as any immigration officer about to arrest two marauding Scots would be. He looked from their passports to them and back again a few long times (*she* wished again that she hadn't had her hair destroyed) while they chatted him up by bombarding him with information about their trip; about Scotland; about how much they were enjoying his *wonderful* country; about the *marvellous* scenery and . . . she was just about to give him her *delicious* recipe for bannocks when he handed back our passports, still unsmiling, and wished us a good and safe trip. We later heard from friends that hundreds of Mexicans try to enter America illegally every year, so there are a number of road-blocks with unsmiling immigration officers placed strategically along the border. Road signs along the border advise travellers not to give lifts to strangers. As if!

We always have cold soft drinks in Ed's fridge and gratefully drank some down tight, dry throats away from officialdom around the next bend in the road. *He* said he hadn't been worried at all, just relieved to find in all that desolation that they were on the right road to Seminole Canyon State Park. Hmm! Comstock[25] loomed in the distance – if eight houses and a store with one gas pump can be said to loom. Eight miles west of this metropolis we turned off the long desolate mountainous US 90 on to an even more desolate but smaller road into Seminole Canyon Park. The canyon in which *he* was clearly very interested fell away to the left (driver's side in the US!). It was with relief (*hers*) that they eventually reached the park office and were given a site. It was an amazing place altogether: miles of desert encapsulated within miles of mountains. A real barren waste, but one which held enchantment and history – and rattle-snakes, according to the literature.

Because this historic canyon was full of Seminole Indian folk-lore, including original carvings in the caves four miles away, no-one was allowed to hike the grounds without being on a guided tour. We knew that hiking this rough terrain was beyond us anyway, and settled for the imaginative exhibition back at the office. There we could also look through binoculars into the canyon which was 300 feet deep; an astonishing natural channel formed by a now dried-up river. The average annual rainfall in this part of Texas is 15 inches per year, making water a precious commodity and to be used sparingly. The people who live here and any visitors must share it with the local wild-life. Even the rattle-snakes needed to drink, we were informed; we were not convinced. We discarded our shorts and open-toe sandals for long pants tucked into thick socks and shoes, despite temperatures in the high eighties.

The sunset was simply awesome at Seminole Park and most of the campers (all wearing suitable snake-proof attire) climbed a small hill to watch it from the best vantage point until it was pitch black. We went out again later to do some star gazing, and the night sky with a sliver of bright moon was as wonderful as Texan skies are said to be and sung about. *Her* version of stars at night being big and bright deep in the heart of Texas kept the rattlers at bay. *He* added a new line, about 'big bright stars being in all the wrong places!'

[25] *Comstock–too small to count!*

True if you're Scottish! The pole star, always in the north, is much lower in the sky because (according to *him*) its elevation is always equal to the latitude of the observer. In south Texas it is latitude 28 (still according to *him*) whereas in Scotland it is 56 (apparently). The Plough is also lower (*he* lectured on) and its handle is almost vertical in Texas. Obviously (*he* continued, in pedantic mode) it will change as the night progresses. *She* progressed on to another chorus about bigness and brightness and we both went in to bed.

Friday 19 February through Monday 22 February

In the morning, the sunrise was just as inspiring but the air was cold – very cold – close to freezing. This proved the point (*he* continued over early morning tea) that big bright cloudless skies in a vast country could bring about these incredible temperature differences. *She* wasn't given to singing much in the mornings, so breakfast was a quiet affair, especially as *he* had run out of astronomical trivia. We were moving on today as we had serious miles to make up. On a good day we had 'striking camp' down to about thirty minutes. While *he* did the outside chores including various tank emptyings and fillings along with water and electricity disconnections, followed by the important connecting of Dolly and Geo to Ed, *she* did the inside things like preparing a movable lunch and washing breakfast things (before he did the disconnectings), then stowing the breakables away into safer travel places (before he got to the bumpy connecting bit).

Balmorhea State Park, still in Texas, 250 miles west and north of Seminole was our next stop-over. This was close to the highest peaks of the Davis Mountains which are at one end of the 450 mile long Big Bend mountain area – one of the absolutely *must* tours, according to the book of what to see and do in the USA. Had time allowed and Ed been a few years younger (sorry dear friend), this could have been a brilliant three to four day part of our travels and one we had enthusiastically planned to take when mapping out a possible route back in Athens. But several miles of constantly ascending/descending twisty roads through rough terrain with dry campsites (see appendix) situated on the top of mountains, might be a bit much for all of us and *one* of us was pretty relieved to admit this frailty on *her* part. The journey to Balmorhea[26] was enhanced by fantastic scenery, but the continuous and

[26] *Balmorhea–750*

silent desolateness was also pretty eerie. It was made even more weird when a cartoon character suddenly shot out of the bushes as we descended into Balmorhea. The road-runner did what road-runners do best and ran with loping gait across the road in front of us. The bird made no attempt to fly despite our closeness to him, judging his pace and the distance to the other side just perfectly. From that short glimpse it was perfectly understandable why this character had first been developed so amusingly by Warner Brothers in 1949. Admittedly the real bird did not appear to be in a competition with a coyote as he didn't emit a *toot-tooting* sound as he raced across the road. And, OK, he was smaller and less colourful than Chuck Jones, the cartoonist, had drawn him for Loony Tunes, but his aggressive road running skills were pretty impressive and unusual. We would soon have a closer look at this member of the cuckoo family.

The RV Park, described as an oasis, was not actually on Lake Balmorhea but had, as its central appealing feature, a two acre swimming pool created out of a natural spring. This pool in turn fed the irrigation systems for several thousand acres of surrounding farm land. The spring was a godsend in an area which had not seen a drop of rain for seven years and had a dry hot desert wind blowing through as we arrived which, at its peak on our third day there, caused quite a dust storm affecting the driving of would-be travellers. This was not entirely unpleasant but took us by surprise. So why did we stay in this blowy, dusty desert oasis with day temperatures in the high eighties and night temperatures in the low thirties? The magnificent views of the mountains surrounding the park, the absolute peacefulness, access to Mount Davis National Park 34 miles away, new sparrows, pyrrhuloxias and road-runners, would all qualify as good reasons.

We were thrilled at our ability to identify two friendly sparrow species who, having sussed out that all Scots don't have a staple diet of haggis, came scrounging for scraps. The first lot were house sparrows, indigenous to Europe and introduced to the Americas in the nineteenth-century in the hope that they would control insects. In some locations, however, the bird proved to be a pest, consuming large amounts of grain and seedling vegetables. It also competed with native songbirds for nest sites and food. The male has a brown back, a grey cap, whitish cheeks, and underparts characterised by a conspicuous black throat and bib. They are bigger than ours back home . . . but then everything in America is! The white-crowned sparrow, however, is indigenous to the United States but only as a migrant in the east. White-crowned sparrows have neatly defined white streaks on their neat heads. Both sparrow families sang a lot, quite beautifully and quite different songs. When they sang together the harmony was quite something to hear! Pyrrhuloxias are members of the cardinal/grosbeak families and resemble the female red cardinals we had seen many times in both size and colour. But on closer examination the colouring is quite different, but equally flamboyant, especially the parrot-like crest. Pyrrhuloxias are a good deal shyer than the sparrows so we did not see much of them.

Shyness is certainly not a characteristic one would ascribe to the roadrunner, curiosity and a strong sense of its own importance being more descriptive. Why the roadrunner is a member of the cuckoo family, heaven knows! It sounds like a chicken with its *took-took-took* call. It also stands on one leg like a chicken, having chicken-like legs. There the resemblance ends, for this 23-inch omnivore has a long white edged erect tail, approximately half its body length. The body is brown streaked and is topped by a weird shaggy crest over large oval magnificently bright alert eyes which have a blue, white and red flash running from the back corner to where ears would be found. The male's flash is brighter and more obvious than the female's. Of course! The first one to visit us came right up to the open side door of the RV minutes after our arrival. To keep her (we amateurs can now sex road-runners) beside us we offered a bit of bread which was shaken wildly before being

The Roadrunner comes to dine

69

swallowed. She kind of danced around the step into the van, head cocked in our direction, running towards us, weighing us up, running away, circling back and running off again. She eventually ran off for good. Hubby then appeared, not to miss out, arriving at a fast run, looking us over very quickly, and being unimpressed by either us or bread – ran off – fast. We were exhausted!

It was shortly after this that the bird expert, mentioned earlier, chatted to us and gave us the very helpful hawk-lesson with illustrations. He (Henry) seemed unimpressed by our excitement over road runners, white capped sparrows and pyrrhuloxias, but was very impressed with our birding enthusiasm. Originally from Michigan but now settled in Texas, Henry spends three or four months at a time in a tiny camper-van just watching and recording birds, a hobby of many years which had become a passion. In his small van it is relatively easy to stop and park by road-sides waiting for the bird population of the chosen place to appear. We could not stop too readily with Ed and had to be satisfied with the species which lived around our chosen RV parks. So far we had been well satisfied with our birding results, but realised that we would never see anything approaching the nine hundred species of birds who either breed in this vast country, visit it regularly, or just drop in for a wee while.

We had learned from our son that the bird-life in the USA was divided into those who inhabited the east and those who inhabited the west and that the Rocky Mountains are generally accepted as what separates east from west – bird-wise. Although these mountains may define where the resident birds hang out, many migrate in either direction during breeding seasons or to winter away from home. This part of America we were currently inhabiting, therefore, had birds from both east and west and we found ourselves using both of our borrowed east and west coast birding manuals to identify anything new we spotted. If a species we identified was not in one book, the chances were it would be in the other. Often they were in both. If we didn't always recognise a particular species, we did recognise that being almost on the central divide was clearly a good birding area for us amateurs who didn't actually much care *where* the different birds called home, but were simply delighted that they hung around here for a time, before going east or west – or even north or south, presumably. Sometimes we amateurs can get a bit frustrated having to spend precious bird watching time looking up map references indicating if the bird we are trying to identify has any right to be there whether in permanent residence or just passing through. Birding, like other things in life, is much more pleasurable if one can just enjoy and not worry about east-west divides. But we remain extremely grateful for helpful birding advice and identification from far more experienced people like Henry, who, seeing our pleasure, are willing to take the time to enhance our birding opportunities. There are, of course, a few would-be experts who can confuse visitors like us by well-meaning descriptions of unlikely species in very unlikely places. But we learned to identify them along with the birds.

During our few days at Balmorhea we went to the nearby lake which was small and had few waterfowl on it, owing, perhaps, to people in boats and on shore competing more successfully for the fish. It will, however, be remembered by us for its astonishing emerald green colour.

The nearby town of Pecos[27] (paycos), which we visited on the Saturday, also gave us something to think about as it was almost a ghost town with many shops and businesses having been shut down or in the process of so doing. Most of the housing was pretty run-down too and we wondered how the mainly Hispanic population eked out a living. Perhaps the present day unremitting drought had something to do with the closure of businesses . . . it was sad. It was in this town that we had our first (and only) laundering laugh. The Park having no facility for clothes-care, we took our week-old bundles into Pecos and handed them over for a service wash to a tiny senior Hispanic lady who offered to do the lot for only $3.00. A bargain! The place was empty when we arrived mid-morning and our hostess very keen to hear all about us. When we returned early-afternoon, the place was quite busy and we were greeted by our laundromat friend in a voice that belied her frame, with caustic comments on *his* lack of hygiene! *'You,'* pointing at *her, 'have 5 pair knicker. You,'* pointing at him, *'have only one!'* We beat a hasty retreat, with *her* accusing *him* of carrying laundry-saving a mite too far! Although *himself* protested all thirty miles back to base that he had regularly changed his underwear *she* did not believe one word of the protestations. Next morning four pairs of newly hand-washed-by-him underpants graced a washing line attached to Ed and a tree. *He* had changed regularly (which of course she had never doubted) but had put the offending undies in the wrong poly-bag. We did not return to the Pecos laundromat to exonerate *him.* Recounting this tale to *all* our friends, *he* would add a punch-line he wished he had thought of

---

[27] *Pecos–12,000*

using in Pecos. 'True Scotsmen never wear knickers under the kilt! True Scotsmen never wear the kilt on Saturdays.'

Although we did not manage the Big Bend adventure we did get up into the Davis Mountains before we left Texas and very high and impressive they are – (very *very* high – *she* pondered). But the 6,000 feet we achieved in the Davis National Park (in Geo) would be surpassed by the height we would achieve (also courtesy of Geo) in New Mexico. Had *she* known about that, she might well have stayed put in Balmorhea – another very different but wonderful State Park. Now there were three great parks which had grabbed our senses. They sure made up for the others – but seemed thin on the ground we travelled.

Tuesday 23 February through Wednesday 24 February

As we breakfasted *he* spotted an unusual-looking bird on a distant tree. The binoculars came out and, still unable to work out what it was, we went out and got closer and closer thinking nothing could have a tail that long on such a strangely-shaped body . . . unless it's a grackle. But it wasn't. The bird flew down and ran towards us fast and with no inhibitions. A tree sitting road-runner . . . *of course* . . . *what else*! This ground-living cuckoo occasionally likes a higher perch. The male road-runner followed *her* back to Ed in circuitous fashion and, once there, almost took a grape from her outstretched hand. She threw it the short distance to him eventually, in case this cuckoo got fed up and left. He looked it over carefully before banging the hell out of that green rubbery fruit; then swallowing it quickly, ran off before he was force-fed another. We will never know whether or not our delightful roadrunners grew fonder of grapes. We do know that many more visitors to this desert oasis will be cheered by their amusing company. It was time for us to drive into our tenth State of this special USA visit. This country is marvellous.

To reach Lake Caballo State Park sixty miles over the New Mexico border we passed through more desert and mountains whose sandy colours changed to ochre, then reddish hues. By the time we reached the big border city of El Paso[28] (3,500ft high) on the borders of Mexico, Texas and New Mexico we were in quite different surroundings. The style of the buildings

[28] *El Paso–515,000*

is unique and called *pueblo* using the Indian name for village, but the houses look very Mexican in manner. Many are built into and on the hillsides and most are built of *adobe*, the Spanish word for a sun-dried brick and for the clay soil from which the brick is made. Adobe soils are found in many arid and semi-arid regions worldwide, notably in North Africa, Mexico, and the south-western United States, where adobe soils cover thousands of square miles. And this clay has been used for thousands of years to build houses and other structures. For example, ancient Babylonians, ancient Egyptians, and some Native American cultures of North and South America used adobe.

The mountains were all around us now, seeming lower and flatter and pinker, yet we were climbing all the time and very high mountain ranges were visible in the distance. The Texas mountain roads with their passes had been replaced by wider vistas, all red as far as the eye could see. The Rio Grande had eluded us as we approached and passed through busy El Paso and *one* of us kept looking for it in the beautiful red undulating terrain. The *other one* worried a bit about this as *she* felt *his* eyes should be only on the I-25. There were many small bridges across dried up creeks and she teased him that the grand river didn't exist either, owing to drought. But, thankfully, ten miles south of Lake Caballo, a larger bridge appeared and spanned part of the still flowing, but narrow, Rio Grande. It was a great relief to both that he finally got his first glimpse of another river he had longed to see. *Caballo* is the Hispanic word for horse and Lake Caballo State Park was divided up into three main parts all with horse names. The one we chose to settle on for a couple of nights was Palamino and looked over yet another beautiful man-made lake – made this time from the Rio Grande himself. If Lake Balmorhea was a delightful deep emerald green, this lake was a delightful deep turquoise blue. The high mountains on the opposite side were reflected in its calm waters and gulls and cormorants circled over it or fed from it.

As *he* went off to tell the rangers which site they had chosen *she* unpacked and (wait for it!) put the kettle on (you-all could write this bit!). A very large white bird with black fringes to its wings flew past the bedroom window as she removed things from the bed, placed there for travel safety. The only bird she knew that was that size and shape was the American white **pelican**, but she had not managed to see its bill clearly enough to make identification accurate. He came back with face aglow to tell her that, according to the ranger, an old white **pelican** was a resident on the lake. Within fifteen minutes they had both seen him – and another seven, who might be temporary residents, but who were there NOW and just wonderful to behold. Unlike their smaller brown cousins, white **pelicans** don't dive for fish but sit on the water skimming them up in their large yellow bills. Over the day and a half spent on Lake Caballo we watched these birds fly and fish and felt very honoured to share the beauty of this bit of the Rio Grande with them.

We both put a toe into this cold river to say that we had done so and to feel the water which is life to so many New Mexicans, Texans and Mexicans, flow over a tiny part of us. We did this on the evenings that we fed the mallard ducks and ring-billed gulls who appeared the instant they saw us, calling loudly for more of their families to come join the feast of stale bagels and bread. The white **pelicans** never came as near to us as the brown ones had in Florida but we were able to admire them even without our binoculars as they flew and fished. How we would have loved to stay there longer, but Santa Fe and our patient friends awaited us. One day we just might return there – our fourth marvellous State Park.

Thursday 25 February through Friday 26 February

By the time we got to Albuquerque[29] (where have we heard that before?) – it was mid-day and we were only 58 miles from the city that folks, on learning that we were making this trip, said we *had* to visit, namely Santa Fe. Albuquerque (5,500 ft) is the big business town of New Mexico and the roads into and out of it teemed with rushing traffic. But although it is just another big city with business blocks and skyscrapers, it is certainly not as unattractive as many others we passed, perhaps because it is in the New Mexican mountains with Pueblo adobe dwellings around its steep perimeters. It is hard to describe, without too many superlatives, the magnificent drive between Albuquerque and Santa Fe. The mountain ranges grew higher as we climbed and the mountain called the Santa Fe Baldy rose before us, the top of its 12,622 ft peak covered in snow. We approached this all-year-round tourist city which we had looked forward to visiting for so long, with slight trepidation. What if it did not come up to expectations? It did, and exceeded them ten-fold. Santa Fe,[30] founded in 1610 to serve as the State capital, is a flat sprawling pretty

[29] *Albuquerque–400,000*
[30] *Santa Fe–56,000*

city in the heart of the Sangro De Cristo Mountains with a character all its own. The buildings, including State administration, stores and businesses, are made of adobe and are designed to fit in with the Mexican-Indian characteristics. It is 7,000 ft above sea level.

We parked Ed etc outside the home of Marjorie and Bryant and were given the warmest of welcomes by our hosts. The delightful guest bedroom with adjoining bath looked marvellous to us RV-dwellers. We accepted their kindness very happily, deciding that Ed, Dolly and Geo could be left to themselves for a day or two. Before she cooked our evening meal Marjorie took us the short walk from their house to the famed central plaza of Santa Fe, which is a small square with gardens and seats at its centre and covered walkways around it, where shops, hotel and cafés are laid out in pleasing lines. One side houses Indian street vendors who sit before their wares, made either by them or by family members, and willingly tell stories about their culture. We had never seen so much turquoise stone before, all local and set in gracefully carved silver as were other stones, either precious or semi-precious. The actual stores are filled with unusual art work, much of it unique to this area and done by local artists. There are galleries displaying sculptures of birds and animals so perfect they took our breath away. We just looked this

Inn of the Anasazi in the central square of Santa Fe. A Typical adobe building

first evening with our hostess, knowing we had time to come back to absorb both the local culture and the history of this town. Well, we nearly only looked. One vendor was selling tiles depicting Indian Mexican art and folk-lore. The tiles are made of different brightly coloured sands carefully sprinkled on to a sticky board, to create scenes or characters. One character stood out. Yep, that road-runner again, the State bird of New Mexico, beautifully sculpted and looking as large as life and definitely wanting to belong to us! How best to describe Santa Fe in a few words? – 'A city different' is how it has become known, Bryant told us over supper – and it most certainly is.

Our delicious meal of fresh salmon, local potatoes and asparagus was also different to any cuisine we'd had recently and a great improvement on anything produced in Ed's kitchen. *She* must hastily say here that Ed's kitchen was marvellous. The unwilling cooks were the problem! The next day we did absorb as much of the city as we could in so short a time and are so pleased that we loved it as much as we had been told we would. We ate Mexican food that evening in a place known to our hosts and listened to their rich stories of life both here in New Mexico, and previously in Iowa. The senior members of this family, like the junior ones, are lovely kindly interesting folk and we were sad to say our farewells to them next day.

Saturday 27 February

. . . but we had to, as we were about to do now what Mark and MaryCarol, who had spent a week in New Mexico two years before, had suggested we do – point the bus in any direction and just drive across as much of this very special State as we could manage. We chose to point it north and ended up at the Oh Kay private RV park at San Juan Pueblo[31] just 23 miles north of Santa Fe. OK, not far, but we had lingered in the outskirts of Santa Fe and were parked in an area we had chosed to be in. The RV park was just about Oh-Kay, but there were no State Parks open at this time of year in this area so we had to make do with one of the less pleasing camping sites once more. It would, however, allow us to leave big Ed and take the twistier road into the mountains in Geo. Although further north, we were at a lower altitude (6,200 ft) than in Santa Fe and, as we had suffered very little from altitude problems

[31] *San Juan Pueblo–900*

other than a slight breathlessness there, we did not expect to suffer any at San Juan Pueblo.

However, the combination of accumulative altitude change with less oxygen than we are used to, along with the exceedingly narrow twisty roads with sheer drops on either side as we climbed higher, combined to make *one* of us nauseous, quite breathless and increasingly panicky. So panicky that *she* begged him to turn round. Turning round on this high narrow mountain pass did nothing for *her* self esteem and even less for *his* ear-drums. By the time we had reached bottom again (back to 6,200 ft) *she* had screamed in real terror for the first time on this vacation. She screamed at every awkward bend, and every time a roadside cross with flowers was passed – and there were many. These roadside memorials are there to honour people who have died in accidents on this tortuous road. Even stopping for a quiet few moments beside the beautiful adobe church called Santuario de Chimayo nestling in foothills just above San Juan Pueblo did not comfort *her* enough and by the time we returned to camp she was in floods of tears made more torrential by *his* apparent lack of understanding. For, although *he* did admit to feeling a bit altitude sick himself, *he,* unfortunately, added that *he* was not a bit upset by the wonderfully scenic terrain, and why could *she* not relax and try harder to enjoy it. Clearly *he* did not understand *her* problem at all.

To be honest she didn't understand it all herself, and began to think more deeply than she had allowed herself to up until this crucial point, about her obvious height problems, and just how many more high roads with chasms below she could actually tolerate. Were her altitude problems real, or purely high-level anxiety attacks? This was not the first time on the trip that she had been scared of heights with legs turning to jelly as we approached a high bit on a road with a big drop on one or both sides. This was puzzling, and had not happened to her before – but then she had never experienced the dizzying heights we were travelling, made even higher by the vantage point of Ed's passenger seat. She had no worries when flying, and few when *standing* above a yawning chasm. This soul-searching was painful, especially as it might compromise their travel plans.

She tried to explain her emotions, but just sounded pathetic and shrill. *He* said that he didn't think he could ever put her through her obvious terror again which, with the Grand Canyon, the Rockies, Yellowstone and heaven knows what other dizzy heights still to come, was a dreadful thought. These places were an absolute must for *him* to see. They had been an absolute must for *her* as well until now. This was the first time during the trip that we had to confront a real problem which could jeopardise the rest of our time on the road, and we felt considerably ill at ease with each other. *She* decided that they were completely incompatible as travelling companions; ignoring the harmony until now. She also doubted that he really understood or sympathised with her phobia – expressed at last. Couldn't *he* see that *she* was knocked sideways by her obvious frailty and by causing him enormous disappointment. She wanted to get a plane home now! *He* was worried about her abject sadness and fears and understandably concerned that he might not after all see at least some of the high wonders of the American west. *He* might well have put *her* on a plane if an airport had been handy. Our possible altitude sickness did not help us to come to sensible conclusions. We went to bed early and separately – feeling very sorry for ourselves. This country and *him* are awful!

Sunday 28 February

This morning *he* offered to go back east, at least for a wee while, to recapture their happiness. *She* offered to go home. *He* suggested continuing west into Arizona but well south of *that* canyon. *She* suggested she should go home. It seemed as if our impasse was worse than the previous day's mountain pass. We finally agreed to leave San Juan Pueblo and go somewhere together. By coffee-to-go time we were down a few feet and heading south (definitely neither east or west). By the time we reached Albuquerque (reprise!) we were talking – just. *She* felt a little more sane and didn't give the airport more than a quick glance. *He* felt relieved that they were not, as yet, heading directly east and pleased that he didn't have to find a parking place for the rig in Albuquerque airport. Over lunch we agreed to continue travelling west together as we had new friends we wanted to visit. Surely we could work out the height thing at a calm lakeside State Park. For once we did not look in much detail at the area around the chosen park, we were just relieved to be going somewhere together. This State Park *was* open, we discovered from a telephone kiosk *en route*, even if it didn't have water on tap at this time of year owing to freezing conditions. Prewitt[32] was the name of the small town with the phone kiosk at a McDonalds which *he* chose to park in, having passed their billboard

---

[32] *Prewitt–400*

five miles back welcoming RVs. *He* presumed that this meant easy parking for large vehicles. It didn't. That particular bit of the parking lot was under construction and we were right in it before *he* realised this. Rapid application of the brakes just stopped Ed's front wheels from diving into a rather large rut in the tarmac. There was no way the driver could reverse the rig (see Appendix for Mechanically Minded), so some necessary unhitching of Geo and Dolly was accomplished, accompanied by some un-necessary strong language. After nifty Ed reversal we re-hitched the wagons and rolled out of McDonalds, away from its burgers and its far from welcome yet-to-be-constructed RV parking lot. We almost smiled at each other!

Blue Water Lake State Park, about sixty miles east of the Arizona New Mexico border, is at 7,400 ft and on the edge of a canyon approached by a narrow road along the edge of another canyon. In between taking deep breaths as we descended to the lake, *she* wondered if *he* had planned this. *He* was both conciliatory and careful to take the bends slowly and with Ed's lowest gear engaged. It was a very beautiful place and, at that freezing time of year, devoid of any other campers. There were a few day visitors boating or fishing on the very cold lake or picnicking in shelters trying to stay out of the icy blast whistling between the high mountain peaks and over the rippling lake. Ed was parked high up (quite close to the not-very-grand-canyon) and the views all around were breathtaking – as was the altitude!

By 5.30 pm it was completely deserted and extremely lonely, apart from the birds which were plentiful and in good voice. We saw our first western meadowlark, a pretty, ground-hugging nine-inch member of the blackbird family with a bright yellow front, and a black crescent on the chest. They build domed nests hidden in the grass, so this was an exciting find for us.

He offered to cook supper – *she* let him while she addressed the computer screen to take her mind off the road they would climb back up tomorrow. We ate to the final exciting chapters of the current talking book and knew by its close that even if we had differences in ability or outlook we were basically on the same wave-length. We would continue our adventure wiser and, hopefully, more aware of each other's shortcomings (although *she* remained completely convinced that *hers* were shorter than *his)*. *She* offered to make their next stop-over at a private park in North Arizona (no State ones open there until May). This park was forty miles west of Flagstaff, and sixty miles south of the Grand Canyon. *He* accepted and offered to visit the Grand Canyon on his own. *She* accepted. We went to bed together and spoke about the five weeks now behind us, discussing honestly the positives and negatives so far. They came out something like this...

Positives . . . Him

- the desert sky at night

- driving Ed

- the friendliness of people in shops & camp grounds

- watching **pelicans**
- eating muffins at a picnic table in gorgeous scenery
- spotting a bald eagle in a tree top
- the high quality of some of the smaller roads
- successfully getting Ed out of a tight parking space

- looking at the long, long trains as they approach level crossings

Negatives . . . Him

- the awfulness of some private highly-rated camp-sites
- the worry about the gas station layout being suitable for the full rig
- feeling let down by a hip needing replaced which prevented walking more than a a few hundred yards at a time – especially frustrating in a place like Seminole Canyon
- no owls as yet
- not being able to have a lie in a hot bath
- missing some wild-life while driving
- the amazingly poor quality of some stretches of interstates
- the anxiety of having Ed in a wrong lane at a busy intersection
- the hooting of the long, long trains as they approach the level crossings at twenty minute intervals

Positives . . . Her

- getting to see so many American States and the different landscapes of each

Negatives . . . Her

- leaving some wonderful places; not spending nearly enough time in others

- meeting lots of interesting people, most of them helpful and friendly

- meeting lots of new wildlife, especially the woodpeckers, coyotes, road-runners and **pelicans**
- eating bagels, muffins and doughnuts (anywhere)

- the night sky at Seminole National Park
- the wonderful diverse scenery seen from the front seat of Ed

- going to sleep in clean sheets with clean laundry in the closets
- having supper in the gloaming on the edge of a beautiful lake
- best of all, being driven by *him* feeling relaxed and like royalty from her high-arm-chair

- having to put up with a few anti-social campers with little regard for their fellow campers or their surroundings
- not seeing ONE owl yet: there are supposed to be many species in this country . . . where are they hiding?
- putting on weight after eating bagels, muffins and doughnuts (everywhere)

- the dark wet day sky throughout Tennessee
- too much high and diverse scenery seen too easily from the front seat of Ed

- waking up in dirty sheets with a day's laundering ahead
- having breakfast in a rest place right on an Interstate
- lack of initiative to get into Ed's driving seat

Tomorrow was a new month with a new State to be tackled and at least *one* of us getting close to that Grrr – and Canyon.

Monday 1 March

She awoke early and slightly nauseous to find *him* awake and, although not nauseous, not feeling altogether wonderful. Over a lighter than usual breakfast we compared symptoms, discovering that both of us were having some difficulty in breathing with a slight but constant pressure above the diaphragm after even a small exertion. Her nausea quickly passed but she felt a bit light-headed and very tired. He did too. A kind of altitude lassitude we decided. The area around the Grand Canyon was also pretty high at 6,800 ft, so the best thing might be to spend a quiet day at Blue Water Lake to see if another twenty-four hours would help us become better acclimatised. This 7,400 ft would probably be the highest altitude of our trip (possibly of our lives). We should adapt and enjoy! *He* was very pleased to stay put as driving 260 miles to Flagstaff seemed a lot of distance, when tired. *She* was equally pleased as it meant that the spine-chilling road up from the park to the I-40 could be put off for another day. Besides, it truly was a lovely place to spend a day in spite of the outdoor chill. The black-eyed juncos agreed as they scoffed their morning crumbs. These juncos, six-inch members of the finch family, have several sub-species which makes them, with the sparrows, a tricky group to classify. The eastern juncos had been a snap to identify as they appeared to be one race. But the ones inhabiting the west were another matter altogether, as there were at least three variations on the junco theme. Mostly they were grey or black with white underneaths and some had rust coloured sides. Whatever their feathered outfit, they are charming little birds.

By nightfall we had also seen a Stricklands woodpecker – otherwise known as the Arizona woodpecker and the only US woodpecker with a solid brown back. Pinon jays, which are smaller than the eastern blue jays with a darker solid blue coat, came to feed noisily on the pinon pine nuts which are abundant at Blue Water Lake. One of the park officials stopped by to say hello as we were absorbed with juncos, jays and peckers and we asked him about the local birds. He mentioned the obvious jays, and then went on to rhapsodise about the 'itty-bitty birds' which were found here. As he enthused about them he described their size with thumb and forefinger. As the space between his gesturing digits was about 3 centimetres we were going to need hawk's eyes to spot these itty-bitty birds. We took Geo to the lake side, about a quarter of a mile away, to give him an outing with two very senior seniors who felt unable to walk the distance. Mountain bluebirds were all around and showing off their gorgeous turquoise blue top with a paler blue belly, very different to the eastern ones which have a rusty undercarriage. Beautiful little birds, but at seven inches not that itty-bitty little. We had a frustrating hour at the lake unable to identify a solitary duck or waterfowl of some sort on the opposite shore. There was no picture in either book which bore any resemblance to this bird which seemed to us an exotic duck which should not *be* here. We think the sun, rippling waves and distance played tricks on us, or we saw a completely new species or sub-species. A welcome hot coffee back with Ed and Dolly warmed us – it was pretty cold by the water.

The landscape at Blue Water Lake was much lusher than the rocky deserts we had passed through further east. There were many trees in the canyons, mostly pines, and quite a number around the park. This was yet again different scenery and most beautiful. We understood why people regard New Mexico as a marvellous State with its varying landscape. It is not called 'the land of enchantment' for nothing! Our dusk stroll, after a most gentle day, took us round the side of the small canyon and we found that we had almost adjusted to the altitude – almost, although neither of us could have run a yard to save our lives had a bear or coyote crossed our path! We looked once more in the direction of the trees for wakening owls, once more without success: the one bird we had expected to see quite often in its many guises given the abundant natural woodland in many States. Still no American owl to be seen. Where are they all? Even without them this country is marvellous.

Arizona

Tuesday 2 March through Wednesday 3 March

Today we left a wee canyon and started on the first leg of the journey which would take us to a grand one. *He* was distinctly excited about this and took the spine-chilling road up to the interstate, which would get us most of the way there, with confidence and skill. *She* hoped, as she opened her eyes on reaching the interstate, that the approach road to Grand Canyon Village would be a bit more amenable than the one to the wee canyon at Blue Water Lake. Fifteen miles along the interstate we crossed the Continental Divide (see Appendix for the Geographically Inclined). We were now officially in the West, and any rivers we saw from here, until we re-crossed it again, would end up in the Pacific Ocean. 'Does this mean that from hereon westward our journey will all be downhill?' *she* enquired hopefully. 'Not quite,' came *his* casual response, 'there are still some steep climbs ahead.' Darn!

We reached another border by noon, having travelled the last lovely seventy miles of New Mexico slowly, stopping for coffee, a talking book, and to replenish food supplies at the Safeway store in Gallup,[33] twenty miles from the Arizona border. To begin with the landscape in Arizona seemed much like that of New Mexico, then the colours of the mountains changed to every hue imaginable, at times from the palest pink through darker pinks, red and purple; at others from light sandy beige through yellows of all shades to a spectacular orange and russet. The mountain shapes changed too, becoming more rugged with lots of high individual peaks resembling church spires and some with snow on top. There were periods when the mountains seemed to recede and the Arizona desert was in evidence with sage-scrub and cacti and succulants of many shapes and sizes – the kind you would pay the earth for in garden centres back home. At this point we lost a few hundred feet. Then more mountains appeared and as we approached Williams,[34] the small town 54 miles south of *that* canyon, the landscape became green and magnificent; forests grew at the foot of the mountains and continued up to their summit.

[33]*Gallup–19,000*
[34] *Williams–2,500*

85

We had climbed once more and the RV park was 6,800 feet high in perfect surroundings. We approached this private park with some dubiety, given earlier experiences. This one was good and we were given a quiet location as requested. Only one request was made to us by the owners – not to waste a drop of water. This liquid gold was brought to this small community by lorry from the city of Flagstaff, forty miles away. In fact, the water supply to the individual camping units was turned off from 7.00 pm-7.00 am daily in case the pipes froze, burst and wasted the precious commodity. We discovered that another Scottish couple were camping here. Nothing *so* surprising in that. The fact that they lived only eighteen miles from our home and knew friends of ours well, *was* surprising, however. Small world! Marvellous country!

The night was very cold, about 20°F, but the day of '*the canyon*' became warm and wonderful. *She* had decided to accompany him in case he fell over the edge and she didn't hear his final words! She will be thankful for ever and ever that she did, not only because *he* didn't fall over and have to say something memorable as he went, but because she discovered the real meaning of 'awesome'! As they approached one of the world's acknowledged wonders, *he* was filled with anticipation and pleasure that at last he was going to see this particular one. While *she,* appreciating the good straight highway free of sudden cliffhangers, wondered why there was all this fuss about a big hole in the ground. The time was 10.00 am and the altitude still 6,800 ft as we stopped at the visitor centre on the southern rim of the Grand Canyon. It was 3.00 pm when we finally dragged ourselves away from one of the many marvellous viewing points in this National Park. Our first sight of the most awesome hole in the ground was after a forest walk of half a mile. We came through the trees and there it was falling away before us; miles of it and yet this was just a small portion of the Canyon's total dimensions. We were simply overcome with emotion as we looked at this mighty multi-coloured ravine and overawed to think that something this big and beautiful had been here, with little change, for centuries and will still be here, with little change, for centuries to come. Gradually, the immense size of the Grand Canyon slowly gripped us and the disbelief that the Colorado River, way below us, started this erosion about six million years ago. The Canyon is 277 miles long, up to 18 miles wide, and more than 1 mile (5,280 ft) deep. It contains gorges, valleys and towering mountains (called cathedrals). Ben Nevis (4,400 ft) if installed in this mighty canyon, would be just one of many and would not reach its top. The exposed rockfaces show nine separate layers, each distinguished by a different shade in the glorious technicolor display. A spectacular section of the Canyon, together with plateau areas on either side of it, are preserved as the Grand Canyon National Park. Opened in 1919, it now welcomes about four million visitors a year. We were thrilled to be counted in the 1999 figures! We took photographs to record this momentous occasion in our lives, *she* standing as close to its edge as she could possibly get. A little fear beat away inside her as she looked downwards, but the fear was cocooned by the sheer splendour of the moment.

At our second vantage point, from a room built a few feet over the canyon's edge inside an old cabin built in 1935 by a resident photographer, we had another specatacular view from a slightly different angle and could just see the Colorado river a mile below – a narrow greenish strip of ribbon viewed from this height. It did not seem possible that this tiny little river could possibly have been the creator of all this grandeur. It is difficult to say exactly how we spent all of our five hours in this magic place, hardly aware of the thousands of other equally dumb-struck first-time tourists. It is not easy to explain how completely awesome the Grand Canyon is and how utterly insignificant one feels beside it.

Wow! . . . he's *about to look a mile down to the Colorado River*

People not only come to look at this canyon, thousands traverse its narrow tracks every week: some on foot; some on mule-back. Some go all the way to the bottom and camp there overnight. Some walk purposefully along the paths at the rims for twenty miles or more. Some walk carefully for just a few yards. Some explore its mighty caverns. Some go white-water rafting in the dangerous river far below. Some are young. Some are old. Some, like us, are content enough to stop a while and stare and shed a tear with the sheer joy of just being there.

As we left, we each had our own thoughts, shared later. For *him* it was a dream realised and the reality was *so very* much better than the dream. For *her* it was last week's nightmare turned into a dream-like adventure and one she nearly missed experiencing. Some interesting personal facts emerged. *She* was less afraid of looking down from views well-over the edge inside the cabin than *he* was. *He* admitted that the engineer in him worried about the structure of a sixty year-old cabin. *He,* however, could go right up to the edge and walk along the rim. *She* could never do that. *He* would have liked to drive along the rim. *She* could not do that. *She* wanted to go back tomorrow. *He* did not want to do that, preferring to remember it as it had been on that day – Wednesday 3 March 1999. We would both like to be able to return another day in a different millennium. We would like to share the awesome spectacle with the younger generations of our families and watch their faces as they too absorbed the uniqueness of the Grand Canyon, being forever touched like us, by its natural wonder and beauty. America is marvellous.

We did not feel like returning to the RV park quite then and opted to take the longer route back via Flagstaff[35] and the quiet country forest scenery we felt would bring us back to earth more gently. It was a good plan, for the quite different surroundings were just what we needed, even when we found ourselves 8,000 ft high at one point. The country roads had a good smattering of unmelted snow at their edges and this pretty white stuff gave the dense woodland around us a Christmas card image. From time to time there were groups of white aspen growing shoulder to shoulder with the pines, giving the landscape a spectacular silvery-green luminosity as dusk began to settle on this astonishing landscape. And, unlike Scotland where trees won't grow on hills above a certain altitude, here they won't grow at low heights, but do grow to the top, giving the mountainsides to their summits an added dimension. We could have been in Scandinavia with high mountain peaks and ski slopes

---

[35] *Flagstaff–46,000*

towering to one side. Not down to earth at all, really! A recording of An Alpine Symphony by Strauss played by the RSNO seemed a most appropriate piece of music to listen to and made the journey back to Flagstaff even more memorable. We were advised to drive with headlights on at all times and watch out for elks. The only thing to rush out from the forest on to the road was a raccoon. It was more easily avoided than an elk. Flagstaff (7,000 ft) is a small historic town set at the foot of Humphrey's Peak; at 12,600 ft it is Arizona's highest mountain. Most of the wooden alpine-styled houses sit above the business section. It is on Route 66 – a very famous road, being one of the first cross-America routes from Chicago to Los Angeles. Much of it is now gone, swallowed up by the big interstates. We found a Flagstaff shopping mall and bought some frozen yoghurt, some hand towels, and a hook for the hand towels. You can't get more down to earth than that!

Thursday 4 March through Sunday 7 March

. . . well, you can and we did – get down to river level, and the Colorado river at that. We got to see it properly at Buckskin Mountain State Park, a mere 546 ft above sea level. The descent had been amazing and relatively slow, for which we were both thankful. There was one very steep bit where all trucks and other large vehicles were advised to keep to the right lane and that there were emergency pull-offs for six miles should they be required. We also had to look out for elks (again!) and falling rocks. It was agreed unanimously that *she* would look out for runaway elks and rocks while *he* and Ed descended cautiously, keeping an eye in the mirrors for runaway trucks. This sharing of responsibilities worked well and we-all reached the bottom safely. *One* of us did notice a good number of large skid marks in the right lane and on the hard shoulder but did not share that with *him* until we were on terra firmer and *she* was able to unclench her teeth and speak through chittering lips. No sooner were we down than we went up again and then down again . . . a bit like the big dipper at a fun fair, only much scarier. Once more the scenery with all its ups and downs was pretty amazing and as we neared our destination, remaining on the level at last, large and varied cacti were all around us in the sandy desert soil, many reaching gigantic proportions.

We passed through the busy tourist haven of Lake Havasu City[36] where

---

[36] *Lake Havasu City–24,000*

London Bridge now sits, looking small and insignificant in this vast countryside. Once we had settled in to our site on the river we had a walk around the park and three things in particular stood out: 1) That we were surrounded on all sides by mountains, which in the late afternoon light, were resplendent in their varying colour schemes; 2) the interesting cactus garden at the entrance to the park which labelled the cacti with their animal names – elephant, teddy bear, etc – so much more descriptive than their botanical names. Chipmunks ran in and out of holes around the cacti. They were noisy wee beasties given their size, emitting loud chip-chip sounds followed by a rapid trill as they moved around their precinct; and 3) the most pleasing attraction for us tourists was to be beside the Colorado River, no longer a thin

She *has a wee paddle in the Colorado at Buckskin Mountain*

green distant ribbon and, as we paddled in its warm waters, we looked across it at this point to – California. A State only about a hundred yards away, and yet with a different time zone to the one we were *currently* paddling in! It was Mountain Time in Arizona and one hour ahead of California which ticked Pacific Time. Fiona, in Tennessee, was one hour ahead of us, in Central Time, while Mark and MaryCarol in Georgia were one hour ahead of that in East Coast Time. Are you with us – still in Mountain Time? We were to get a bit confused at one time-crossing point. This country is marvellous!

That evening as we left the still warm river's edge (so much warmer than it had been just two hundred miles back and one mile higher) we met a man from Oregon walking his two Irish red-setters. Naturally we stopped to say hello – to the dogs! Half an hour later we were ensconced in Art and Diana's motor home sipping lemonade (the *shes*) and beer (the *hes*) while the dogs lay around our feet. Two hours later, the topics of conversation had dealt with politics and politicians on both sides of the ocean, careers, education, motor-homes and gardens. Art, having retired from the US Airforce, is now involved in things botanical and has many UK plants in his five-acre yard (garden), including a boundary of five hundred Douglas Firs and a large rose garden which we were invited to inspect on our travels through Oregon. We hoped very much to do that.

Not all Americans are like Art and Diana, quietly enjoying recreational pursuits in this country which offers so much space and so many opportunities. Many choose to be much noisier about it. The Colorado river and its water creatures had a lot to endure over the next three days, as had the folks who came to enjoy its blue beauty without making pollution or a disturbance. The week-end noise of the many water-sporting vehicles, from large power boats to small skidoos, that plied its short navigable course at this point, was bad. The disregard shown to this natural resource was worse. Many boat engines were far too big for the size of the craft they powered. Most were driven by young men with more speed than sense, showing off to the impressionable screaming young women they had enticed aboard. The large wakes from the too-powerful craft showed all too clearly the erosion of the river's edge. How the large bass, seen leaping when the river was empty of thoughtless joy-riders, fared, one dares not imagine. Nesting sites of waterfowl were likely to be swept away. Did they contain more charming families than the ones yelling in their boats?? More than likely! River revellers come out to play at weekends whenever the weather is good. It was a relief to many of us when a cold wind hit Buckskin Mountain resort on Sunday afternoon giving the river, its wild-life and its quieter recreationists a bit of peace. There were moments when both of us (and other like-minded souls we later found out), viewing with distaste several yelling water skiers and leaping skidooers ducking and diving out of each other's paths, wished that they and their craft would become severely entangled causing not a little damage to enormous and over-powered egos. There are, apparently, no laws in North America governing who can use a natural waterway, or how it and its natural dwellers should be respected. Pity.

But it was the birds who gave us their gift of presence and made the time on this side of the Colorado special. There were great-tailed grackles who came visiting with their friends – red-winged blackbirds, and they are *something else!* If you can imagine our UK blackbirds (male-coloured) but bigger by a couple of inches, with red epaulettes fringed with gold then you have the common form of the US red-winged blackbird. The red is not evident when the birds are still; it is the yellow fringe which first catches the eye. But when they take off the red is simply splendid to see and so much of it. The vermillion red of the small exotic vermilion flycatcher really caught *his* eye as it sat on a wire waiting for flies to show. *She* was talking to an eight month spaniel/West Highland terrier cross at the time and at first was annoyed at having to cut the absorbing conversation short – until she followed his excited finger. The six-inch male vermilion flycatcher was not perturbed at being watched and showed off his flaming vermilion crested head and flaming vermilion underparts without any noticeable flush of embarrassment! What a wee stotter as they say in the west (of Scotland). There were spotted sandpipers on the river's edge with a large family of moorhens. But it was the great-tailed grackles who demanded most attention, even waking us up at dawn for their breakfast by walking over Ed's roof right above his very sleepy inmates. They have a marvellous way of strutting with their bills raised heavenwards: one eighteen inch male was particularly adept at this strut – almost as proficient as us seasoned RV-strutters!

Monday 8 March through Wednesday 10 March

By the time we got to Phoenix[37] we were hungry and ready for a new talking

[37] *Phoenix–983,000*

92

book. The plan had been to cross the border and the time thing through the city of Yuma into California today, but we were not ready to leave Arizona and Mountain Time quite yet. It was our favourite State so far, and could well keep that place in our hearts. Nowhere else along the road we travelled had such a diversity of terrain; where mountain foots (should that be feet?) climb gracefully to reach elevations of 12,000 ft with pine forests and snow at their summits; where grass plains with rivers turn into desert; where lakes sparkle in the sun just a few hundred miles south of barren wastes. And then what about its many canyons, both Grand and less grand? This preamble is by way of saying that we went back east instead of continuing west as had been our norm since Louisiana.

Phoenix (elevation less than 2,000 ft) was where we would find the last Cracker Barrel, with its talking book exchange system, for a while – they are not too common in the west. This city is BIG and had lots of roadworks around its perimeter that day. Nothing much to sing about really! More road construction continued between Phoenix and Cottonwood, our destination, and much of it seemed to be on tight high bends on the I-17 at places where one would rather have had at least two lanes and a hard shoulder, instead of one lane and no shoulder. How could someone, *she* wondered, clinging to Ed's comforting arm-rests yet again, who found travelling along mountain tops even on interstates a bit worrying, possibly consider Arizona such a great place? She closed her eyes so that she need not contemplate canyons to the right of her – canyons to the left of her – volleying and thundering downward, ever downward. *He* of course, loved it all, apart from the delaying road construction, although even that presented a driving challenge which gave Ed and him a chance to show off their cornering skills. Just when *she* thought that one more hole in the ground would be one too many, another long descent came to an end and the I-17 and road works were left behind for a neat State Route and the pretty town of Cottonwood.

Dead Horse Ranch State Park just outside Cottonwood,[38] was a pleasant place to unwind after a long day on busy interstates. The name of this park is thankfully not synonomous with equine slaughtering, but came from a family of early settlers to the area. The story goes that this family, with young children, had spent a day looking round several ranches in order to purchase one. At one of them the owner's horse had just died and the carcase was waiting to be picked up. When the children were asked at the end of the day which ranch

---

[38] *Cottonwood–5,900*

93

they liked best they replied the one with the dead horse. That name has remained to this day and the estate's title deeds contain a decree that the name must remain in perpetuity. The park was devoid of horses alive or otherwise but very busy indeed and we were lucky to get one of the last three available spaces. Ed had two other motor homes chasing him round the park to get the best of the three. He won! By nightfall the overflow park (with no water or electricity) had twenty-one recreational vehicles waiting for a space. In the morning there was much early activity, for, as soon as an RV moved out of its space, one of the vans-in-waiting quickly took possession of it. We were discovering that the RV parks are much busier in south-west USA in March than they had been further east and north in February and in fact we had been one of the 'overflow rigs' at Buckskin Mountain for our first night there. Being seasoned RV-ers we had been up and ready to move to the pick of the emptying spaces by 7.30 am the next morning, eating our cranberry and almond breakfast cereal a little later than usual, but as the proud occupants of the best site on the block.

The reason for some of the busy-ness of the RV parks, we were told, is that the 'snowbirds' were beginning to return to their permanent homes in the north as the weather improves there and it gets a bit too hot for them in the south. In fact, we would meet quite a few doing just that from here, in the middle of Arizona, to places north as we travelled along.

But back to Cottonwood and the Dead Horse Ranch where we met our first hummingbirds. It was a totally unexpected meeting as far as we were concerned. We thought we would see some in Southern California quite soon where the days are hot and the nights warm. But here, 3,600 ft up, although the day-time temperatures are quite hot in the sun but cool in the shade, the night temperatures drop to 25°F. However these Anna hummingbirds are the only ones to winter in these parts, the other varieties sensibly wintering in real tropical climes. These itty-bitty birds appeared perfectly happy to be in Arizona in late winter, at least during the day. How they kept warm at night without duvet or blanket we could not imagine. It is absolutely marvellous to see a tiny humming-bird for the first time as it concentrates on finding its food from the centre of flowers with its incredibly long needle-like bill. Their tiny wings go so fast as they feed that they seem blurred and it is this wing-beat that makes the hummers hum. We also saw one of these 3½-inch long male birds sitting on a telegraph wire with the late afternoon sun striking his ruby red crown and throat making those iridescent feathers sparkle so brilliantly as he turned his head around from side to side. It was almost like a minature neon sign flashing on and off. The rest of this Anna hummingbird was coloured dark green on the back with a paler shade underneath. His plainer wife has no ruby crown, just a tiny necklace of these stones at her throat. By the time our journey ended we would meet other species of hummingbird. But those first ones were special and so colourful.

She was a bit more colourful than she wanted to be that evening as the determined sun-tanning exercise of her morning agenda turned into a sun-burning experience in the evening. *He* on the other hand never experienced the glowing ruby-red phase. *He* became a splendid sun-tanned brown without ever having to think about programming a sunning slot into *his* agenda. Tomorrow *she* would take more care, she decided, as she gingerly stroked cream into her ruby throat.

Cottonwood has to rate as one of the loveliest of America's small towns as far as these travelling Scottish seniors are concerned. Of course it is in a gorgeous part of the country, but it had a charm of its own in this outstanding setting. That setting stopped us dead as we left a supermarket at dusk on our final evening there. We came out with our trolley and were making for Geo when we were overwhelmed by the view in front of us. An encompassing mountain range bathed in subtle sunset colours brought tears to our eyes as it dazzled us with its extraordinary spectral grandeur. 'Beats coming out of the Dalkeith Tesco,' *he* remarked as he wiped his eyes.

California

Thursday 11 March

California, here we come – today – and reluctantly. Although we were looking forward to staying with our friends, met at lovely Lake Ouachita, Arkansas, we were somewhat hesitant to enter California, for inexplicable reasons. We would cross the border near a small town called Needles.[39] (We knew it was a small town by the *pin*-prick on the map!) It was a beautiful day, but very windy, as we left Arizona and its remarkable landscape; the last fifty miles of which became a red desert backdrop. The cacti growing in this desert region were as tall as telegraph poles and we remembered old western movies with scenery just like it. An occasional bridge spanned a waterless creek. An occasional cow looked for something green to chew on. Arid Arizona compared to the green Arizona of two hundred miles back.

We spent our first Californian night on the Colorado River looking back across it into Arizona, which was still in Mountain Time. We, of course, were now in Pacific Time. OK? We had not cleverly planned this cross-river backward view to Arizona; it was just coincidence – but a nice one. It had been a warm afternoon as we arrived, but still a bit breezy. The river was wider and flowing much faster on this side of the border, but that didn't deter two Canada geese, one snow goose, several coots, a flock of feeding swallows and three large white ducks? No – didn't look quite like ducks. Geese then? No – not geese either. Then what? Once again, as in New Mexico, the pages of the bird book were searched desperately, to find an eastern or western duck or goose fitting the description of these large white birds – and they were not **pelicans**! We decided that getting closer to them might help and on the way to the shore chatted to two couples who were leaving soon to return to Idaho and British Colombia having wintered in Needles for four months, real snowbirds who had been coming here for the last four years together. Three other couples, with similar habits, had just left this riverside park for their summer homes in various other northern places: one big happy family, we

---

[39] *Needles–5,200*

97

thought, but a family who never strayed from the town of Needles and its immediate surrounds during their southern sojourn. They were about three hundred miles from the Grand Canyon and had never seen it. Quite extraordinary. To invest in expensive motor-homes in order to move about, but then to not move from the road connecting their summer and winter homes, seemed crazy. We know folks back home who are just as happy to repeat their holiday location year after year too – and why not, if that's what floats your boat! Talking of floating, our unknown feathered friends turned out to be far from home also! They were imported Chinese ducks, pets of the park owners! We budding ornithologists could relax.

Later we chatted to another couple from Oregon who had sold their home two weeks earlier and bought a splendid large motor one so that they could eventually see *all* of their great country. Takes all kinds, huh! This couple who had observed the goings and stayings of the others over the last week also told us, with evident enjoyment, that the big happy family – wasn't! The couples who had left had fallen out with each other and with the couples who had remained. It seems that living in such close proximity (and these vans were *really* close to each other) year after year and doing nothing significant together, can lead to family feuding. Petty jealousies, like who had who for coffee yesterday and *why* weren't *they* invited, *needle* some family members until minor irritations become a bit more major. Perhaps next year they-all should try new locations with new companions.

Two things we therefore acknowledged would be impossible for us to contemplate: we would never spend four months of every year with the same people in the same place, nor would we sell up a permanent home and spend the rest of our lives moving from place to place, no matter how marvellous the country. Besides, we could see all of Scotland a lot more quickly than it would take to see all of California . . . and think of the Scottish weather . . . Brrrr! . . . don't think Ed, Dolly and Geo would rhapsodise about that!

Friday 12 March

The serious wind from upstate Arizona replaced the breeze in downstate California in the early hours and blew along the river and into and all around Ed, Dolly, Geo and us seniors. *One* of us seniors had picked up a cold or virus in New Mexico and *he* had been struggling to keep it under control for the past few days. Not with great success! His cough was making *him* fed up and *her* anxious as she remembered the pneumonias he'd succumbed to during recent Scottish winters – and always in March! At this point *he* was in denial that he was other than perfectly well and *she* knew perfectly well that *he* was not perfectly well. Whatever, the last thing he needed right now was a gale blowing into his lungs. So we left Needles to seek more acceptable weather conditions further west.

The Trailer Life Guide highly recommended Orange Grove Park in Bakersfield,[40] and we believed it – but for the last time! This private park invited guests to enjoy its large country-style vista with outstanding facilities like picking your very own oranges for breakfast from your very own orange trees which gave you privacy from your neighbours in your very own spacious spot. We had been in enough private RV parks by now to know that spacious meant just about enough room between vans in which to swing a cat. This one had that facility. It did not, however, have a country-style vista or many good looking oranges on our one scrawny orange tree. There were some sad looking shrunken ones at its base which had evidently dropped to the ground in disgust. True there was an orange grove at one end of this 300-site concrete park, with a rail track beside it and the inevitable train hooting its way noisily towards the already challenged oranges. The absolutely most maddening thing, apart from the unsubstantiated over-indulgent words about Orange Grove Park by *The Guide's* insane editor, was that the countryside during the last fifty miles of our journey, before this – this – this – *place,* had been absolutely stunning.

Shortly after leaving Needles, we saw groups of large wind machines on the Sacramento Mountains, most of them turning fairly fast in the prevailing wind. We then drove for about 150 miles across a dreary flat prairie plateau with little scenic excitement. Then suddenly we found ourselves climbing up and across a wonderful green land of hills and vales which was almost fictional in its verdant beauty. It looked like the pictures in a storybook where princes court princesses, then live happily ever after in a magic kingdom. There were orange groves by the dozens, and vineyards, and almond and cherry orchards to heighten the senses as we bowled along its pretty paths. To come down to this awful concreted earth made us very sad and, incredibly, we had to queue to get in! This Park was on a major west-coast route from southern California

---

[40] *Bakersfield–175,000*

to northern Washington and western Canada and used by snowbirds as they headed north and home. If you just want somewhere accessible to rest *en route* then this kind of park is ideal and this one had very good facilities along with cable TV (all 80 channels). But it was not the place for us, and would do little to help chase coughs and colds away. We scanned Bad Sam's book of lies, but could not find a spot back in that magical place which would accommodate our weary heads and sore hearts. We would move on tomorrow and hope to find that ideal spot. If not exactly ideal, it could be no worse . . .

Saturday 13 March

. . . but it was – in a very different way! At first, Oakwood Lake resort at Manteca,[41] round about the centre of California and fifty miles south of Sacramento,[42] did not seem too bad. For, despite its size, it was relatively quiet and the receptionist gave us the really isolated spot we requested close to the alleged lake. This man-made lake was an old quarry: no beauty spot and not the ideal retreat we craved. As we established earlier in the journal, being a private park, it had permanent residents. As it was not a school day there were dozens of residential children zooming around the entire park on their bikes, not limited to their own back yards. There were also dogs by the dozen, barking frenetically and leaving their calling cards for all to see. As you enter many private parks the residential part hits you and some of it not in great condition. If camp-site owners require regular rent to boost their living then it would be better for all if the permanent homes were quite separate from the places set aside for people out for recreation purposes. Oh, for some good State Parks where the maximum stay for *any* visitor is fourteen days. But the few in this part of California did not provide either water or electricity and, although Ed was fully equipped to allow us to 'go dry' (see Appendix 6), we were not convinced that the noise of the generator which was an integral part of 'dryness' would appeal to us – unless absolutely necessary. Perhaps absolutely necessary was *now*. We drove off in Geo to seek a nearby State Park to establish if the noise outcome of changing from a full-hook-up system to a no-hook-up system was a possibility. This proved a pointless exercise as

[41] *Manteca–41,000*
[42] *Sacramento–370,000*

we forgot to take the directions to the 'dry' park with us. Back at Oakland we settled down to total darkness and quietness – the children indoors and the dogs hoarse. But hark – *owls* were hooting somewhere near. This is not so bad! But would we see one?

At around 8.30 pm a dull thud hit Ed's coach door followed by another sharper one. On investigation, hoping not to find a hurt owl, we discovered a hurt Geo – his feelings, that is. Our wee pal was whitely visible, being completely parcelled up in yards and yards of white industrial toilet paper. Not physically damaged, but trussed up good and proper. We had not heard anything until the bangs on the door and *almost* admired the silent skill of the loo-paper-parcellers. It was the empty loo roll holders which had been thrown at the door. We decided it was a childish prank and, after freeing Geo from his tissue decorations with a few words of comfort and, unable to see anything or anyone in the inky darkness other than distant lit-up motor homes, we went indoors. There was another lot of scuffling noise a little later and some giggling. This no longer felt like either a childish prank or comfortable. The giggling continued and was augmented by some human owl-hooting. *He* went and sat in Geo, hoping that the security guard would come past in his van while *she* peered through Ed's curtained front windows. No security van came near, only a private car hurried past, ignoring the camp-ground speed limit. The office with security guard was a long way from our spot and we did not want to leave Ed or each other to get help. Eventually, scuffles, giggles and hooting stopped and we went to bed, not too relaxed, but not too worried.

We both woke early, upset by the night's events, and made preparations to leave Oakwood Lake Resort with its unfriendly environment as soon as possible. It was a great shock to find that eggs had been thrown at Ed's passenger door. When this happened, we did not know, but it completely changed a perceived prank into a threatening experience. It was not a nice feeling! We were both pretty angry as we confronted the park's managing director who, in the absence of the owners, dragged himself out of bed to listen to our complaint. *She* did most of the talking as the night air had not helped his cough much; besides *she* had plenty to say about slack management and lack of security as she shoved yards of unusable toilet tissue into the astonished young director's arms. She was vaguely aware of sounding like another Margaret (an English one!) as she demanded regally that someone clean the offending egg off the van – and soon! The park director (wishing it was his weekend off no doubt) kept apologising as he dealt with copious unravelling loo-rolls while trying to organise, via his mobile phone, the removal of Ed's uncooked omelette. Parrot-fashion, he kept repeating that nothing like this had ever happened before. So, why them? *she* countered – and went on about the disgrace that visitors from Scotland should be treated like this! Who-all knew of our nationality? Was this an anti-Scots attack? The director managed to get a word in as *she* drew breath and herself to her full height of five feet two inches – and the word he got in was – Georgia! It was much more likely, he declared, that we had been hassled (*hassled!*) because of the Georgian vehicle plates. Could the inhabitants of the deep-south still be regarded as the enemy by some other Americans?

We were not going to get into an inter-State argument, so drove off feeling dejected to Interstate 5. As we left the loo-roll remnants were being deposited in the garbage can, where they belonged. We began to wonder why we had come to California if the past two days were examples of its hospitality, whether to Scots or Georgians, it made no difference. This rich State, we reckoned, could learn some manners from poorer southern ones like Miss Sippy and its kindlier folk who had shown no inclination to offend us in any way. As we turned Ed northwards to a 'dry' State Park, we felt pretty low and just hoped that we would find the peace we needed to recover from ill feelings both physical and mental and have our faith restored in this great country – which right now was far from marvellous!

Sunday 14 March through Wednesday 17 March

. . . but a place called Corning proved it still can be! We arrived at Woodson Bridge State Park in rain, the first for weeks, and found it deserted. Ed took care of us nicely with the noise of his generator being a pleasanter one than those disquieting sounds of the night before. Large valley oaks throughout its acres gave a tranquil shaded comforting feeling to this park, despite the fact that in mid-March the trees were leafless. The bit of it we chose out of the forty-two well spaced out empty sites, was under one of these magnificent trees, looking out over a green square with many other oaks surrounding it. We heard woodpeckers and wrens, but the only birds to visit us that damp afternoon were scrub jays (larger birds than their varied cousins with dark blue overcoats and pale buff bellies with light blue and grey markings). They are so pretty to look at and so remarkably cheeky. No owls hooted that evening. It seemed ironic that the first place we should be really close to owls had been in that far-from-birding-paradise of Oakwood! But quite enough of *there*. Here was heaven and the sun shone brightly for the next two days as we absorbed all it had to offer and found our feet and voices again. Woodson Bridge State Park was a birding paradise – as long as we recognised that we would never identify *all* the species for whom it was home. We would have needed our own resident ornithologist for that. (Where is Bill Oddie when you most need him?) Those we knew we recorded and, better than that, we enjoyed them! Spotted towhees arrived when they heard the toaster go on, along with white-throated sparrows and, of course, the jays. Towhees are widespread across America and the ones living in California strongly resemble the eastern towhee with its rufous-coloured sides, black hood and back with white marking on the wings. As far as we could tell the main difference is that the spotted variety has more white bits. Three species of woodpecker were around: the red-bellied flicker, the ladder-back and, joy of joys, the acorn woodpecker. Well with all those magnificent oaks around, they would be daft not to consider this a great place to hang out! Acorn woodpeckers make holes in the bark of oaks in which they store their winter supply of acorns and then they carefully insert an acorn into

Woodson State Park, just us, the birds and the Valley Oaks

a hole, taking lots of time to make sure it fits exactly. If not then it will fit another hole. During the winter (quite warm in mid-California) they check the acorns to keep them secure, turning them around and sometimes moving shrinking acorns to more suitable holes. Fascinating! Presumably they eat some too! The oak trees at Woodson had pecker holes all over them. We also saw western flycatchers, hawks, phoebes, nuthatches and European starlings. The jays saw us prepare our meals and came right up to the door demanding sustenance. One time, when *he* went off to shower while *she* added another few pieces to the communal jigsaw, a rustling noise made her ask – 'Good shower?' No reply – but more rustling, 'Did you—' she repeated, looking up to see a jay in the kitchen area, head on one side contemplating a bag of potato chips, trying to work out the way in. She scolded him as he had scolded her earlier in the day, and for less reason. Mr Jay reluctantly took his leave.

The Sacramento river runs right through this State Park and is a large, fast flowing turbulent river which caused a slight unease as we stood in the comparative safety well above it. Warning notices tell you it is deep, cold and fast with strong currents and you'd better *not* fall in. It rose so high in December from rainfall and snow melting on the northern mountain tops that it burst its banks and flooded most of the park. The trees in a nearby orchard still had their roots in river mud. But a great blue heron, a smaller Louisiana one and a great egret fished its waters. We heard an owl one night, but didn't see it.

The small town of nearby Corning[43] is idyllic, with its neat streets, pretty buildings and friendly inhabitants – unless you upset an important inhabitant by cruising slowly along a parking area in your car in front of the one belonging to a local sheriff (armed) who sounds his siren (gently) behind you. What you do then is stop immediately in panic mode. 'And how are you folks doin' today?' was this ever-so-young sheriff's opening gambit. (It isn't only British policemen who look younger every year!) 'Doin' OK till you stopped us,' was the male driver's too-quick response. 'We are looking for a pharmacy, officer,' *she* broke in, 'my poor dear husband here is suffering from a nasty, nasty bug and we need something to make him better, and . . . em . . . we're from near Edinburgh, Scotland . . . and . . . em . . . your country is marvellous . . . and em . . . would you like my recipe for bannocks?' *She* didn't really say the bit about bannocks. After some charming chit-chat about many things, excluding bannocks, we were shown the pharmacy and parked ever-so-

---

[43] *Corning–6,000*

carefully outside it. Small town America is marvellous where on-street parking is so easy, and sheriffs give directions without shooting first.

Before *she* puts this lap-top to its bed on this March Wednesday evening in Woodson Park she feels she has something final and personal to record. *His* cough is now abating and with two lazy days of sun-tan he looks fit again. *Her* mental equilibrium is more even (for *her*, that is!) than it was two days ago . . . and we – well, we are back in each other's good books and don't talk about the lows behind us or the highs to come (but not *too* high *she* hopes) . . . And this country? Well, this country, including California, is marvellous. Tomorrow we meet up with Rich and Jan in Dixon,[44] a hundred miles away. From their home we will visit San Francisco. We will see the Pacific Ocean. We are having a great time.

[44] *Dixon–10,000*

A vociferous blue jay hoping for some left-overs

Thursday 18 March through Sunday 21 March

Sometimes in life you meet folks with whom you are immediately comfortable. You even wonder if a new friendship could develop and whether, if that happens, it will be a transitory thing or a life-long thing. It had been some weeks and some States since we had met Rich and Jan along with their kinsfolk Judy and Ron. This first meeting took place, you may recall, on a lovely day on Lake Ouachita, Arkansas. Now, we were about to meet Rich and Jan again, in their place this time and we were both excited about that, if a trifle nervous. Would we really get along for a few days rather than a few hours? They might soon wish they had ignored us on the boat and not extended this warm invitation to visit with them. We worried unnecessarily as it quickly became apparent to all four of us that the easy relationship begun on that lake was going to become something rather special. Rich and Jan's home has a marvellous family atmosphere where five children were brought up not so long ago, and where our hosts made us feel so special that we relaxed within minutes of meeting them again, quickly forgetting frustrations of travel and health. This pretty house is a veritable treasure trove of their amazing handicraft skills. Sadly,

Berryessa Lake, California, with its sink-hole to stop the water level getting too high

106

Jan was working that day but came home to greet us and produce a tasty lunch, after which Rich took us out in one of his restored cars to look at the dam on Lake Berryessa. The countryside we drove through was resplendent with orange, almond, walnut and olive groves as we climbed up to the lake. *He* and Rich were very interested in the dam, such a long way down, and its particularly unique over-flow system. Several photographs were taken. *She* took more of an interest when they got to the visitor centre and shop where a pretty mug, with the California Poppy painted on it, and some postcards were duly purchased, while *he* and Rich happily read *all* about the dam . . . again! Jan was busy in the kitchen when we returned home, and dinner that evening was superb and a great deal better than we ever managed in Ed. Our post-prandial conversation took up where we left off in Arkansas before we four retired for the night, happy in our renewed friendship.

The second day of our visit Rich took us into the Californian vineyards of the Napa Valley as Jan was busy at the office once more. It began to rain as we left Dixon and the waterworks did not abate until we returned there. However it did not dampen our spirits one bit and may even have helped our chilled palates to savour the grape better when it came to the tasting part of a winery tour. Although we are not great enthusiasts of the crushed and fermented grape, we learned quite a lot about wines and the making thereof. For folks who are quite lacking in knowledge when it comes to the best years for wines, we were pleased to learn that old wines are seldom good wines and that most wine on sale is ready to drink *now* and does not have to be stored in dusty cellars or kitchen wine racks. That evening we went out to a local eatery which Jan and Rich frequent occasionally. We had clam chowder, sour-dough bread and dinner salads (very large plates of mixed nutritious raw vegetables with nuts and seeds – all in the dressing of your choice) and . . . boy was it ever delicious! No room for desserts! Aw!!

Saturday 20 March, we went to San Francisco; not requiring flowers in our hair to make it memorable. (We use some words in this journal again and again like memorable and awesome. We make no apology for this as these particular words so succinctly describe our feelings as we travel across this land.) The first part of the day was spent in the Muir Woods National Monument named after a great Scot – John Muir. His monument here is a large beautiful forest of giant redwood trees that just go up and up and up. They are the tallest trees in the world, and grow absolutely straight. One of them in this park, a colossal tree 252 ft high and 14 ft in diameter, was already

Her and him posing under a giant redwood in the John Muir Park

a hundred years old in 1776 when the first thirteen American States came together to form the start of the United States of America. Some of these giant redwoods, found on other parts of the California coast, are more than a thousand years old and the largest recorded is 367.8 ft tall with a diameter of 22 ft and still growing! The giant sequoia, another species of redwood found inland in the Sierra Nevada of California, grows larger in diameter (40 ft – recorded) but is shorter (311 ft – recorded). One of *this* species has been discovered, aged 3,200 years old and still growing!

The Muir Woods were full of people on this beautiful warm March Saturday morning, most of them, like us, having photos taken under towering giant redwoods. There was a stillness and gentleness in the air which was pure magic. Generations of people had walked through this place and these trees, generations old, had made a canopy of quiet welcome above them. A wee burn played downstream as we walked alongside folks from many nations on paths of soft pine needles. It did not matter which mother tongue any of us spoke, we were all using similar words to compliment Mother Nature on her creations. The Grand Canyon, with its rugged size and ornate colours, took our breath away. This giant redwood forest, with trees of gentler size and gorgeous hues of red and green, did the same. We could not possibly say which one had impressed us most. Thankfully we don't have to. All we had to do was enjoy each of these wondrous spectacles while being grateful for the chance to see and love some of America's natural national treasures.

While millions of this earth's citizens do appreciate its natural treasures, a few want to destroy this particular one and turn its scarred remains into hard cash. Apparently, some unthinking people want to cut down these giant redwoods to make modern furniture from their tough flame-resistant wood. It is hard to conceive of such thoughtless disregard for one of nature's more remarkable and long-lived specimens. This irreparable criminal act would deprive countless numbers of thoughtful people of an exceptional experience, in order that a few privileged people might sit at redwood tables on redwood chairs. The protection of these red giants is surely a worthwhile aim, and we hoped, as we left the John Muir Park, that the more thoughtful folk of this great country would endeavour to be the custodians of this natural heritage, preserving it for all time and for all-comers.

Approaching San Francisco[45] from Muir Park is quite incredible – certainly the way we did it. The road was very, very, *very* hilly, winding through high forest with deep gorges on *her* side which made that occupant of the large roomy car, being skilfully driven round hairpin bends by Rich, talk nineteen to the dozen as she looked hard at the opposite bank. She gathered that the view on *her* side was particularly spectacular. Suddenly the bay on which San Francisco sits was there in front of us and, of course, the Pacific Ocean. *He* was ecstatic. *She* thought it looked pretty cool and looked forward to admiring it from lower down. Our hosts were enjoying our delighted reactions and determined that we should see this extraordinary city from every conceivable angle. The first view was as we came out from a tunnel in the hillside and saw the Golden Gate Bridge with San Francisco on the opposite headland. The

[45] *San Francisco–725,000*

109

The Golden Gate Bridge, San Franciso. A little bit like the Forth Road Bridge?

next one was from a hill above the bridge looking across the entrance to San Francisco Bay where ships were making their way to the Pacific Ocean. That was an amazing view and we gazed at the ocean for a loo–oong time. We then crossed the San Francisco Straits, called The Golden Gate – first called this, we understand, around the American gold rush era and long before the bridge was built. Those of us expecting the bridge to be golden in colour were, therefore, disappointed to find it the same dull oxide red as the Scottish Forth Rail Bridge! However, the city on the other side was a little more dramatic and picturesque than North Queensferry! Before we got there we had another spectacular view to absorb. This was the underside of the bridge from an old fort called the Presidio of San Francisco which had been carefully preserved when the bridge was built over and around it. There we had a real taste of the Pacific as its waves crashed on the rocks on which we stood. Just marvellous! From this vantage point we looked eastwards to the island of Alcatraz and its infamous prison, now closed, but a tourist attraction reached by boat.

It was now time to see San Francisco itself and Rich drove us into the town which, although we had known it was built on hills and used for film sets to good advantage, still surprised us by the dramatic steepness of its streets.

Rich showed them off with great adroitness and we climbed up and teetered on the edge of some, unable to see the down side of the road before beginning the descent into what seemed like thin air. The cable cars (trams to us), seen in many American movies, are basically used for tourist travel and have right of way. What a city San Francisco is! There could not be another like it and we were seeing it with experts who knew it well and loved it all. Our next stop was up another narrow street to the Coit Memorial Tower on Telegraph Hill where the city was spread out below us with bay, bridges and sea beyond. It was from here that we saw houses built into the hillsides and the high winding roads between and around them. So much had we to see that food had been forgotten and we hungrily ate at a fast food place in Fisherman's Wharf – a fun part of San Francisco which was packed with people having a good time. Our final view of this remarkable city was from a high spot called Twin Peaks and we watched the sun go down over the ocean and the city lights come on gradually, with other like-minded souls and with tears in our eyes.

We returned to Dixon by the Bay Bridge, tired but rejoicing in a most wonderful day having seen San Francisco for the first time. It will not be the last! Thank you, Jan and Rich, for your unstinting care to ensure our enjoyment of your city.

Sunday we-all relaxed, had Sunday breakfast out (an American custom we love!), then the menfolk did macho things with Ed who was greatly made up by Rich's automobile knowledge and attention. The womenfolk shopped and then one cooked while *one* wrote. Our last evening together was enriched by chat and promises that this special friendship, made on a boat on a lake in the east, would continue. Hopefully, the next leg will be in bonnie Scotland near another great city with hills.

Oregon and Washington

Monday 22 March through Thursday 25 March

Saying goodbye is never easy so we said '*au revoir*, see you soon' to Jan and Rich and left quickly for the very north of California and into Oregon. We reached dear old Corning by noon and, after failing to get a reply at the State Park we had chosen further north, and failing to get anyone in the Californian State Park system who knew anything about it, decided to remain in Corning, turning Ed in the familiar direction of Woodson Bridge State Park in the valley oak woods. It was absolutely deserted again.

It was in this peaceful atmosphere that we reviewed our American coast to coast journey and began, reluctantly, to consider the return leg back to Athens. (*So soon?*) We also recognised something which had gradually become fairly obvious – there was no way we could travel all of the distance originally planned and continue to enjoy more of the pleasures which the USA has to offer. New England, we concluded, would have to wait until another time . . . maybe with Ed? Was there any way we could keep part of the trio in Athens and have Scottish family and friends enjoy some of this marvellous country too? Not if we dealt in reality!! Boy, was it hard to realise that our future was unlikely to include any of our travel companions. The weather would determine which interstates and US highways we took through which of the States heading east in about ten days time, after our visits to Oregon, Washington and, possibly, British Columbia.

Our evening stroll was well timed before the rain came drizzling down, and before the immature bald eagle, sitting on a tree near the even-faster flowing Sacramento river, flew away. How incredible to see our third bald eagle so unexpectedly and while we were in sombre mood in need of a little cheering up. He was BIG and showed little inclination either to fish for his supper or to go home to bed. We watched him despite the increasing rain, reluctant to end this moment. Our first bald eagle had also been immature, living in the most south-easterly part of the US. Our second, an adult with brilliant white head feathers, had been in the centre of the States. This big baby was in the north-west of the country. Would we see more – and where? This majestic bird was thriving all over its vast land.

But not in Valley of the Rogue State Park situated on the Rogue River in south Oregon, quite a bit busier than Woodson Bridge, now 220 miles to our south, on this blowy March Tuesday. The journey here was adventurous to say the least, as we climbed through high green mountain passes only to descend again on 6% declines and up again, through even steeper passes and down again via longer declines. It was raining, which made driving less pleasant and spoiled the view of range after range of beautiful mountains encompassing the I-5, many of them snow capped. The highest is Mount Shasta at 14,000 feet and as we ate lunch it loomed over us in a moment of brilliant sunshine. For a while we drove across an almost treeless plateau where cows and horses grazed together in green pastures . Green fertile land is the dominant feature of Oregon and we could quite understand why it is described as having the most beautiful scenery in the USA. Along with the enveloping greenery a tremendous amount of spring blossom filled the landscape with masses of multicoloured flowers and rich perfume. The edges of the highways in both northern California and Oregon are lined with oleander bushes which at this time of year have their new growth complementing their evergreen leaves. Daffodils were just everywhere in Oregon but now past their best in northern California and long-gone in southern California. Amazing what a difference a few hundred miles can make – flora-wise.

We found the miles also made a difference to the late afternoon temperature and we went off to do our now customary 'spot the bird' within the welcome warmth of sweatshirts. As we arrived at this park we had noticed birding enthusiasts with glasses around necks and cameras in action, so we walked the way they had been along the Rogue River, hoping for a special sighting. Robins, juncos and jays were plentiful and then *he* spotted a Californian quail sitting on a nearby branch with his funny floppy crest bobbing at us. We got very close to this weird chap before Mrs Quail joined him for a few moments and began ushering him off the branch to get on with supper arrangements. As we returned to Ed and our own supper we met the birding enthusiasts who told us of the osprey they had seen sitting on a branch very close to where the quails had been, and consuming a large fish. There was a nesting place arranged on a tall pole near our site with the beginnings of a nest on it; would he/she add to the furnishings, we wondered, and watched the nest until it became too dark to see. No osprey was in building mood that day or the next morning as we left Rogue River. About a dozen quails were scurrying busily about with plumes a-flutter at the exit of the park.

The destination today, 25 March, was the small town of Corvallis[46] only 203 miles due north and in the agricultural Willamette valley, about three quarters way up the State of Oregon. The scenery was as splendid as yesterday's, only the heavy rain stopped us from seeing it properly. We were visiting Diana and Art who had kindly invited us to do so when we met them in Buckskin Mountain, southern Arizona. Their five-acre garden was a pretty sight for the eyes of us Scots who were missing the blooms of our early spring garden back home; especially the daffodils which nestled under the varied trees and shrubs of this delightful garden. Art and Diana welcomed us into their charming airy house with hot tea and insistence that we make ourselves at home there. After we had parked Ed and Co we walked round the garden with Art, its designer and cultivator, admiring with enthusiasm its content and lay-out. The Irish setters and elderly golden retriever ambled around with us – a reminder of our first meeting with Art and of what a large part animals can play in our lives.

Next day *she* had a day without *him* and *he* had some respite from *her.* Diana is a lady with many talents and some of her beautiful sculptured pottery was shown to advantage around her home. Another of her great pleasures is being an active member of the local American quilting society, whose volunteers make quilts for children who are either affected by circumstances which take them away from their natural parents for a while, or who have other special needs. Each child is given their very own quilt so that they might be comforted by the wrap-around warmth of something special just for them. The quilters' work is quite wonderful, in the uniqueness of their giving, the quality of the quilts and the happiness that quilting for the benefit of others brings to them. Diana both makes quilts and is the main fund-raiser for this group. She was taking two of her colleagues to a quilting exhibition in Portland,[47] eighty miles north of Corvallis, and had invited her guest to join them. The guest was thrilled! It was a marvellous day of chat and getting to know some of the people involved in quilting for pleasure and quilting for exhibiting. *She* learned a lot about colour, major design names and technique and forgot most of it as she wandered round the exhibits, stunned by the ability of the quilters and the beauty of their colourful exquisitely designed handicraft. This was the second time she had been privileged to view quilting

---

[46] *Corvallis–45,000*
[47] *Portland–440,000*

and she fondly remembered Essie Buck back in Mississippi and her '*Two by Two*' quilt. Just as on that occasion, *she* wished that she could whisk a few quilts from their hanging places to take back home. Even more she wished *she* could quilt!

He had gone with Art to another high place – the deep Columbia River gorge with stunning waterfalls – and enjoyed the whole experience without *her* anxieties, while Art did the driving and the tour guide thing. We would spend more time with Diana and Art after the next stage of our travels north.

Friday 26 March through Sunday 28 March

We made the State of Washington today after driving through the Oregon city of Portland, much of it sprawling over and by the Columbia River. It was hard to make out the city's docks beneath the high bridge spanning the river because of the driving rain. This bleak wet outlook made us so fed up that we stopped earlier than intended at a wooded State Park in the small town of Battle Ground;[48] so called because of a battle between an Indian tribe and some settlers which never took place. Seem reasonable? The ground was sodden, the trees were dripping wet and the lake well below our camp-site looked particularly wet and cold. We felt sorry for the tenters battling in the elements to control their canvas homes and were ever-so-glad we had Ed with his furnace.

The rain which had pattered down on the roof all night had cleared a bit on Saturday morning so we moved out of these gloomy wet woods into another lot! But at least we had reached yesterday's proposed destination today! It was the little town of Castle Rock,[49] made famous almost twenty years ago when the volcanic Mount St Helens erupted, spectacularly blowing the top off its head, all 1,500 ft of it, moving an entire lake to another area and changing the landscape around it completely. Those of us who saw this disaster on our TV screens on 18 May 1980 will remember the horrific scenes as lava descended on a community, changing their lives for ever. Nowadays, Mount St Helens is a National Monument and the visitor centre at Castle Rock tells the story explicitly by film and pictorially in a small

---

[48] *Battle Ground–3,800*
[49] *Castle Rock–2,000*

museum which also houses bits of volcanic rock and other artifacts from this time. A seismograph records the fact that Mount St Helen is still a live volcanic mountain and this week alone, seven shocks have been recorded. Mmmm! As the geographers amongst us know, cities like Los Angeles and San Francisco also lie on this geological fault along the American west coast where earthquakes occur, creating havoc and leaving a trail of disaster. One lady we spoke to in a gift shop which sold, amongst other things, ornaments made of volcanic ash, told us how she felt on seeing her home landscape so changed by the eruption that she didn't recognise it. Tears were not too far away as she explained how bereft everyone living there felt in May 1980 – and still do. In fact many residents, who just could not cope with the after-math of the volcano's scenic changes and the all-pervading volcanic dust, moved away to live elsewhere. Because of the misty rain we could not see the now flatter, lop-sided top of Mount St Helens with its new peak of solidifying lava rising out of its centre. We decided not to drive the 37 miles to near its summit as the visitor centre with viewing facilities there was closed due to adverse weather conditions. We were not surprised!

It rained through Saturday evening as the screech owls screeched in the tall redwoods, but remained out of sight in their high branches. We went to bed early to get under the covers from the drumming water and also in order to be fully alert next day, and not appear *Sleepless in Seattle!* – tomorrow's destination. It dried up a bit around breakfast and we hitched our trio together and set off for the city. The air was as cold, misty and damp as any March day in Scotland, and still we could not see the top of Mount St Helens as we left the National Park. There was snow on the mountain range to the west, seen through a short-lived gap in the clouds as we rejoined interstate-5 once more. It was not long before the bleak misty rain returned. Bits of the 106 mile journey to Seattle were very reminiscent of Scotland, apart from the billboards advertising **Sam's Eagle Casino . . . Open all day and night – for *your* delight!** We gave the casino a miss. We were surprised to find that Washington State had gaming houses – not sure why. We were also surprised to see George Washington's sillhouette on every State road sign – other States usually have their State map outline on road signs. Somehow it seemed disrespectful to use the profile of America's first president in this manner. But what would we know?

Our proposed camp site was a private one, as none of the State Parks in this area are open before mid April. We hoped it would not be too—ooo bad. It was worse than bad – it was dreadful! Situated on an industrial park, the owners had herded the happy campers in like cattle awaiting the slaughter-house truck. Our next-door neighbours were within touching distance had we felt inclined to lean out and do so. They were in the fortunate position of having our waste disposal pipe by their doorstep. We did not have one next to our doorstep, having obtained a site at the end of a row. We were, however, next to the much-used restrooms which made our lunch seem a little less appetising. Geo took us to Seattle,[50] a city we have been eager to see since we first started to watch the American sit-com *Frazier* some years ago. At first sight the Seattle skyline was impressive as we approached but not, however, the much-made-of *space needle,* so called because of its architectural appearance, the tower with sight-seeing facilities. The needle had seemed huge in the opening credits of *Frazier* but turned out to be quite small and ordinary when viewed next to the Seattle skyscrapers. *He* felt quite cheated and decided not to go up. *She* had never intended going up anyway. They both felt that the opening of *Frazier* would never have the same appeal again. We drove along the cold windswept quay-side and saw the ferry to Victoria, Vancouver Island, British Columbia. We drove through city streets, very like city streets anywhere, only this one did not believe in city road signs to help its tourists along. We came across a Sunday market by chance, and the Chinese Quarter, which we had been told was attractive – and wasn't – by perseverance. What was wrong with us? Well, we were discovering, yet again, that most cities anywhere are just anywhere cities, with the exception of one or two which have totally unique qualities like Santa Fe, San Francisco and Edinburgh. (A wee sad homesick sniffle, here.) We also finally admitted that American cities were not 'what floated our boat' whereas small town America did – with sails on. However, talking about floating, we did come across some of Seattle's famous house-boats, but did not recognise the one on which gorgeous Tom Hanks was *'Sleepless'*!

We returned to camp dreadful, reunited Geo with his travel companions, and left. It was only 2.30 pm, Seattle had been a big disappointment and it was way too early to spend the rest of the day too close to people we did not know, and definitely too close for comfort to people requiring the comforts of

[50] *Seattle–516,000*

restrooms. We had paid $28 for parking the rig for five hours. It was damp and too cold to spend the rest of the day trying to find other places to visit around Seattle. If Washington was awash with water, it could be even wetter and colder further north. March was clearly not the best month to visit this wet State or, indeed, Vancouver, British Columbia, either. We headed back south through rain which quickly became torrential once more. Interestingly, the city of Seattle is renowned for its high rainfall; it was the only place which did not rain over us in Washington!

Back beneath Mount St Helens, in the now extremely wet National Park, we reviewed the past nine weeks of our American journey over a bowl of hot soup and recognised that we had begun our journey back east. We had come a long way, 6,027 miles, since we left Athens, Georgia. As we sat supping soup in Washington, we were diametrically opposite Florida, the warm dry State where we welcomed in 1999: States diametrically opposed both weather-wise and map-wise. If a bit of rain is the worst thing we have to record today (other than camp dreadful) then we have been lucky indeed. Lucky to have been able to make a coast-to-coast journey like this in our senior years. Lucky in the people we have met and the friends we have made. Lucky in the things we have seen; some of them wondrous indeed. We need to keep luck with us as we look forward to another two months on the highways of America. This country, coast-to-coast, is marvellous!

At this point *he* went to offer assistance to a young couple who had come into a site close-by and who were obviously struggling with the newness of RV-ing. We experienced motor-home travellers should give of our expertise when necessary, *she* felt as she encouraged *him* out into the rain. *He* was gone a while. 'Did you have to help a lot?' *she* enquired on his return. 'No, talk a lot,' *he* replied. It turned out that the female of the duo came from Birmingham (England, not Alabama); the male from Edinburgh (Scotland, not Indiana). Small world! Marvellous world!

Monday 29 March

The screech owls screeching and the rain raining wakened us quite early and we considered the options of the day ahead over the warming cuppa. If the rain lessened, we decided we would drive eighty miles to a wild-life reserve/ safari park where native American animals roamed fairly freely. As we had only seen five American species roaming absolutely freely (one red fox, two racoons, several chipmunks, a few tree-squirrels and one or two ground squirrels) we thought a day admiring them would be a day well spent. The rain did not lessen, it increased, so we went for option two – returning to the garden in Corvallis. We prepared to leave and a chipmunk and two stellar jays came to say goodbye, enjoying the remains of a delicious twelve-grain loaf. Stellar jays, close cousins to blue and pinon jays, are also crested but are a darker blue with black and no white. They are gorgeous, but noisy. If we felt rained out, we wondered how the overnight tenters had fared. All had gone, we discovered, and faint wisps of damp smoke from the individual camp fires were the only evidence of their ever having been there. We also discovered that bits of pine trees had come down in the night and that a wind was blowing hard.

That rain just kept increasing in severity and the wind turned quite gusty as we drove back down the I-5 being sprayed at by all the fast-moving trucks. Part of the journey was close to the very swollen Columbia River which rushed turbulently north. It was not a journey to enjoy. Diana and Art's garden was indeed a welcome sight and the rain, if not totally turned off, was just a mere trickle compared to that in Washington State. It came on quite hard during the evening, however, but Art announced enthusiastically, after checking with the Internet, that we were to expect only an 80% chance of showers the next day. Somehow this did not strike us as a wonderfully great percentage of improvement.

Tuesday 30 March through Wednesday 31 March

. . . and it still seemed poor odds as we breakfasted to a pitter-patter we were becoming accustomed too. Isn't it a good day to give Ed his well-deserved oil-change *he* enquired of a gloomy partner. *She* muttered something about well-deserved climate change, but agreed. *She* got to do the laundry in the nice warm house and send some e's while *he* and Ed went to town – Huh! Mind you, she also got to spend time observing the many birds who came to the verandah feeders or just flew about in the lovely (if somewhat sodden) garden. Watching the hummers come for their sugar water took up a good deal of time. Rufous-sided humming birds, to address them more formally, are tiny hummers at 3.5 inches maximum. The male's upper parts are bright red-brown, his tail and throat flaming orange. These bright colours sparkle vividly as they feed. The female is a lot less showy but very pretty with her greener colours and speckled rufousy bits. At one point when the 80% rain opportunity had eased off a little, she sat with hot mug in hands on one part of the verandah to see the bird-life at closer range. A sudden whirring noise made her jump a bit as a male and a female hummer arrived to feed just two feet away. The humming noise of their wings is pretty startling at close quarters for creatures little bigger than a butterfly.

The Oregon coast is one of *the* most spectacular coasts in the world, our host enthused. Fortunately for us, Art was much better at geography than weather forecasting. It is indeed a stunning place, we discovered on 31 March, with the vistas around this part of the mighty Pacific Ocean ranging from rugged rock faces with high pounding waves through enormous sand-dunes to long quiet golden beaches. The journey from Corvallis was a most beautiful one through the deepest of green hills and dales. Oregon could rival Arizona as our most favourite State if only the rain would go away – and it did – quite suddenly. Once we had traversed the passes across the coastal mountain ranges the sun was shining on the wet green landscape making it return the compliment. Once we had established our place in another completely empty wooded State Park we set off to view the ocean from a high rugged point with a spectacular overlook to the crashing waves below. Quite breathtaking, but also quite sobering, this cruel-looking sea. Waves could reach twenty-five feet here, we were told. That day they rose to nearer fifteen feet and were still amazingly big to us. We were distracted by a barking noise and looked to the rocks and beach below for a dog or two. No dogs were daft enough to be exercising there. This loud continuous barking came from a rocky sandy islet about a quarter of a mile out to sea and appeared to be coming from huge jutting rocks in the middle of the cove which on closer binoculared inspection turned out to be very large sea-lions: sea lions who barked for the sheer enjoyment of being alive on this Pacific coast; or sea lions who barked because it was *that* time of year when Mother Nature gives them a procreative nudge. As we became accustomed to their size and shape we made out more and more large animals. Some were sporting in the waves, some were lying on their backs with faces and flippers sun-wards, others were just sitting in conventional groups barking. We watched them for what seemed like hours until a red-billed water bird fishing just below us with a blue heron for company, caught our attention. This unlikely creature had flesh-pink legs and feet, large black body and well-shaped head with eyes rimmed in the same startling red colour as its long laterally flattened bill. What could it be? There was something familiar about it and we felt that we *should* recognise this stockily built coast bird. The near-by State Park information board told us it was an American oyster-catcher and as soon as we read this we knew why it had seemed familiar. The oyster-catcher we know rather better is smaller and sleeker than this seventeen-inch cousin and has a fair amount of white feathering. The now familiar blue heron fishing in a pool beside the oyster-catcher got scant attention from us.

Thursday 1 April

... and we were completely April-fooled by finding bright sunshine wakening us for the first time in Oregon! Wonderful! We moved on, northwards this time along a very scenic part of the Oregon coast and after following the ocean on roads both high above it and along its pretty golden beaches we came to a State Park with secluded sites right on the beach. At last we were truly on the west coast of America, and we loved it. It was just over two months since we had stood looking at the Atlantic ocean with Connie and Leon on the American east coast at Charleston, South Carolina. What a lot of water we had seen flowing under bridges since then! What an amazing experience. We spent the remainder of that day pottering about and walking along the sands well wrapped up; for, although there was no rain, the April ocean breezes were somewhat brisk! The sound of the mighty Pacific waves breaking over the beach was our background music. It lulled us to sleep and it wakened us gently in the morning. This country from east coast to west coast is marvellous.

Friday 2 April through Sunday 4 April

We might have stayed a little longer, but it was Easter weekend and this ocean State Park was fully booked and filling quickly with holiday-makers by the time we were ready to say our goodbyes to this little haven on the Pacific coast. We might not see this ocean lapping on the North American continent for some years, if ever again, so we felt a bit sad and nostalgic. *She* tried to cheer them up by saying it was not *that* much different to *any* other bit of coastline and they *did* enjoy their walks with Harris-dog along their local beach in east coast Scotland. But we both recognised that the Forth estuary of the North Sea with the Fife coastline so near was not quite in the same category as the Pacific ocean with no coastline as far as the eye could see. And yet, it's all part of nature's bounty, and it's all pretty fantastic wherever the coastline.

Talking of coastlines – nine lighthouses adorn the Oregon Coast, most of them established in the nineteenth century and standing high on the cliffs above the ocean. These sentinels are now all automated, but many of them are open to visitors. We had a look at Yaquina Bay lighthouse from the outside; sadly it was not open to week-day visitors before May.

Back at Corvallis the sun was still shining and it was warmer and more sheltered than on the coast. No-one was home so we parked the trio and got out the garden chairs. No sooner had our bottoms hit plastic than the sun went in and stayed in for the rest of our visit to that dear small American town. Corvallis has kept its old-world values of yesteryear, not moving on dramatically as many towns have nationally and internationally, and we liked it very much, apart from its affinity to water! So, Cottonwood, Corning, Corvallis – all three beginning with 'C' and all three the most 'C'aptivating small towns of America – so far!!

Art assured us it was normally a drier area with only 36 inches of rainfall per year . . . pity they all came within ten days! But our host will never forgive us if we don't add the following climatic postscript: every twenty years this very green and pleasant Oregon valley has an on-going rainy season from January through April and guess what? That's right: the last one just happened to be *exactly* twenty years ago!!! Funny…huh? Come on, Art, April Fool's was yesterday! However this wet tale was told again and again by shop-keepers as we spent a more expensive afternoon than planned in local stores, rather than in the sun-worshipping our bodies coveted. The Carrie tans, acquired in hotter southern climes, were fast disappearing and the wrinkles, disguised more tolerably under a neat brown colour, were fast reappearing on pale faces. (*One* of us would like to point out here that *she* should speak for herself!) Hmmm!

Before we found the Uniquely Oregon Store selling exquisite wood carvings in nearby Philomath[51] and became bankrupt, we went to find one of Oregon's

---

[51]*Philomath–3,000*

covered bridges.[52] This one, called the Harris Bridge, was built in the very unique year of 1936 when the apparently more wrinkled one of us came into the world! The Harris family still live there in a very attractive wood-green painted house beside it, and have gifted the bridge to the State. The afore-mentioned wood carving store and workshop was quite close by, and two young, talented, male members of the family who owned the business and produced many of the goods on display, explained that the carvings were all made of durable Oregon myrtlewood. This evergreen tree, a member of the laurel family, grows uncultivated only in a small area along the Oregon coast. We spent a long time choosing some goodies to take home and *he* spotted a lovely painting on carved myrtlewood of the Harris Bridge. Well, to cut a long story short, both the year and the name of the bridge (we are quite fond of a flat-coat retriever back home with that name) seemed to be telling *her* to part with more dollars. If *he* was less enthusiatic about the disappearing dollars, he was equally enthusiastic about the beautiful art work. Besides as *she* pointed out, it would make a marvellous gift for her birthday in five days time (hoping that *he* had already made purchases for that historic event!).

Saturday and Sunday were spent with Diana and Art. Once more, we knew we had forged a friendship that would last and grow with the years. It was also good to be with friends as we prepared to head back east, in the knowledge that the first exciting leg of our travels was over and, although we had so much still to do and see, we were aware that some of the excitement had inevitably gone as the coast-to-coast-thing had been completed. There can be no better time than this to say thank you to Diana and Art and to the many other wonderfully warm American people who made this half of the trip so special. Thanks, guys!

Monday 5 April through Tuesday 6 April

Art and Diana left for work before we left for pastures new, thus giving us time to bid a private fond farewell to the hummers, the pine siskins, the jays, the finches, the doves and all the other birds fortunate to live among the

---

[52] *There are hundreds of covered bridges in many of America's States, some of them, like the fifty-three in New Hampshire, dating from the nineteenth century. These wooden bridges tend to span small creeks, some long dried up. Indiana reckons it has the most and holds an annual Covered Bridge Festival every October.*

Geo and him *at the Harris Covered Bridge near Corvallis, Oregon*

Douglas firs, flowering cherries and numerous other trees, shrubs and plants which made this garden such a wonderful retreat. It was raining a little, so no surprises there, but the greenness and tranquility of it all, which had reminded us so strongly of another house and garden way to the east over that big pond, delighted our Scottish senses. We were now relaxed and ready to assimilate whatever fate had in store for us both on the trail east – at least that is how we persuaded ourselves we were feeling. It was surprisingly hard to turn the rig in an easterly direction and recover that pioneering spirit we were both enveloped in a few short weeks ago.

Geographically speaking we actually went north first for 85 miles back towards Portland on the Washington State border, picking up the I-84 which would take us all the way to Utah. This led us alongside a much more tranquil Columbia river than the one we had travelled along so recently, and would follow part of the famous Oregon Trail taken by pioneer settlers from Kansas 160 years ago, if in the opposite direction (see Oregon Trail appendix). The first hundred miles of this part of our journey was through the Columbia River gorge where waterfalls tumbled into the river from the high mountains above: quite spectacular. It was this gorge that Art and *he* had explored the previous week. The sun came out as we settled for one night in a camping park in a tiny hamlet called Maryhill, which bears as much resemblance to the Maryhill estate in Glasgow as the Forth Estuary does to the Pacific. To get to it, we had to cross the Columbia river over a half-mile bridge. Halfway across it we were welcomed into the State of Washington – again, but rain-free this time! The camping grounds were in a lovely parkland area full of history (which is recounted in the Trail appendix), made more interesting because we looked across the river back into Oregon.

Next morning we were up with the crows to get some serious miles in which would take us to the eastern edge of Oregon and the western edge of Idaho. As we recrossed the bridge back into Oregon we had a superb view of snow-capped Mount Hood. At 11,239 ft, it is the highest mountain in Oregon and one we had failed to catch a glimpse of through the persistent clouds as we moved around the north of this State. The scenery changed once we had left the Columbia river behind and climbed gradually up to 4,100 ft in warm sunshine. Oregon was trying hard now to be remembered by us as the Western Sunshine State! No way! This area was treeless and, although the geography of this part of the State is described as more arid, plentiful crops grew in this plain; well irrigated certainly, as rows of gi-normously long irrigators testified.

That evening we camped by the calm twisty Snake River at a place called Farewell Bend where thousands of settlers had arrived tired and exhausted after travelling 1,600 miles from Kansas to their promised land now known as Oregon. They still had another 400 miles more to travel to the verdant Willamette valley we had so recently left behind. Wonder if it was raining when they got there? However, history records that it was *not* raining when the first emigrant wagon train arrived in 1842, as it was the fall and drier (allegedly). Our pioneering spirit had returned with the sun as we sat at Farewell Bend, so called because the settlers had to leave this river, with its life-saving water, at this point to head across the hills to the Columbia River for the last part of their long trek. Once again our view across a river was of another State; Idaho this time. This made the fifth time that we had camped on a river in one State looking across it to another State. Pretty clever of us you may think, until you suss out that rivers often form the boundaries between the American States. As we made supper that night in our well-equipped, fully loaded Ed, getting our water from an indoor tap, using the micro-wave and gas stove to cook food from the freezer, pouring milk from a carton in the 'frig, we paused to wonder how the Kansas settlers had managed with so little other than their determination, in tiny wagons not built for either warmth or comfort. What, we also wondered, would they have made of our Ed, or of the couple in a very prestigious motor-home fifty yards away struggling with their essential satellite dish which would bring them some evening entertainment – a film about pioneer settlers, perhaps!

Certainly, no settler would have had our earlier experience of switching time zones two times in as many minutes. For, as we reached Farewell Bend at 2.10 pm, Pacific Time, we were advised that we were now entering Mountain Time. *One* of us put *her* watch forward an hour. At this point, we left the interstate, doing a U-turn on to the minor road leading to the State Park which ran parallel to the interstate. At 3.12 pm Mountain Time, we were advised that we were now entering Pacific Time. *She* put her watch back an hour. Later in the afternoon, still in Pacific Time, we were in the sleepy little town of Huntington[53] five miles north at 4.40 pm, and found the clock at the country store declaring it was twenty minutes to four. Had we somehow missed a time change to some unrecorded zone west of Pacific Time? NO!! The proprietor had not yet got around to moving his store clock forward an hour to Daylight Saving Time (good old British Summer Time). Confused? We sure were! The storekeeper commented, 'We don't bother much about clock-time, we just go by when the sun comes up and the sun goes down.' Pretty much how those early settlers lived. As our sun went down, back in Carrie-time, we couldn't help thinking about the first Oregon Trail pilgrimage, and imagining their little wagons, of which two are preserved on this Park, coming around the Idaho hills long ago on the tracks still marked by wooden wheels. In this isolated place, you could feel the history, and see the people and the wagons splashing into and across the river – not so terribly long ago.

It did not seem so terribly long ago either, *she* considered, since the year of her birth. 1936 – a good year, but it made her an impossible sixty-three tomorrow. Didn't feel right at all! She went to sleep wishing the last two digits of the year of her birth and her actual age could be switched so that born in '63, she would be a mere 36 – cool! That meant *she* could do this trip with *him* in Ed again and again, except that Ed would just be a spark-plug in '63, and *he* would still be the junior senior. But, interestingly, son Mark would be thirty-six soon and he was born in '63. What a weird coincidence!!! Trouble was, this late-night thought made her feel *very* senior now!

[53] *Huntingdon–500*

Wednesday 7 April

He agreed, over breakfast, that it was an odd coincidence about the *her* and Mark 63-36 thing and then pointed out, in youthful disdain, that *he* would be ninety-three before he had *his* year reversal thing. *He* should live that long! However, she couldn't be nasty as his gift to her was a silver and enamel ruby-throated humming bird swinging on a long silver chain. Perfect! Another enormous parcel revealed one of Jan's gorgeous hand-made and exquisitely dressed bunnies *he'd* purchased from her before leaving Dixon, and it was wrapped in Jan's gift – a beautifully quilted Christmas tree skirt which she had admired above all of Jan's handiwork. This gift, with the hummer and rabbit, made *her* day, and the tree-skirt would make our future Christmases extra-special. So she brought *his* sixtieth forward a few weeks, giving him the special gift she had purchased from Rich and something *he* had admired inordinately the first time he saw this beautifully hand-crafted pen and pencil set, made of chocolate coloured cocobola wood. We sat surrounded by gifts and memories of new friends and years gone by. This was a good day and the sun was shining. Were we still in Oregon? To have a long leisurely day in this

A lovingly restored wagon once used by folks as they travelled the Oregon trail

sunny historic landscape of Farewell Bend seemed a good plan and with the sun hotter than it had been for a few weeks, we relaxed in shorts and T shirts looking over the Snake River to Idaho – tomorrow's State. We could also turn our chairs round and watch some of the happenings of a western cattle ranch, situated behind the camp-ground, where ranchers worked on horseback: something we had previously seen only at the movies.

She relaxed in the sun's warmth a trifle too long as by late afternoon *her* wrinkles were well disguised by flaming red colour. Yes *again* – you'd think by the time she got to her age (*really* old now) she'd know better. *Him* – you ask? Yes, *his* less remarkable wrinkles were now covered by golden brown.

Most State parks throughout America have volunteer camp hosts, and at most parks we managed to have a blether with them. Today was no exception. Somehow the birthday got a mention, and to our surprise and delight Mrs Camp Host came by at supper time with some home-made birthday cake, and it was just delicious. Yet again we felt embraced by the unexpected warmth of the American people we met.

Earlier in the day we had had a chat with the Park Ranger who invited us to become camp hosts at Farewell Bend during August and September as this slot in their calendar was still to be filled. The thought of camping free for two months in this beautiful place was an attractive proposition until we realised that there might be work involved with being camp hosts. *He* did not fancy taking on any camping deliquents, *she* could not imagine being pleasant to everyone, or having to bake birthday bannocks in the August heat

We sat at dusk overlooking the Snake River for the last time (Pacific Time) in Oregon across to Idaho (Mountain Time) and wondered what our next stop would bring. We went to bed prepared for the morrow, sensibly putting our watches forward to Mountain Time from Pacific Time in Daylight Saving Time. Still with us?

Idaho, Utah and Wyoming

Thursday 8 April through Saturday 10 April

. . . good. So we were up and away from Farewell Bend at around 8.30 am by our watches, while campers had another hour or so in bed. And it was *raining*. Oregon couldn't let us go without a few tears. Or were the tears ours, as we left the Snake River for a while? Although we had seen some of the foothills of Idaho across the river, it was to be twenty-five miles by road (I-84 still) before we received the official State welcome. The rain in the potato-growing plain of Idaho did not seem very different to that of Oregon and to begin with the State itself not particularly enthralling, scenery-wise. Potato growing and foul-smelling sugar refining were the basic industries of this bit of Idaho. But it did get better. The rain stopped and the views improved with mountain ranges to east and west of us – all icing sugar coated (very refined, of course!). We stopped at Boise[54], the capital city of Idaho, for two reasons: to see it and to have a brunch at the first Cracker Barrel since Phoenix, Arizona. Cracker Barrel stores are like red cardinals, definitely an east coast attraction. We could now exchange our three-week old talking book and get back into the realms of fantasy as we drove along. The scenery and weather really improved when we got back in touch with the Snake River again and we could scarcely believe the serious weather warnings issued for some parts to the south and west of us. Severe gales and snow were likely to disrupt our eastward travel according the *USA Today* weather-man.

The Three Island Crossing State Park at Glenns Ferry[55] was very much still on the Oregon Trail and again the ruts of old wagons were evident on the hillsides as we overlooked the Snake River once more – but not back to Oregon, or forward to Utah, but to another part of Idaho. (Can't always get it spot on!) As you can tell from the appendix, this pioneering story made an enormous impact on us as it does on the present-day inhabitants living along it today. Glenns Ferry is another tiny hamlet and its inhabitants are very proud to live in this historic place. They re-enact the pioneers' story on a special August

---

[54] *Boise–126,000*
[55] *Glenns Ferry–1,300*

day each year and do it by the book. The rain increased its downward volume during the evening. A very wet end to the day.

We were wakened shortly after 4.00 am by a howling gale. We managed to ignore the strengthening gusts until about six when we felt (*one* of us, at least) that the *other* should inspect and murmur comforting words to Ed, Geo and Dolly. They were all intact and grateful for *his* caring commitment, in the face of the now quite upsetting, gale force, wind. We drank our tea unhurriedly, huddled under the covers knowing that we would probably have to stay put in Glenns Ferry until the wind abated. A forty-foot rig like ours would be hard to steer in these conditions, especially as the I-84 would be ascending most of the way to the Utah border. What worried us even more was whether or not we were on that predicted snowfall line. We did not have snow chains. There were four other sets of campers on the park; two of them left as we ate breakfast. They obviously had no worries: had snow chains, or were headed west! Some phone-calls were made confirming that our almost-made decision to stay put was a sensible one. The ranger at our proposed Utah campsite said that they had three inches of the white stuff and it was still falling. The Utah road-report advised that snow was falling all over the State and although roads were open they were 'slick' and to take care. We decided that the best way to do that would be to stay in relative safety and hope the wind abated and the snow stayed away. Fortunately both of these wishes went our way and we spent a pleasant morning indoors with Ed's central heating keeping us cosy!

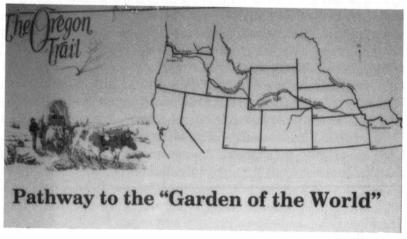

Quite a way to travel in an old covered wagon . . . thank goodness we had Ed

Another set of campers left at lunch-time and then there were two. Felt as if we were in the midst of an Agatha Christie novel! By mid-afternoon the wind was calm enough to allow us to visit the village of Glenns Ferry and its tiny library where we were allowed to send some e's. It was there we learned that the I-84 to Utah had been closed since mid-morning owing to blowing snow giving zero visibility. There had also been a spate of accidents and many vehicles were stuck. We knew that at least one set of overnight campers went that way and hoped they had made it OK.

At this point we had no idea whether or not the roads to Utah would be open the next day. We knew that the current low 40°F temperature would rise to a mid-50°F in Idaho. But Utah? We were now victims of that severe American weather we had worried about from armchairs – and we were coping brilliantly. This country is fascinating!

Fascinating is how *he* would describe the half hour spent stuck at the Glenns Ferry level crossing while an engine chuntered leisurely over the crossing back and forward, back and forward, and back and forward yet again, as it collected together its looo-ooong train of freight wagons! *He* counted to 103 wagons being hauled by three engines when eventually the engineer had his flock assembled and set off along his version of the Oregon Trail-way! *She,* on the other hand was distinctly un-fascinated by the whole looo-ooong operation.

We would not have objected to spending another day or two in Glenns Ferry had it not been for another small factor to add to our delay dilemma. Apparently the town water pump had failed a few days ago, allowing the water pressure to fall and some of the Snake River into the water system. At first boiling all water had been enough to keep health officials happy, but river mud had now got into the settling chamber (whatever that is!). All water had now been turned off and was being trucked in to town but not to the camp. Our white water tank was full of the healthy Oregon liquid when we went round its last bend; it would last until the next day – if we were careful! Makes you think about the Pioneers again though, doesn't it! The water from this river was their *main* means of healthy living. Pollution was not a word found in their vocabulary. The water from this same river in April 160 years on is a health hazard, with pollution being a common word we 1999-ers hear vocalised only too often. So if the road east is still closed tomorrow, and water still in short supply, we might well be returning west, saying 'hello' again to Oregon back there in good-old Pacific Time!

The good news this Saturday morning was that the I-84 was open and snow-free as was the Willard Bay State Park fifty miles north of Salt Lake City, Utah (Utaw!). We were about to cross another border and enter our sixteenth State since leaving home (thirteen on the road) and would be very glad to be parked on a bay of the enormous Great Salt Lake, with a worrying journey behind us. Our first thoughts that morning, on seeing the snow piled up at the sides of the mountainous I-84 along with some of the unmoved accident debris, was to be thankful that we had not attempted this journey yesterday. Today's travel of 220 miles, though not hazardous, was full of ups and downs and not just hilly ones. The road may have been snow-free, but it was not road-work free and we sat for ever in a long vehicular queue, made worse by the increased volume of weather-affected traffic. The road construction was fifteen miles long – which we never got to see. After taking an hour to do two miles and, with the sign ahead telling us that the beginning of the road works was still five miles away, we decided to follow some trucks which exited at a small road junction. At first we thought we had made an awful mistake, for much of this small road was not yet completely snow-free and we drove for some miles over rutted slush and ice, trying to keep the faster, more shock absorbent trucks in our sights. We hoped they were not all making deliveries in the area but taking a route that would eventually lead back to the I-84 east. Fortunately, that proved to be the case as we rejoined the interstate behind one of the slower east-bound trucks and thankfully east of the actual road works. East suddenly sounded good! Now on the almost empty carriageways of the road to Utah and with our insides returned to a less-shaken state, we congratulated ourselves on a bit of clever thinking and a lot of nerve.

As we left Idaho we crossed a desert plain before the large and rugged mountains of Utah grew suddenly skywards before us. It was the most dramatic scenery change, with the snow covered mountains growing from the roadsides; this was the closest we had ever been to such a high rugged mountain range. As someone keeps saying – *awesome!* And the mountains stayed with us to Willard Bay and one of the highest towered above the Park on the edge of the lake where white **pelicans** were fishing on our doorstep. Quite, quite wonderful, and very, very cold. But not too cold to go look at the white **pelicans** who, at this time of year, were in breeding plumage, having a large protruding 'centreboard' in the middle of their enormous yellow/orange bills – quite fetching if you like that sort of thing and, presumably, other breeding **pelicans** do, being clearly enamoured of the 'bodgers on the bonces' of their mates!

The osprey sitting on the dead branch of a tree overhanging the lake seemed more enamoured of himself as he preened the salt out of his feathers. The local starlings and robins sang their lullabies as dusk fell rapidly and the temperature fell dramatically with it – well below freezing. Although our daylight hours at this pretty place had been curtailed by matters beyond our control, we really enjoyed the short time we had there on the Salt Lake with its osprey and **pelicans** . . . Marvellous birds; marvellous country! Unless *one* is expected to stand in the cold evening air while the *other one* continued *his* fascination with things that travel on rail-roads. Against a picturesque snow scene for a back-drop, rail-wagons were making their way south. The same ones *he* admired at Glenns Ferry? Could be – except this lot was much longer – 127 wagons being hauled by five engines. *His* excitement was barely contained: the biggest train-scene yet. Definitely worth freezing for!

Sunday 11 April through Monday 12 April

We were in front of the next bad-weather front which the *USA Today* weather map indicated had descended on States behind us, and was about to reach

Ed admiring the view of the mountain towering above Salt Lake City

135

States we were in and going to *be* in before too long. We had a big decision to make which we decided to delay until we reached the capital city of Utah. As we approached Salt Lake City[56] the mountains followed us for most of the way. The State Capitol and the spires of the Mormon Tabernacle, sitting high above the city, were the only attractive things we saw as we hurried through this city, which was busily preparing for the 2002 Winter Olympic Games with tons of concrete.

Serious roadworks were everywhere, it seemed, and these very much detracted from what might, otherwise, be a lovely place. By the time we had found our route through the mess of concrete and metal which would eventually improve the city's roads, we chose to take the I-80 north and east into Wyoming, an interstate we would become very familiar with as we travelled ever eastwards. We were a bit sad at not discovering more of Utah's undoubted splendours, but the combination of bad roads and bad weather were too much for all of us seniors. Ed was pretty fed up at having his innards bounced about so much and roared his disapproval at the constant gear changes. Dolly and Geo were not having that great a time either. In fact Geo, who had been bathed with loving care at Farewell Bend, was now unrecognisable in his mud-bespattered grey-blue coat. The joys of endless ring-route up-grading with the up-gradients being pretty high continued long after we left the city behind and was nerve-wracking for all of us. Even the driver was concentrating harder than usual on his route through road construction on narrower than expected roads via high Parley's Canyon which, allegedly, makes this a scenic route into or out of Salt Lake City. Snow was all around on the mountains as Parley's Canyon gave way to East Canyon at the summit of a tortuous ascent. A notice at the top declared that the scenic road round East Canyon was closed today. Well, we took that major disappointment on the chin! The roadworks ended near the top of this mountain pass, at a tiny Alpine-like village which had a much-needed source of succour for Ed. No mention was made of the lack of octane opportunities through the long miles of road construction. If ever *coffee-to-go* would be more welcome in the whole of the US of A, then *she* for one would be amazed. *Her* offer of a straight swop of bannock recipe for tranquilisers didn't cut much ice with the patron of the pump station. The name of this high spot in our lives was called Highline Quick Stop, as we later discovered tattooed on the gas bill. We probably each had *his* or *her* own

---

[56] *Salt Lake City–160,000*

thoughts at this moment in time, both along the similar lines of '*what on earth will the Rockies be like?*' We still hoped they would be accessible to us, despite the adverse weather which would keep us, and many others, away from Yellowstone National Park situated in the snow-bound borders of north Wyoming and south Montana. Now this *was* a major disappointment!

The part of the Rockies we had chosen to cross was in Wyoming and on the I-80. This was the preferred route *he* advised after carefully considering the best possible one for a partner who preferred looking up at mountains rather than being on top of them. *She* had also been advised, at numerous times during the past few days, that, '*no,* there is *no* way round them, without going back down the Utah Canyons and south to Texas'. *She* felt that perhaps *he* just wasn't trying hard enough to find one! When *she* looked at the map there seemed to be lots of empty un-rocky-like places in the State of Wyoming. There were, *he* concurred, but, pointing firmly at the Rand McNally, showed her that there was also a long string of black dots through the middle of the empty spaces which were (according to *him)* both the Continental Divide *and* the Rocky Mountains.

But there was still some way to go before the black dots would be joined up into Divides or Rockies, and we met another startling change of scenery soon after entering Wyoming where mountains wearing white turned to desert wearing a dusty sage green. This desert plain exhibited some amazing rocks which jutted up in weird formations; with names like Boar's Tusk, looking very like a large molar, and Pulpit Rock, looking very like a large pulpit. Then the ground became flatter, even although we were up at 6,200 ft (most of it reached via *those* canyons and in anticipation of *those* Rockies). The small industrial town of Rock Springs,[57] set down in abandoned isolation in this empty landscape, was our home for one night at a KOA RV Park (Kampgrounds Of America – a coalition of grounds, individually owned). We had stayed in two others: the very likeable one at Williams near the Grand Canyon, and the very un-likeable one near Seattle. But we had no choice here where hundreds of miles can separate camp-grounds and few State Parks open before May. It had been a tough day and we were so relieved that this KOA proved to be a good KOA, if not scenic. It was close to the interstate but not busy, and extremely well kept by Bonnie, the lady who welcomed us to her part of wild spacious Wyoming. Bonnie's looks and nature gave credence

---

[57] *Rock Springs–19,000*

to her name. She put us at the end of the park, near her house, so that we would be undisturbed by new campers. This we appreciated, as we did the wonderful laundry room, the immaculate showers, and the shop with essential catering supplies. Compared to the Seattle KOA which allowed only inches between motor-homes this had lots of room which, in peak season, its guests would appreciate. Bonnie told us about her family's move from their home in Oregon four years earlier, when the lumber industry there had all but collapsed. At first she was nostalgic for that greener land, but now she just loved the Wyoming wide open spaces: giving 'a body elbow room'. Bonnie also ensured that her permanent residents had lots of elbow room in their own space, neatly fenced off from the RV part. Everyone was happy! In fact we met one of the residents in the laundry room in the evening, and *she* exchanged a lot of family details with her as they happily folded sheets together. Would this happen back home, we wondered? We'll find out next time a laundromat experience is necessary. *He* thought some of the poorer private parks we'd had the misfortune to encounter could do with some Bonnie input.

Next morning, on the way to find out how those black dots were joined, we appreciated Bonnie's sentiments regarding the wide open spaces we drove through, where even the cattle have elbow room. We ascended from our already elevated position quite gently, but definitely in an upward direction. Amazingly the ground all around the I-80 ascended gently too. It did not feel as if we were climbing mountains and, although we were to reach 8,000 feet before the day was over, we never felt anything like as precariously high up as we did ascending the road up the sides of the Salt Lake City canyons. At first the snow-capped mountain peaks were in front and to the sides of us, becoming closer and closer in this high plateau until we were travelling right across the middle of the Rocky Mountains as they ran north to south in a long majestic line, and what a remarkable feeling that was! It is very hard to describe our overwhelming emotions at finding ourselves 7,000-8,000 feet up in the midst of this chain of mountains known world-wide, which conjure up the American wild west in the imagination of every child, and is recognised by more geographically adept grown-ups as the great Continental Divide of the North Americas. We ran along the Continental Divide for some two hundred miles and across it at least three times, wondering why we (well, *she*) had ever feared crossing this glorious part of a marvellous land. How best to describe this pinnacle of our journey and the thrill at being on America's roof-top even though it was only for a little while? . . . *Awesome* would do it!

One last comment before we descend to reality. The Rocky Mountains are high but did not seem unusually high from our point of view. But we must remember that our point of view was from approximately two thirds of the way up to the summit of the highest peaks of the Wyoming Rockies at this point of their centuries' old journey through this and other States such as Colorado. The next stage of our journey into the Rockies would be in Colorado but, before that, we made a small descent of 1,500 feet and an even bigger descent into reality when we saw the RV park we had singled out for the evening of the day we crossed the Rocky Mountains. Bonnie, where are you when we need you!

Drawing the curtains at home on a cold early dark evening shuts out the reality of winter. Drawing Ed's curtains on this particular warm April evening, at least two hours before dark, shut out an ugly world which we did not want to think about, never mind see. This park on the outskirts of Cheyenne,[58] capital of Wyoming, close to the northern border of Colorado and the western border of Nebraska, was built in the middle of a run-down mobile-home park whose entrance ran through the middle of **A.D.** RV park, described by its owners (**A**line&**D**rew) and the misguided *Trailer Life Guide* as *'the best for hundreds of miles'*. There were a few others closer than a hundred miles, like Tex's Bison Ranch Park, which advocated that *it* was the best, as you could live, for a time, beside his bison. Tex's bison, however, when we passed his ranch, which nestled on the busy I-25, sensibly roamed the hills well away from the park and any masochistic campers. They could, perhaps, be seen on a good day, through strong binoculars! We had discarded it and one other also by the I, in favour of **A.D.** – **A**bsolutely **D**iabolical, thinking it would be less noisy two miles away from the interstate. And it was – after midnight, when the constant automobile noise from vehicles being driven at speed through the RV park *en route* to the residential park, stopped.

---

[58] *Cheyenne–50,000*

Colorado and Nebraska

Tuesday 13 April

We breakfasted with the curtains still drawn, pulling them back only as we left **A**cutely **D**epressing park around 7.45 am with little in our tums. It was a lovely sunny morning as we joined the I-25 south, and it continued this way as we were welcomed into the State of Colorado. Our final destination was the Rocky Mountain National Park, the pride of Colorado, which has almost 1,100 Rocky Peaks above 10,000 feet and 55 over 14,000 feet. WOW! One can understand why Colorado's nick-name is *'The State nearest heaven'*. We checked into Riverbank Private Park, about twenty-two miles east of the entrance to the National Park, which, thankfully, was a great deal more up-market than that **A**wfully **D**ownmarket park of 50 miles earlier, and we finished our breakfast at 10.30 am sitting at our table in the sun by the riverbank. The river, called Big Thompson, was responsible for the huge gorge we drove through (at its bottom – hurrah!) on our way to the famous National Park. Once upon a time Big Thompson must have been a mighty chap to carve this

She *loved the Rocky Mountains too, and Geo provides the perfect perch*

141

deep narrow gorge through the foothills of the Rockies whose sides were 1,000 feet high to the left and right of us at some places. It was an amazing drive on this narrow twisty road and what was equally amazing were the number of homes along the route, some built right into the rock-face, and with their own personal bridges across the present-day narrower, shallower, Big Thompson. We fancied one as a holiday home...we can dream! The road opened up at Estes Park,[59] a small very pretty town 7,600 ft high, enveloped in the peaks of the Rocky Mountains. Literally hundreds of peaks made an astonishingly beautiful backdrop to the town. Those inhabitants of Estes Park whom we spoke to, emphasised that they never ever take for granted their good fortune to live and work in this outstanding place, even when some serious weather hits town, which it does often and suddenly.

Right then we wanted to go five miles beyond Estes Park into the Rocky Mountain National Park, while the sun kept shining on the range of mountains before us. We stopped at the visitor centre for advice as to which of the car trails in this 150-mile park we should concentrate our time and Geo's climbing abilities on. The route we chose was past a hundred-strong herd of elk and at

[59] *Estes Park–3,200*

'Hi, how are you? I'm not a Gnu, I'm an Elk.'

142

last we got to see what we had been told by road signs throughout many western States to avoid, if possible. And we are so pleased that we had, until now. We sat in Geo watching some of these camel-coloured north American elk or wapiti (their proper name) grazing quietly, while others ambled past us crossing the road for the greener grass on the other side. Not only are these elk the colour of camels, they look quite like camels with their long curving necks especially as they have no antlers at this time of year, shedding them in March and growing them from a starter kit every spring again! They are much shorter than camels, but grow much longer ears, and don't have the camels' obligatory hump. But they do have a camel-like quizzical expression as they chew their cud with yellow teeth and large floppy lips. Some members of this herd were quite happy to pose for the camera, not always giving us their best profile, however! We took a fairly high road after this, getting up to a steep 9,000 ft at one point (ridiculously high, *she* felt) to reach a pretty little lake called Sprague Lake where we lunched with the birds and the fishes on two stale crackers, a banana, and a bottle of water, having forgotten to buy anything more substantial in our rush to the park. All the time the snowy Rocky peaks were above and around us. It is so hard to describe adequately our feelings at this moment in time: time which seemed to stand still in this gorgeous, majestic, American National Park. Stellar jays, scrub jays, tricoloured blackbirds and woodpeckers made their presence felt and a fluffy grey bird, new to us, perched on a pine branch nearby. We could not identify him, despite scrutinising both bird books. So which robin-sized bird was this in the middle of the Rockies?

As we stood on a bridge by a little stream beside the lake, frozen round its edges, one of the locals pointed out some green-backed trout, telling us that they had been an endangered species for a while and that all fishermen had to throw back any they caught. We spent a lot of time just driving slowly around the well-travelled lower roads of the park, one of us very glad that the top road was closed until mid-May giving no pressure, therefore, on Geo to climb to 12,500 ft up the road descibed in the brochure as the 'Oh, my God!' road! Some hikers could be seen making their way up this hazardous ascent. Neither of us seniors was sufficiently upwardly mobile to climb the foot-trails to these dizzy heights, and *she* for once, was quite okay with this age thing! *He* also seemed quite comfortable with our low-ranging abilities at this point in time and place. Had we climbed, according to the leaflet we might have met a grizzly – sobering thought. By staying low we met marmots (large rodents also known as woodchucks or groundhogs) and a coyote hunting for his tea –

probably an unfortunate marmot. The coyote was very close to our road but was completely unconcerned with people, smaller mammals being his chief concern right then. *He* was pleased to observe this canine *she* had seen solo back in Mississippi, and *she* was pleased to observe this more laid-back one at closer quarters.

Back at the almost closing information centre, we bought some cards and a small booklet on the *Birds to be found in the Rockies*, discovering in its pages that our unknown grey bird was a grey jay. Had us fooled, this un-crested quieter jay which doesn't strike the more-familiar pushy pose of its cousins. We were ecstatic about this as we had now seen all named jay species coast to coast. This country is absolutely blooming marvellous, we agreed as we ate an early supper in a small bakery restaurant in Estes Park with our final view of the magnificent snow-capped mountains before us, at first glinting in the evening sun and then suddenly disappearing in clouds. Full of snow we guessed as, according to the Rocky Mountain's forecast for the following day, the precipitation there was to be heavy and snow-laden. Rain then sleet came on as we left Estes Park for the 2,500 foot descent through Big Thompson Gorge to Riverbank. Our evening drive through Big T was lovely and the precipitation stopped almost as soon as we began to descend. We enjoyed the high contours of this gorge from a different angle and it was every bit as amazing as the morning journey. That night we slept soundly, dreaming of Rocky Peaks and being rocked by a wind which now had heavy rain in its increasing velocity.

Wednesday 14 April through Saturday 17 April

These four days were the most consistently windy of our travels so far, and here *she, Dolly* and *Geo* would like to pay tribute to Ed and his wonderfully skilful driver who brought us patiently, carefully and safely through endless days of buffeting gales with sleet and snow. We travelled windswept on interstates and US highways into RV parks where the wind did not abate and where we were rocked to sleep each night more agressively than we care to be rocked to sleep, with the howling wind singing a constant tuneless lullaby.

An abbreviated description follows of places seen in more whirlwind fashion than usual as we tried to escape the weather and spot some unique birds as they left their stop-over in Nebraska for calmer northerly climes! We drove north from windswept Colorado back into windswept Wyoming to rejoin the I-80 east for windswept Nebraska, straining our eyes and craning our necks from the Wyoming border onwards looking for cranes – sandhill cranes to be precise. Thousands of these huge light grey birds with long thin necks, a big well-feathered rear bustle, and a bald red patch on their heads settle on the sandy shallows of the Platte River, Nebraska, for six weeks every year on their migration route from the south to the north. They arrive at the beginning of March, eat all the remaining corn in the cornfields through the day, roost noisily in the river at night, become more intimately reacquainted with their lifelong mates, and generally enjoy life flying about their daily routine, often in the high warm thermals. *Our* warm thermals, brought in a last minute life-saving decision from Scotland, were unearthed from the bottom of closets. They helped, especially the driver who got a bit pipped when the draughts getting in through Ed's door reached essential parts – for driving, that is!

Two sandhill cranes flew over us and the I-80 into the wind, struggling to keep in a northerly direction. We did not get a good view of them but recognised their distinctive flight described in the books. That Wednesday afternoon we parked ourselves on isolated gusty Lake Ogallala State Park, by the small town of Ogallala,[60] Nebraska, and hurriedly got into Geo to see the bunch of sandhill cranes who had chosen the sandy beach around the larger next-door lake called McConaughy as their final Nebraskan stop-over. This exciting news was given us by a lady in the parks information department. She was wrong – or the birds had moved off since she last saw them. After a fruitless cold search we returned to base in the angry wind accompanied by snow flurries. A great blue heron cheered us up as he paraded in the freezing lake water in the biting wind determined to get some supper. Blue herons are so pretty with their grey/blue feathers and head plumes (male) during the breeding season. They are 44 inches tall with a wing-span of six feet, flying with neck tucked in. They walk sort of hunched forward, like old men, with their long, long necks outstretched and long, long bill pointing the way – almost comical to watch. This blue heron stopped his stooped perambulations, stood stock still for several seconds, and then lunged forward quite suddenly, his bill and neck disappearing into the lake water. His huge wings opened out to steady him as he fought with his evening meal. His head reappeared with a large fish, a good eight inches long, in his bill. Much too large for him to hang on

---

[60] *Ogallala–5,100*

to, we thought, but he did hang on as the fish supper struggled in his clenched bill. He eventually felt steady enough to take the fish, still wriggling, on to the shore and his top half disappeared for another few seconds. He must be breaking it up into pieces small enough to swallow, we decided. But no, the head came up, the fish was thrown in the air and went down the long neck, head first, as the heron intended. It took a lot of gulps to get his supper down but Mr Heron managed without choking to death as we observers, with glasses pressed to eyes, stupidly thought he might. He stood absolutely still then,

A contented Blue Heron digesting his fish supper

presumably digesting his enormous meal, before taking to the darkened sky and bed. *He* wondered aloud whether the heron would have obeyed the conservation rules and thrown his hard-won supper back, had the fish been a green-backed trout. Daft man!

Next morning, before we left Lake Ogallala (what a great name!), we interrogated the entire staff at the information office about the sandhills. One of them obligingly phoned around discovering, as we had by now expected, that all but a few stragglers of the sandhill crane variety had left despite bad flying conditions – their homing instinct, apparently, stronger than their common sense. However, when you have rushed across three States to see sandhill cranes then the sight of a few stragglers is better than nothing. We left the office with a great deal of paper on these maddening cranes, the advice to come back earlier next year (if only!) and the best travelling route across Nebraska and the Platte River to find any cranes sensible enough to wait for improved flying weather and the Carries. We saw not one, either *en route* through gusty-force wind and snow, or at Thursday night's deserted campground, Fort Kearney State Park. Neither did we venture out to look for cranes that evening, preferring to keep warm inside Ed, with the deafening wind accompanying our supper, bed preparations and the little sleep we managed. Oh and we were in a new time zone, Central Time, having crossed into it from Mountain Time somewhere between Lake Ogallala and Fort Kearney. This had not been noticed. Another hour – gone with the wind!

Kansas

It had been our hope to have left the storm behind by now and to stay here for a few days, especially as the driver could do with a longer break from the elements and had admitted, for the first time during our travels, that he had not enjoyed driving for the past two days. Friday morning was no better, but we opted, after careful consideration, to move on again, preferring to be buffeted on the I-80 and hopefully out-distancing the wind, rather than sit indoors camped on a particularly bleak spot. The first part of the journey was **bad** but it gradually improved, particularly when we turned south on to US 83 towards Kansas. But it was still blowy enough for us to feel a great sense of relief when we arrived, Friday evening, at Lake Kanopolis State Park, in central Kansas. Why we did not instantly recognise this as being another paradise we can put down to exhaustion. The Park Rangers agreed that weather conditions were less than great, but that today was much calmer than yesterday when some trucks had been blown off the US 83 we had just come down. If the weather wasn't exactly on our side, luck certainly was, we felt. After endless driving through adverse weather, we slept soundly in the most sheltered part of this huge park under trees well away from the exposed lakeside spots. It had only been three days since we had sat at 9,000 feet in shirt-sleeves amongst the high Rocky peaks. It felt much longer ago, and in a different country!

Saturday morning it was definitely calmer and we inspected the rest of this Kansas State Park with a view to finding the perfect spot to stay put for a while, and we found it – by the edge of Lake Kanopolis in part of this large parkland, but in a piece of it run by the Engineering Corps who had engineered the dam on the Smoky Hill River to create this beautiful lake we were now camped alongside. Lake Kanopolis is one of ten such recreational lake parks in Kansas and the first to be built. It was quiet because poor weather had kept people away from recreational pastimes, and we appreciated that quiet more than a little! That evening, it was warm and pleasant enough to sit outside, looking across the lake and admiring the water birds, including white **pelicans,** around its shore giving voice to the calm weather. There were also some land birds singing along. *She* found herself making up a daft final verse of the better-known Christmas song and it's written in, so that you can get an idea of the wonderful bird-life we were privileged to see. In this Kanopolis version as we-all sing along together, leave out the variety, and instead of partridges in pear trees, and pipers piping try:

Name		Variety
12 seagulls	mewling	(ring-billed)
11 starlings	chattering	(European)
10 **pelicans**	floating	(great white)
9 coots	a-swimming	(American)
8 geese	a-flapping	(Canada)
7 robins	feeding	(American)
6 ducks	a-diving	(tufted)
5 cormorants	flying	(great)
4 meadowlarks	singing	(eastern)
3 bluebirds	preening	(mountain)
2 blue-heron	fishing	(great)
and a Martin	a-cooking her tea	(greatly-ruffled)

As we locked up for the night, we heard the most amazing noise coming to us from an inlet across the lake – a very loud repetitive, shrill, orchestrated bird symphony. A cacophony of cranes, we wondered, having read of the night-roosting noise a flock of sandhills make as they settle down for sleep on their sand banks. They sing (not a truly descriptive verb, however) especially loudly on the eve of the continuance of their migration trail. Should a colony of cranes exist over the lake, we would sleep more easily – if only that *shrill din* would cease.

Sunday 18 April through Tuesday 20 April

The morning sun woke us, streamimg in through the curtains of our bed-space. It was very quiet, not a breath of wind and no crane concerto. Ah well – guess they left early. But at 1.00 pm we realised that they had preferred to remain at Lake Kanopolis for lunch, before setting off. The sky over the lake became crowded with long silver birds flying in a totally haphazard fashion, criss-crossing over each other in complete chaos. 'That's sandhills for you,' *one* of us said (the *one* who had read the literature heaped on *her* two days before), 'they seem at first to have no leader or sense of direction, but soon' – she shut up and we both sat gripping our chairs, while hundreds of cranes sorted themselves out, electing group leaders before forming long lines. Silvery birds with necks outstretched sailed across the sky northwards to Canada and Arctic regions. 'So' *he* remarked, 'not *all* sandhill cranes have their spring break in Nebraska.' 'No,' *she* who had waded through the literature patiently explained, 'only 80 per cent of them.' Well, we were in the right place at the right time to witness the mid-west exodus of some of the remaining 20 per cent. Sadly, for us, they took the white **pelicans** with them, but it was quite something to see the elegant stream-lined formations of sandhill cranes

Next stop Nebraska then off to Canada for the summer. Don't I look elegant!

disappear, with a big V of larger more robust sea-plane shaped **pelicans** following behind. Were the **pelicans** waiting for the cranes to make the migratory decision for them too? It seemed more than coincidental, this sudden leaving-togetherness. We imagined a beach conversation earlier that morning between the head **pelican** and the chief crane. 'I say, my good fellow, are you chaps heading north today?' enquired the **pelican** of the crane. 'Sure are,' was the crane's response, 'but it may still be too breezy for you heavier chappies.' 'Could you possibly wait till after lunch?' the crane was asked by the **pelican**, 'I could do with a few more fishes in my belly-can.' 'OK, old chap,' said the crane to the **pelican**, 'set your watch to 13.00 hours and lift-off will commence at that time preee-*cisely.*' 'Would that be West Coast Time, Mountain Time, Central Time or East Coast Time?' enquired the **pelican** of the crane. 'Mmmm . . . ah . . . yes . . . well . . . why don't I just give your lot a whistle, old thing,' said the crane to the **pelican**. 'OK and out-a-here,' said the **pelican** to the crane. *He* thinks she is being very unkind to the **pelicans** who seem to *him* much more organised than the cranes....*they* took off in a perfect majestic V! But they left one of their number behind. Why? Guess a perfect V can't have eight **pelicans**! Was it Grandma who got left? Will another **pelican** group (even-numbered) show up and take this one with them? We would never know and we would see no more **pelicans** on this trip, brown, white, single or senior. Had *she* known that as *she* wrote this – the tears would have flowed then, as they did later!

We visited the nearby small town of Marquette[59] which informed its visitors, by road-sign, that the four churches of Marquette welcomed us. This was a pleasant surprise; not only the ecumenical welcome, but also that this wee town could support four churches. But sure enough there were four, all well maintained and all looking very welcoming. There was also a wonderful mural on a side wall near the Marquette supermarket which depicted the important activities of this part of Kansas. On the way back to the lakeside, we went to an area within the State Park called *prairie dog town.* These small rodents, related to marmots and ground squirrels, prefer to live in social colonies, but none of the Lake Kanopolis prairie dogs were socialising that day or even sitting singly on their sand heaps in the sun. Pity. We did see red cardinals for the first time since leaving Arkansas and were delighted to hear the unmistakable song of the Carolina wren, who had caught up with us again –

[59] *Marquette–600*

at last! But the glorious song of the eastern meadowlark made the day; telling us in her sweet voice that we were definitely back in eastern birdland once more. It seemed like only yesterday since we left it.

There was one other couple on this part of the large well-designed park. Gene and Linda lived just sixty miles away and had brought their new 1999 motor-home to a place they knew well, before venturing further afield. This magnificent modern large 5th wheeler (see Appendix for the Mechanically-Minded) was very posh indeed and Linda, while proudly showing us around, demonstrated its slide-out. We had seen many of these on the outside of upmarket RVs and had wondered how they worked inside. This one worked with the touch of a button and almost doubled the living space. Modern technology is wonderful. We told Gene and Linda that *our* Ed was a fabulous bus and we loved him dearly. They completely understood, as they had not long parted with a motor-home ten years older than Ed. Later we recounted this story to Ed, emphasing our affection for him, adding that we did not covet our neighbours' property! (Ed especially loved the bit about being younger than the neighbours' previous mobile home.)

By Monday morning, we had caught up with some writing and spent most of the day just sitting around in the sun by the lake watching birds and people fishing. The only thing to slightly spoil the day was the intermittent noise of jets flying over the lake to a military target range a few miles away. But it only lasted a short time. Our depleted sun-tans were topped up, and the lazy lovely day passed in doing nothing, very skilfully. Linda and Gene came to visit in the sun and we talked about many things including the planes and the war our troups were involved in. It is quite astonishing to us how often, in fact almost always, that we were in complete agreement with our American cousins on things political and environmental. No-one we have spoken with on this side of the Atlantic has much time for this too-late over-aggressive military action by NATO troups in former Yugoslavia. By the time this reaches print it will all be over, and at what cost? We will find out! Once again, we would like to say what a real pleasure it is to meet and talk with the folk who live in this vast country. We did not spend long in the company of Linda and Gene but we will remember them with their quiet reasoned opinions and their gentle courtesy to strangers in their land. This country is marvellous.

When our bodies could absorb no more sun, and *she* had removed the protective towel from her un-reddened face (*she's* learning) we went to aptly-named Mushroom Rock State Park. Rocks which had been carried here by glaciers millions of years ago had been deposited by the melting ice; natural erosion over many ages had worn away the softer rock underneath, sculpting the original rocky deposits into imposing mushroom shapes. This five-acre Park is an exceptional place.

As nightfall gradually turned the lake a deep dark purple we listened to the very different sounds of a woodpecker (unidentified in the dusk) and two belted plovers, called killdeers, who wear charming black rings around their plump pretty necks. The plovers were engrossed in hunting along the shore, their long legs engaged in the running to-and-fro dance which makes them and their cousins, the rails, so delightful to watch.

Tuesday morning came in with the woodpecker telling us it was another great day to be alive and don't knock it! His advice to stay around in his State, to appreciate it some more, was easy to accept. Well, we didn't need much persuading and we had earned this sunny break after battling with the Colorado, Wyoming and Nebraska elements. After a blueberry waffle breakfast (out-of-the-freezer and into-the-toaster kind of waffles), a trip to the nearby town of Lindsborg,[60] to catch up on things domestic, was undertaken. We also called in to the local library to deal with e-mailing and spent a small fortune at their

[60] *Lindsborg–3,100*

Him *wondering if this mushroom would improve tonight's dinner*

book sale. Books we were glad to have; but books we had little or no room for in our already over-loaded suitcase space? By now we had resigned ourselves to either ditching all of our clothing in order to find room in our four large suitcases for our new possessions, or buying more air-line luggage-space. *She* felt the latter option more suited to *her* needs and the needs of her new American clothes, so was therefore less inclined to worry than *he* did if something special caught her eye, demanding to be purchased – within reason of course, like the fifteen inch wooden straw-hatted black Kansas crow with bright yellow beak and feet seated nonchalantly on a large wooden swing complete with rope. How could *anyone* not see that he was a must for the gardenroom back home? Ten books, mostly hard-backed, illustrating some of America's marvels, also seemed a perfectly reasonable purchase, packing-wise. *He* was in the laundromat at the time, transplanting the clothes (*she* was taking home) from the washers into the dryers. Lindsborg, another of America's most delightful small towns, retains many aspects of its Swedish origins with chalet-type houses, and with Scandinavian gifts in its stores.

During the twenty-two mile drive back to the lakeside through a lush green prairie where horses and cows roamed, we rejoiced at being alive in the center of the USA. The State of Kansas is the centermost State and exactly as we imagined it to be: rolling green fields with some hills and dales; its lakes an added bonus. We had just discovered our Ed was born near here fifteen years ago, even though his *parent* company no longer exists. He loved this story too, when we told him about his coming into the world for folks like us to love him. Ed, Dolly, Geo and we two just love Kansas. Saying goodbye to Gene and Linda that evening was sad, but could not dampen our exuberance. What did, was news of the massacre of teenagers in a high school in Colorado. It seems there are trigger-happy idiots everywhere in this world from Scotland's Dunblane to America's Denver. Guns! – Who needs them! – Really?

Wednesday 21 April through Friday 23 April

Saying goodbye to Lake Kanopolis was not quite as difficult as we expected because, by morning, the lake was as grey as the sky and the accompanying breeze encouraged waves to lap noisily as we packed up. We felt so much better for our time here and will remember another American lake with fondness. In fact we found it a neat coincidence that our two most favourite lakeside State Parks were in Kansas and *Ar*kansas. We said goodbye to the couple who ran the small store at Venango which sold food, fishing bait and the licences to use the latter. We collected some information about an ancestor of theirs who had graduated in medicine in Edinburgh. *He* had promised to try to look him up in the old medical school records. However, *he* might have quite a problem with this, as this ancestral medic graduated around 1660 from the University of Scotland! Mmm-hmm!

The clouds were gathering as we began this 305 mile four-State trip (the longest of our journey), taking the scenic route to the I-70, passing the little town of Brookeville[61] with its historic hotel where Wyatt Earp stayed and formed posses on many of his baddie-catching outings. Real wild west stuff in this part of Kansas. This State does have that old mid-west feeling where time ticks slowly and one can imagine Wyatt's gals being all his *'in buttons and bows'*. Of course, it has its fair share of modern cities and we passed by famous names like Salina, Abilene, Junction City before stopping in Topeka,[62] renowned in history and song for being part of the Atchison, Topeka and Santa Fe Railroad. We lunched in a Cracker Barrel (where else?) in Topeka's suburbs. Our intention until then had been to go over the Missouri River into the State of that name and camp for a day or two near that river. However, *USA Today*'s weather picture showed a great belt of rain with thunderstorms from east Kansas right across most of Missouri and even into south-west Iowa. *One* of us does not particularly care that much for thunder and lightning storms so prevailed on Ed and *him* to keep going north and cross into Iowa to an RV Park about twenty miles over the border with Missouri.

---

[61] *Brookeville–too small to count!*
[62] *Topeka–120,000*

Missouri, Iowa and Illinois

So, we headed north to enter Nebraska again, this time near Falls City[63] before making a right to cross the Missouri River at Rulo, thus entering the north-west corner of Missouri. We hugged the Missouri/Nebraska border up the Missouri valley on the I-29, crossing into the most south-westerly part of Iowa near the small town of Hamburg[64] and the State Park of Waubonsie. The weather remained fair and the thunder rolls were quite gentle and far off, we reckoned. Not much lightning to speak of either. That came with nightfall – and without thunder. It was absolutely spectacular. Unlike the type of forked lightning we are more used to back home with thunder, this was like a continual noiseless firework display. The whole sky was lit up by great sheets of sparkling colour – from blue through green to yellow. It was all around us and not the least bit frightening. It didn't frighten the white-tailed deer strolling close by or the 'possum looking for scraps previous campers might have left. It illuminated them brilliantly, so that we could observe the night wild-life more easily. This, oh joy of joys, included the first American owl to be seen, as well as heard. This sighting was worth the wait, for this bird was the biggest of the American owls and easily distinguished as the Great Grey at twenty-seven inches tall with dusky grey feathers heavily striped lengthwise and a very large round head without ear tufts. Not only did the lightning help us to see him clearly, he obligingly sat on a low down branch of a tree close by us and a path light. The binoculars enabled us to see every feature very clearly, including his small bright yellow eyes with large feathered circles round them, and his yellow beak with two white discs underneath – for all the world like a military moustache. This was a real treat. The great grey owl swooped to the ground several times to collect a nourishing morsel, always returning to the same branch, and then one time – he didn't.

The 'possum (a cousin to our badger) did return, hoping, presumably, that

[63] *Falls City–4,800*
[64] *Hamburg–1,200*

the new campers might have put out some scraps by now. We hadn't and wouldn't, as all State Parks request strongly that folks don't feed the animals as they can become too dependent on human delicacies; stop fending for themselves; forget how to hunt and could die when the convenience-food runs out. It had been quite a night. Earlier, we had phoned Connie, our friend from South Carolina, to be told that she and Leon would be in St Louis, Missouri, at the weekend for a wedding. Were we anywhere near? St Louis was a mere 450 miles away, a snap to reach in two days for travellers of our ilk! To spend a day with our friends in a city they knew, was an attractive prospect. So let's go for it, we decided, much to Connie's delight! It did mean that we would not get into Des Moines, the Iowa capital, or into other than the most southern strip of this State. But there would be opportunities to do that on our next trip for, by now, we both knew that we simply had to come again. There is far too much to see and do in 4½ months in this vast country.

So, we rose early and left Waubonsie State Park with its grey owls, 'possums and deer still fast asleep. We drove across half of Iowa in a slight drizzle, on a real scenic route by way of US 34. This gave us a golden opportunity to appreciate another countrified State, more agricultural than Kansas, where corn and other crops would soon be sprouting through the chocolate coloured earth. Iowa is said to be the US bread-basket and we had expected that part of its production would require vast flat fields. But in this south-west corner of the State the fields are small, only a few acres at most, and terraced. The soil here is fine grained, like sand, left behind by melting ice and blown by the wind into dunes. By terracing the fields the farmers prevent this light soil from being washed away by the rains. The farms themselves are also quite small, but most have elegant farmhouses with wrap-around verandahs. The towns we passed through had an old-fashioned look and feel. Well-preserved old wooden buildings had wooden board-walks in front of them. Rodeos are common-place family gatherings in the mid-west; sadly we had no opportunity to go to one. So the sign outside an office in the old-world town of Sidney,[65] not far from Waubonsie State Park, offering Rodeo tickets for sale was as close as we would get to one. The fields not allocated for crop culture were full of horses, sheep and cows with cowboys in attendance. We appreciated this mid-western culture and also could appreciate why Lorry and Jack, now in North Carolina, found it so very different to their home-State. We managed

---

[65] *Sidney–1,200*

to spend a little time admiring one of *The Covered Bridges of Madison County* – film buffs will understand the significance of the italics; for the significance of covered bridges – see footnote on p 124. This part of Iowa is much prettier and less flat than we had imagined – a green and gentle State – apart from another thunderstorm, with loads of crackling lightning this time, which caught up with us by evening and we unhitched our modern horse-power in a downpour to thunderous applause with electric back-up.

This Iowa State Park, called Honey Creek, was very large and on a lake which we could not see too well, given the elements. It was completely deserted. Only two mad Scots, three deer, and a wild turkey ventured out in the evening storm. The storm began to abate a little just as *she* stated that they would simply *have* to move on and just as *he,* Ed, Geo and Dolly thought *she* must have completely flipped to consider moving in this storm. A discussion, which brought a little warmth into an otherwise cold household, ensued covering the unlikely possibility of them dying in an accident in a torrential downpour on a wet road with zero visibility (*his* theory . . . unsubstantiated) to the very likely probability of them dying as the next lightning flash struck them down (*her* theory . . . full of substance). So, they moved – to a different, less lightning-exposed, part of the empty park (in *her* opinion, quickly agreed with by *him).* 'Neat compromise,' thought a relieved, dripping Dolly, Ed and Geo. The storm did stop completely in time for us to hear the nocturnal whip-poor-will. His call rang out clear and strong – in a higher key and a faster rhythm than we had expected the call to be, but quite unmistakable . . . *whip-*oor-***weel*** – *whip*-oor-***weel*** . . . the first and last notes emphasised, the last more so and ascending slightly – wonderful! Goatsucker or nightjar are the other names for this brown nocturnal bird which rests horizontally through the day, camouflaged in dead leaves, and if disturbed will flit away like a large brown moth – one of its favourite foods.

Friday's journey began early. We wanted to collect and send a few more e's, so stopped off in Centerville,[66] calling at a gas station for gas, *coffee-to-go,* and directions to the library. However the friendly ladies in the gas station offered us a phone hook-up there and then. It was this kind of friendly interest in us, along with a willingness to ensure that we should '*have a good day'*, which made our journeyings so pleasurable. After Centerville we proceeded along State Route 2 before turning south on to US 63 to take us into Missouri.

[66] *Centerville–6,000*

A surprise pleasure was in passing through an Amish community. Seeing members of this religious order driving along in their horse-drawn buggies reminded us of the first time we had encountered these folk in Pennsylvania years before. We would meet up with two members of a friendly group later in this journey. Before getting on to the more familiar I-70, we continued down US 63 to another Columbia. It is amazing how many town/city names are repeated across America – or is it, given that many are imported with immigrants from other countries? Seventy miles remained of this leg of that day's journey before we entered the outskirts of St Louis – and here there was a minor fallout between *him* and *her* with Rand McNally being the arbiter. OK, so inevitable road construction clouded the driver's vision but *she* did tell him to make an earlier right than *he* considered seemed correct. However *she* was right (mmm-mmph), which *he* reluctantly conceded after the longer more tortuous route *he* made Ed take them on (made even longer by *her* crowing noises). The dispute and journey ended at the Dr Edmond A Babler Memorial State Park. The morning had been cloudy, but dry; the afternoon cloudy and wet; the evening just cloudy again, with the odd thunder-rumble in the distance. This park was thirty miles from St Louis and we would be there for two nights while visiting with Connie and Leon. These friends will be interested to hear our tourist tales and how we have visited nineteen States with the rig, bringing our total mileage, since leaving Athens on 24 January, to 9,427. If we count all of the States we have spent time in since setting foot on American soil last December, the grand total is twenty-two. No wonder we are tired and off to bed! Good night – marvellous country.

Saturday 24 April through Sunday 25 April

We found our way into St Louis[67] with little trouble and meeting up with Connie and Leon again was as happy as expected. The day was warm and sunny, the storm now to the south of us, and we spent the first part of our day at the St Louis Zoo which has a wonderful range of animal life, most of it non-American, exotic, endangered, species. But there were some American prairie dogs happily socialising and munching carrots in their prairie-style town; one almost expected them to be sporting stetsons. They are bigger than

---

[67] *St Louis–400,000*

we had imagined, sitting about twelve inches high on their haunches, ginger coloured and resembling large gerbils. We all got to see our favourite creatures and, for us Scots, the birds are still top of the bill! For Leon it was the reptile house, to which he went solo, but then insisted that we all go see the Kimodo Dragon – impressive! We all watched the 'gators and caymans for a while (safely enclosed), waiting to find out if they were real, as not one moved any part of its terrifying body, or even seemed to breathe. Then one big 'gator did blink one eye and we knew *real* when we saw it!

The second part of our get-together was spent in the city of St Louis, which is an appealing city, mostly along the waterfront where the very full Mississipi River had barges plying their trade – especially for *one* of us, it seemed, who was thrilled to bit*s* to see *his* favourite American river again and at work. There is also a lot of *play-time* on this river which, for gambling purposes, is deemed here in St Louis, Missouri, to be part of the State of Illinois all the way to the Missourian river bank. This is a very beneficial thing for gaming house owners, given that gambling is illegal in Missouri, but not in Illinois. Pretty neat thinking, huh? So, floating casinos are part of the lure of this St Louis riverside. We thought about rolling a few dice, our reason being to win enough money to allow us to keep our precious rig! But the look of despair on the faces of Missourian gamblers with temporary Illinois State-*us* descending from the Illinois paddle-steamer casino on to the Missouri wharf, made us move along quickly. So, we (*one* of us) contented *him*self with taking an inordinate number of photos of the river (again) from innumerable angles, encouraged by Connie whose love of this river and city is huge. Leon and *she* preferred to shop.

We left our much-loved friends as the late afternoon sun glistened on the Gateway Arch of St Louis (much more impressive than the Seattle Needle) and drove out of the city back to our park, knowing that we would all meet up again at the end of our adventure in about five weeks' time. *Five weeks*, was that all the travel time we had left? Oh dear, how fast time had flown! Far too fast for us slow Scottish seniors.

Sunday, we moved up the map of Missouri to a State Park on Lake Wakonda – this lake not man-made but Mississipi-made, thousands of years ago. The old man still overflows on a pretty regular basis whenever he flows through low-lying land. We remembered the folk of Fort Coburn, Mississippi, telling us in February that they got flooded nearly every year in March. By the looks of things here, the river spent much of its time flowing merrily across fields

The Gateway Arch, St Louis, Missouri. He *took a really neat picture here!*

and into villages and towns. *One* of us is completely enthralled by this river and so it was no surprise to the *other one* to find *her*self on its overflowing edge in the tiny town of Canton[68] while *he* photographed it and its barges and its lock and its ferries from positions almost in the river from what *she* could make out from inside Geo as she sipped a vacuum mug of red-zinger herbal tea. The zing in red-zinger didn't have much effect on her really, as observing the Mississippi was, in *her* opinion, almost as thrilling as watching paint dry. He was grinning in sheer delight as he walked back to Geo with Old Man snapshot 203 in the can. Connie and floating boats came to mind! Unfortunately this particular lock on this particular stretch of the great river was closed to visitors, being under repair, so *he* could not see the barges go through it. *He* did not seem unduly traumatised by this. So it came as little surprise when she learned over their evening repast that tomorrow's State Park campsite was a little further up *that* river and had *two* locks on it! 'Let's hope, dear heart,' she said as she swallowed her last mouthful of lasagne carefully, 'let's hope, that at least *one* of them is open to at least *one* visitor.'

But a couple of conversations we had in La Grange,[69] a small town close to the RV Park, are worth recording. The first, with the owner of the local gas station, who knew the actual town population down to the latest baby, informed us that the river was actually pretty low and he hoped it would stay that way as his house was only five feet above the current level. He had been flooded out a few times in the past. Our second conversation took place in the small supermarket where the topic was not so much about the price of fish, more about the price of tables. The check-out girl was explaining to a friend all about a new oak table arriving soon to her home, complaining about its exorbitant price. We became involved in this chat when we told the girls what a similar table might cost back home. The check-out girl was left happy thinking anew about her bargain purchase, and we left, thinking how terrific it must be to live in a country where wood was plentiful and the cost no great deal!

The day closed for us in a most delightful manner when we took ourselves down to the lake's edge in the twilight to see what we could see. Two Canada goose families were having a wee stroll by the water. One set of parents were shepherding two tiny goslings across the grass; the other set had six slightly

---

[68] *Canton–2,600*
[69] *La Grange–1,100*

older offspring to contend with, but all the youngsters were exceptionally well-behaved, following mum and being helped along by dad. This atmosphere of shared care was most pleasing and we watched them for a long time. The birdie chorus was getting in to full swing as we made for Ed; there were the usual robins, mourning doves, starlings, blackbirds and wrens, but no owls and, even more unsettling, no jays. We hadn't heard any vociferous jays for a few days and wondered why.

Monday 26 April through Wednesday 28 April

We left Missouri, re-entering Iowa in mid-morning, travelling along the Mississippi for a hundred miles to the town of Muscatine and a State Recreation Area called Fairsomething which was beside *his* locks and close to a wildlife centre which *she* particularly wanted to visit. Fair-anything would be a most unsuitable title for this park as fair it certainly was not. It was very small with three thin rows of dejected-looking RV sites on uneven concrete washed by the swollen river. It was about a hundred and fifty yards from the busy State Route 22 across a level crossing on a busy railroad. This was the first State Park we had come across which was unbearably awful, and we were back across the railroad and on to the highway before you could say disappointment! It was impossible to find another park open, either State or private, on this stretch of river in Missouri. The nearest most likely stop-overs were well away from the Mississippi River in Illinois. Saddened, we finally left the great river behind at the city of Davenport,[70] crossing it for the last time into the State of Illinois. We would never know whether its locks or its wild-life were accessible to us woebegone travellers.

Back on the I-80 once more, and once more it was a windy road to travel. Because, we concluded, much of this interstate ran from west to east or east to west depending on your travel direction through the flat prairie country-side of Wyoming, Nebraska, Iowa and now Illinois, it would always be a bit breezy. We reached the Johnson-Sauk Trail State Park near the small town of Kewanee[71] by late afternoon and this *was* a bit of all right! Our fantastic outlook was over a wonderful nature reservation area with prairie and

[70] *Davenport–95,000*
[71] *Kewanee–13,000*

164

woodland surrounding a small un-named lake. This 1,361 acre recreation area is beautifully laid out for the public to enjoy with many trails, some bearing Indian names like Potowatomi and Ojibwa. So we stayed for three days and if one of us was missing *that* river, it wasn't evident. The first evening we drove around the lake, stopping at various viewing areas to watch the water birds. One pink-foot goose and two snow geese mixed with the much larger number of Canada geese. There was quite a lot of arguing going on amongst the noisier Canadians, many of whom had clutches of wee ones, while others sat in the man-made nesting boxes in the middle of the lake. Suddenly two of them, making a heck of a din, flew across the water and landed right beside us. Probably they were as surprised as we were at the sudden close proximity of man and goose. The gander was very protective of his lady-love and tried to shoo us away with a little hissing and a lot of weird neck language. We decided to ignore this hassle (well, we were there first!) and got out the camera to photograph them. As often happens with wild-life used to the eccentricities of people, they posed for us, drawing up their long elegant necks as far as possible and staying absolutely still. But Mrs Goose got hungry and began to pull up her favourite weeds out of the grass while he

Our friendly Canadian Geese in Illinois.
One guards while the other eats. Seems reasonable!

stood guard beside her. Then it was his turn for some supper and as he gobbled she was the sentinel. A loving couple.

The dusk was settling around us as we negotiated a bend further along the lakeside road and a large owl flew silently across Geo's bow to settle on a nearby tree. It was *big* and at first we thought it could be another great grey but as we cautiously walked towards the bottom of the tree where it sat, we recognised it as a barred owl which, at twenty-four inches, is at the smaller end of the great grey's stature. This was such a truly lovely bird, one of only two large US owls with brown eyes; the other being the barn owl which we in Scotland are more familiar with. This chap was quite relaxed, looking intently down on us with his large limpid eyes, showing no fear as we sat beneath the tree watching him through our binoculars which picked out the perfectly matching chocolate brown bars on his chest. We were ecstatic – our second large American owl in a week and at a time when we were finding it a lot trickier than it used to be to *'spot that tuneful bird'*. This was due to the

An Illinois round barn with 'no dark corners for the devil to hide in'!

summer foliage opening out on the trees, which made a good screen for our feathered friends to hide in. Birding in winter, when the branches are bare, is much less hassle, we decided, and, not for the first time, we realised that for this and other reasons we had chosen a good time of year for our trip. However the early summer rainy season which had followed us intermittently from North California caught up with us again on Tuesday morning. So the neat town of Kewanee had a wee visit from us and we dashed from foodstore to gift shops trying to keep as dry as possible. But back, for a moment, to Monday evening and the owl. As we were absorbed in watching our barred acquaintance, a car came close, went away and came close again and stopped. The owl, fortunately, stayed. The occupants of this extra-large old American car were a young man, his mother and his baby son. We struck up a conversation which included a question from us about stuff to see in the near-by town of Kewanee. This took some thought on their part – but – 'Walmart's' was the eventual reply as neither mum nor son could apparently think of any other highspots in their home town. 'It's a 24-hour Walmart,' the young man enthused. He also commented on Geo by saying, 'So, it is true that you English [some gritting of two sets of Scottish teeth here] have itty-bitty cars.' *One* of us pleasantly pointed out with a well-emphasised Scottish accent that Geo was American, having been purchased in Georgia. 'Oh,' was the rejoinder, 'but I'll bet you searched and searched to get an itty-bitty one.' We hastily agreed with this, for it was true, and we didn't want Geo upset further. Nice people. Hope they see more to their town, though, before too late. Because Kewanee was another great if 'itty-bitty' American town, despite its 24-hour Walmart.

It brightened up on Wednesday and we spent a relaxed day exploring the park and just generally being slobs. There was a wonderful round barn near the entrance of the park and, although we were unable to see inside it, we could appreciate the endearing reason given for making barns round. Apparently if there are no right angles to a barn then *'there are no dark corners for the devil to hide in'*. Mmmmm . . . *She* felt particularly lethargic and the cold post-rain air seemed to get into her aging bones more than usual. Even the passing white-tailed deer, the red fox sighted as it dashed past with an itty-bitty small mammal in its jaws, and the sweet bird song did little to cheer her up. The cold bug hit in the night and by morning it was *her* turn to have snuffles, sneezes and soggy-tissues.

Wisconsin and Minnesota

Thursday 29 April through Sunday 2 May

We drove 220 miles through the pretty and prosperous farmlands of Illinois into the pretty and prosperous farmlands of Wisconsin in glorious sunshine. And, even if we are being a bit repetitive vocabulary-wise, we must say how much we enjoyed travelling through these arable States in early summer. The different greens of fields and trees unfurling their summer leaves, combined with the newly sown brown earth, made for the kind of landscape painters enjoy capturing on canvas, and tourists sigh over between sneezes.

We arrived at Country View RV Park in mid-afternoon, near the small town of Mukwonago[72] and close to Waukesha,[73] its larger neighbouring college town, where our Arkansas acquaintances, Judy and Ron reside. It was a really lovely warm day with temperatures in the mid seventies in this private park – the best private RV park of our entire trip, with its woodland sites and loads of Wyoming elbow room. The twenty minute journey into Waukesha was past loadsa money in the shape of big houses, well-to-do farms and perfectly trimmed golf courses – a very pretty drive. Ron and Judy welcomed us into their lovely, tastefully decorated condominium, with an English afternoon tea procured from a local English store. As the scones smothered in clotted cream were eaten with relish (these English can do *some* things well, but Judy might like *that* recipe of *hers*) we renewed the friendship made fleetingly on Lake Ouachita, relieved to find that we did enjoy each other's company a great deal. Just as their cousins, Jan and Rich, way back in California, had made us feel special, Judy and Ron did likewise, and our Wisconsin days with them were super days. That evening we drove round pretty and prosperous-looking Waukesha, stopping to eat a dish of custard ice-cream (heavenly) before meeting their delightful family of daughter, son-in-law and three soccer enthusiastic grandsons who, despite their busy lives, were extremely hospitable and friendly.

---

[72] *Mukwonago–4,500*
[73] *Waukesha–57,000*

Friday morning Judy had arranged a visit round Carroll College, her old alma mater, which was most interesting and conducted in a relaxed and knowledgeable manner by one of the students sitting his final exams. He had one to come later that morning, but that did not stop him from taking the time to show us proudly round his college with its graceful buildings. Our hosts had stuff to do that afternoon so we relaxed back at Country View, *one* of us still snuffling a bit but hoping the sun's rays might get rid of the bug and that *her* partner did not succumb to its tenacious affinity for her upper breathing apparatus.

Saturday we met up with Judy and Ron in mid-morning and, after discussing the day before us, had a typical Carrie lunch of ham and cheese rolls at the picnic table back in the woods of Country View, before driving to the city of Milwaukee[74] on Lake Michigan and a ten degree drop in temperature. BRRRrrrrr! Milwaukee is a lovely city with its parks on the lake where hundreds of people of all ages were enjoying the sun and water. All sorts of recreational aids can be hired here from kites to roller blades, from bikes to boats. We declined the urge to roller-blade, enjoying instead the drive through a city understandably well-loved by Ron and Judy. There was also the pressing matter of procuring new tyres for Dolly whose biggest attractions were looking a trifle frayed at the edges. She never complained about her towing responsibilities or the wear and tear to her outfit, but we could see how pleased she was at her new rig-out when she was finally attired in fresh rubber! Our delicious meal that evening was produced by Judy and we ate and drank in such fun and friendship that it was hard to realise we had only known each other for a few weeks and that this was just our second get-together. MaryCarol had asked, during a phone chat back in Oregon, if we went round the RV parks picking people up and inviting ourselves to stay. Well, of course! But we didn't make the right moves at every RV park as, sadly, only three couples had succumbed to the Carrie charisma. Well, we still had a few eastern States in which to try our luck and on the way back to Country View we practised our chat-up techniques. 'Hi, we're from Scotland, are you from Minnesota, Michigan, Ohio, Pennsylvania, Kentucky or West Virginia by any chance?' Might work!

She did not have the best night Saturday through Sunday as *that* cold moved from nasal cavities to ones in her chest. So Sunday's outing to Old World

---

[74] *Milwaukee–630,000*

Wisconsin, near Eagle,[75] was shortened by a couple of hours as she caught up on some sleep. But, despite the shorter time, we spent a lovely few hours in this unique 576-acre parkland, where sixty-five original historic buildings laid out in farm and village styles of yesteryear told the story of early settlers to Wisconsin from foreign lands like Norway, Sweden and Germany. The village we most enjoyed was the early Yankee one where actors in clothes of that era showed us round the blacksmith's, the County Hall, the shoemaker, the village store and a rich Yankee home. It was intriguing to see all the old equipment used in cobbling, iron-foundering etc and the mix of late nineteenth century goods on display at the store. The current store-keeper was delighted that she now had soap (awful lye stuff) to sell along with her bolts of cloth and four different types of coffee beans!! The present mistress of the posh home was delighted with the new big iron cooking stove (*circa* 1865) and gigantic square piano (*circa* 1860) which must have taken some shifting with its iron frame encased in heavy oak-wood. We marvelled at how on earth it had ever been moved there in the first place. Mrs Posh announced that it could not be moved to spring clean! Tut, tut! Altogether a delightful step back into old-colonial American history and our thanks to our friends for a lovely day and lovely visit which ended at their son's home close by our camping ground. There again, we were accorded a warm welcome and were just thrilled to know that our Wisconsin friends wanted us to meet their families and vice versa. Never easy to say goodbye, we hope to say 'hello, have a dish of haggis' when Judy and Ron with cousins Jan and Rich come to visit with us in Bonnie Scotland, 'ere long we hope and, in case it stops them coming, they don't *have* to eat our national dish as long as they enjoy *her* bannocks!

Monday 3 May through Thursday 6 May

We drove north-west through Wisconsin to Mirror Lake State Park near the town of Baraboo[76] where we camped for one night and then onwards and northwards on Tuesday to Pattison State Park close to the twin cities of Duluth – Superior: the Superior[77] bit still in Wisconsin and the Duluth[78] bit over the

---

[75] *Eagle–1,200*
[76] *Baraboo–9,200*
[77] *Superior–27,000*
[78] *Duluth–85,500*

St Louis River which runs into Lake Superior at the Minnesota border. Both parks were pleasing, but not meriting too many words as we have described similar lake-side State Parks during this journal, and these two were in the category of places to cook supper and rest our cold-filled heads. Yes *he* had stupidly caught *hers,* and inconsiderately given it back again. Sniff!

By Wednesday, when we actually crossed into Minnesota, the wind and rain forecast for the area had arrived in force and we were blown north-east along the great lake to Temperance River State Park, 74 miles south of the Canadian border and right on the edge of Lake Superior. The river is called the Temperance River because, unlike most others flowing into the lake, it has no *bar* at its mouth! Ouch! The Indians called it Deep Hollow River because of the gorge with large waterfalls it flows through. The cooperative bi-national agencies which look after the conservation of this great lake and its surrounding area, *and* are determined to restore and protect their heritage, have produced a great leaflet entitled *Making a Great Lake Superior.* A great lake it certainly is and as *he* remarked, between sneezes, 'it is unbelievably big'. This is encapsulated in that leaflet by a quote from Reverend George Grant during an expedition here: 'Those who have never seen Superior get an inadequate, even inaccurate idea by hearing it spoken of as a lake. Though its waters are fresh and crystal, Superior is a sea – it breeds storms and rain and fog like the sea – it is wild, masterful and dreaded.' The Indian name is *Ojibway chi gumig,* the Great Water, the sweetwater sea, within which dwells the spirit of *Nanabijou.* As we stood on its north shore the lake, or sea, in front of us was displaying its dreaded un-calm side, as high grey waves broke on the rocks sending spume twenty feet up into the rainy grey skies. In the late evening the wind and rain stopped for a while and the sun came out in time for us to appreciate the sunset giving a red glow to miles and miles of calmer sea. Once more we felt privileged to be in a special place with all the beauty and magnificence of a truly Superior Lake. Marvellous country!

Thursday dawned with sunshine, but colder and breezy. The sun didn't last too long as showers soon joined the wind and once more the lake we looked upon from inside Ed's cosiness was fearsome. Thankfully, the night-time had not brought any of the visiting bears or timber wolves who, we were told, roam the surrounding wooded hillsides and lake shores. In fact the local news was all about a black bear attack on a man who objected to it taking off with his dog for supper. We wondered how brave we might be in his shoes! Fortunately there aren't too many bears in East Lothian for Harris-dog and his walkers to worry over. We had come across the remains of a deer on our previous evening's stroll and hoped that the appetite of its killer would be satisfied with venison for the next two days. However, we were regularly visited by huge crying seagulls who circled the rig and occasionally sat on bits of the boys and Dolly, in the hope of a snack. We ignored them, but less stoically than our rig-mates! What we most desired to meet on one of our woodland strolls, was a moose, as they also live here. We had to make do instead with the purchase of a wooden and wax replica of a very laid-back moose reclining on one elbow with '*Made in Montana*' stamped on his rear.

By now *his* sneezes were out-shining *hers,* and paper hankies were much in evidence as we tried, while one of the more distinctive showers was in evidence, to finish the jigsaw puzzle of a New Hampshire covered bridge started weeks ago. We had really enjoyed relaxing over the puzzles of Mount Saint Helens and the Grand Canyon even if they were a mite tricky at times. This one was an un-relaxing nightmare – a thousand pieces of varying shades of black, dark green and grey forest around the sensible vivid red, simple-to-do, actual bridge. Perhaps it was as well that we would not be visiting New England this time, as we might want to change one of its scenic views slightly! This was also a good time for us to plan our final four weeks on the road and to think most reluctantly of some necessary words to put into an ad in the *Boat and RV Trader* in order that some other lucky people would spend time with Ed. His friends (and ours) would be dealt with in similar fashion, but later, in a different publication. Oh boy, was this ever hard to do! The pile of wet paper hankies was growing by the second. We phoned dear Connie, now back in South Carolina, and arranged to spend our final May days with her and Leon before returning to Georgia for our final June days with Mark and MaryCarol. *She* had begun to think about Connie as her wee sister and was cheered up considerably by the sisterly love and consideration coming over the phone. Connie even made *him* smile again with recollections of the recent St Louis day and plans for a return trip to, and even on, the mighty Mississippi one day.

This was also the time to prepare for entry into Canada tomorrow where the rain and fog around Lake Superior in Minnesota might be replaced by a sunnier outlook. There were passports to find, return flight tickets to find and bananas to hide! Bananas? Well *she* had, allegedly, tried to smuggle a banana into Canada on an earlier solo excursion to Thunder Bay, Ontario. This unsuccessful importation had involved a sniffer dog, a man in uniform and the swopping of her bannock recipe for permission to stay out of a Toronto jail. (Fuller details supplied on request!)

Ontario

Friday 7 May through Monday 10 May

The day we both went to Thunder Bay[79] started bright but cool. That soon changed to dull, wet and down-right freezing. The rain came on just before we crossed the border without mishap, and with the banana cunningly disguised as a sandwich. It was a deluge by the time we drove into the yard and the open arms of our friend Carol. It decided to give us all a break as we set off for a very special dinner auction that evening. This Benefit Dinner was to help raise money for Carol's pet voluntary project called *Magnus in the Park*. Time and space do not allow for us to go into the detail this project deserves;

[79] *Thunder Bay–114,000*

Him, her *and The Sleeping Giant of Thunder Bay. Cold but calm*

175

suffice to say it is about taking a small cramped theatre, moving it to a larger revamped building, and landscaping the whole area around it into a public park. The evening's dinner and auctions raised a lot of Canadian dollars for this venture and was a real fun event.

Saturday and Sunday were beautiful sunny, but cold, days and the superior lake and Thunder Bay looked marvellous. *She* had seen some of it five years before, when she attended the first-ever International Respite Conference and she had been looking forward for some time to seeing again the bits she remembered, and showing the bits she remembered to *him*. Most of it looked very different as it was mid-March when she came alone, and there had been several feet of snow everywhere, from the out-lying Kakabeka Falls (higher than Niagara, though narrower) to the area around the Inn where the conference was held. To be honest, she didn't recognise that much. Thankfully Carol and husband Rob were great and patient tour guides. By the time the weekend was over we *both* felt we knew this Superior city pretty well; a city which is isolated geogaphically and is, therefore, self-contained. It is Canada's third largest port, and largest grain port, and is sheltered from the storms of Lake Superior by the Sibley Peninsula; known by all for generations as 'The Sleeping Giant'. The peninsula does look remarkably like a giant sleeping on his back with arms folded and, according to Indian folk-lore, he was an Indian Chief who laid down his imposing body to protect Thunder Bay from unwelcome storms and incomers. Native American names and stories abound in and around Thunder Bay. Some streets and areas also have a very definite Scottish feel with names having prefixes of *Mac* or *Mc*. One Thunder Bay street is, however, far more important than the others, but with no *Mc* or *Mac* – just plain *Carrie Street*. How's that for making *us* feel superior!

One of the places *she* particularly wanted to revisit was the memorial to Terry Fox, a young man who had lost a leg to cancer at the age of eighteen but who decided to run across Canada, starting from St John's, Newfoundland, to raise funds for cancer research. He called it his *'Marathon of Hope'* and, chalking up twenty-six miles per day, intended to run all of the 5,300-mile route. Terry didn't make it all the way across; sadly his cancer returned at mile 3,339 close to the spot of his memorial in Thunder Bay. He was forced to return home to Port Coquitlam, British Columbia, where he died a few months later in 1981 aged twenty-three years. Not only is this courageous story of a very determined young man worth telling, but the memorial sculpture to Terry is a work of art and all who see this nine-foot bronze statue, with determination etched in every facial line, are witness to Terry's valiant struggle and hope, like him, that the $24 million raised by his inspiring story will go some way to finding a cure for cancer which curtails so many lives. Terry's words are on the carving – 'I believe in miracles . . . I have to . . . because somewhere the hurting has to stop.' It is the belief of many Canadians that the strength and devotion of Terry Fox united them as never before.

We also paid a visit to Old Fort William, named after the Scottish town, of course, which depicts the lives of the early Scottish settlers who made their living by the fur trade. Mmmm! But that was years ago – we have learned to behave more courteously to our furry friends nowadays – at least some of us!

Fame at last. One man and his *Street in Thunder Bay*

177

Sadly the fort was closed until 15 May, the day when Thunder Bay and Ontario open most of their public places to the public. Just five days too early *he* mumped on 10 May as we-all sat eating Finnish pancakes in the Hoito Restaurant on the morning of *his* sixtieth birthday. *He* would have mumped anyway on this auspicious ageing occasion. The Hoito pancakes are a local delicacy, the recipe imported by the Finnish people who settled in this lovely bay on the big lake. They are quite different to the American pancakes we were more accustomed to eating – and very, very good too. People queue patiently round the block at weekends for Hoito pancakes for breakfast.

There was, however, not one moose to be seen anywhere. They were around, apparently, but not willing to make an appearance for us. Perhaps they were

Cheers! With Coffee to Go *at Pancake Bay*

also waiting for the magical date of 15 May before they became part of the tourist attractions. We truly loved every second of our time in Thunder Bay, with friends who seemed like family. So caring were Carol, Rob, and daughters Colleen and Shelley. Thanks, dear kinsfolk! Thanks!

Tuesday 11 May through Thursday 13 May

There are many parts of this wonderful trip which we will talk about again and again, even again! Paddling in azure blue crystal clear Lake Superior in May on a sunny but coolish day is one, especially as *he* put his feet in too – *eventually* and without his wellies! Sitting with warm, glowing, even clean, feet looking for miles across a calm lake is another. The miles across this lake, from east to west, measure almost four hundred: about the distance from Edinburgh to London. It is a BIG lake. From north to south it is 160 miles across; the surface area is 31,700 square miles; average depth 489 feet (maximum depth is 1,333 ft); it contains 10 per cent of the world's fresh surface water. If the lake water rises by one inch, the volume increases by 553 billion gallons. The water is so clear that visibility is 65-75 feet. Flushing rate (time required to 'change the water') is 400-500 years with the average time one drop of water remains in the lake at 191 years. The highest wave ever recorded is 31 feet and shipwrecks number 350, with the loss of 1,000 lives. Some Superior facts to think about!

But on this May day it was like a mill pond, and it was not the scientific stuff that made us sit till it got too cold to sit any longer, but the sheer joy of being in Canada on a completely deserted beach by the greatest of the great lakes. Ontario is marvellous – and Pancake Bay Provincial Park, where *him* and *her* paddled, was a great place to spend our last night in Canada. Earlier, as we drove along the Trans-Canada Highway, we had seen not ONE but TWO moose (or should that be mooses?). They are certainly not 'wee courin', timrous beasties' but are HUGE. Like the Rocky Mountain elk they didn't look quite real: big long-legged heavy-bodied creatures with long, heavy, comical faces. We bought a postcard of a moose having a bath, looking at the camera a bit dishevilled . . . the caption: 'You don't look so cute yourself.' Well we reckon they are kinda cute but HUGE! We were thrilled to have seen them – and before the 15th!

Our journey through this bit of Ontario was delightful, most of it by the lake and from time to time climbing up into wooded hills and then down again to get yet another spectacular view of Superior. Travelling the miles of pretty forests broken by the great lake, with rivers cascading down to it along this route, called the Superior Circle and quiet in May, is just an outstanding experience, and one we valued. The vastness of this part of Canada, with so few populated areas to disturb its undulating on-going greenery, can be physically felt. Yes, the United States of America is a huge country and parts of it are devoid of people, but we didn't ever get the overwhelming feeling of silent spaciousness, as we crossed State border after State border, that crossing this part of the Province of Ontario brought. All in all, we travelled two thirds of the Superior Circle, driving more than 600 miles along the lake's north shore from Duluth to Sault Sainte Marie and, as Canadian mileposts are in kilometres, it seemed even longer. Only one thing marred this journey and

It's no joke being a tourist attraction before May 15!

that was the charred remains of a serious forest fire which had closed both roads going east from Thunder Bay over the weekend, leaving no alternative route out of this part of Canada other than to return to Duluth and Wisconsin. We were, therefore, relieved when we heard that our road had been opened again, but absolutely devastated to witness the results of human carelessness.

Michigan

On Wednesday, having sadly left Lake Superior twenty-nine miles behind, we passed through Sault Ste Marie,[80] the city where the Canadian and American borders meet. To be exact, the borders meet halfway across a two-mile long and quite devastatingly high (*she* felt) bridge, across the Saint Mary River and the canal and Soo locks which join Lake Superior to Lake Huron. We negotiated the immigration point with no mishaps, and no bananas, and drove for about fifty miles across the Upper Peninsula of Michigan, before the next bridge hove into sight. This, assuredly not so high but devastatingly long, five-mile bridge, called Mighty Mac and the longest suspension bridge in the world, crosses the Mackinaw Straits at the merging of Lake Michigan and Lake Huron. Three great lakes in one day. How's that for a geographical climax?

On Wednesday evening we camped by Lake Huron and all we knew about it then was that the waters of Lake Superior flowed into it at a rate of 73,700 cubic feet per second. (For further information see Appendix for the Geographically Inclined!) Our journey was less spectacular than the previous day's, through a more populated part of Ontario and then into a new State – Michigan! Time for a bit of a recap, as much for our bemused benefit as for our readers. We were now in our twenty-third State with Ed and co: our twenty-sixth since arrival last December and, if you count the Province of Ontario (but just for the records, dear Canadian kin), then it's twenty-seven great places so far! North America is simply marvellous!

Driving through the northern part of Michigan we were aware of two things. First that it is a flat, pretty, agricultural area much like Kansas and Iowa with wide open spaces, and scenic small towns. The second was how wonderfully quiet the I-75 seemed compared to many other American interstates we had bowled along. By Thursday evening when we set up our domestic arrangements at Proud Lake State Park about thirty miles north-west of the city of Detroit

---

[80] *Sault Ste Marie–81,000*

we felt quite differently. The volume of traffic had increased dramatically from Saginaw and had kept on increasing at an alarming rate, finally sweeping us through an enormous area of roadworks. We had entered a commuting time frame, the first for thousands of miles, which made us wonder how folks all over the world cope with this inevitable commuting race-track scenario *every* working day of their lives. Interestingly, we had read in *USA Today* that peak travel time is no longer between 7.00 and 9.00 am; it has grown steadily earlier and earlier and peak travel is now between 5.00 and 7.00 am on many major US city routes. One media quote: 'I can now sit in a traffic jam at 5.45 am and when I can drive I can barely see for all the headlights.' What a weird world we live in. The Oregon settlers came to mind yet again, as they often will from now on, and we wondered what they would have made of it all. Perhaps death from unremarkable and untreatable infections was preferable to death from high blood pressure, pollution, conjestion maladies or road traffic accidents. Fortunately, the city sprawl has not yet engulfed Proud Lake, and it was good to breathe its unpolluted air; long may it and all of the world's greener and more pleasant land remain green and pleasant. This was a busier park than recent ones, and by Saturday evening it would be filled with families and young people enjoying a weekend under canvas; filling the pure air with nothing more lethal than songs around the camp fires. But this was Thursday. Tomorrow we would get to spend some time with MaryCarol's parents, Agnes and Chuck. We had waited almost nine years for our second meeting and we looked forward to it very much.

Friday 14 May through Saturday 15 May

Agnes and Chuck live in a most desirable condominium in the charming small town of Northville[81] about 15 miles west of Detroit.[82] It was a real pleasure to see them again and to catch up with all of their family news. After lunch, we emerged into the sunshine and drove to the historic Greenfield Village in the suburb of Dearborn[83] with its collection of reconstructed Early American houses and workshops, and the Henry Ford Museum. Its vast acreage depicts life of yesteryear, capturing the chapters of American history as its natives

---

[81] *Northville–6,200*
[82] *Detroit–1,000,000*
[83] *Dearborn–88,000*

and immigrants toiled together to be part of that great American Dream. It was financed by Henry Ford whose name, of course, is synonomous with Detroit. Much of the village, and especially the museum, pays homage to the automobile industry and its effect on our lives. Wonder if Henry would have a solution for some of today's traffic problems? Probably privately owned jets. An interesting fact: Henry Ford built the first American airport and airport hotel (the one we had lunched in) at Dearborn, so that he could fly in other automobile giants and customers.

He liked the part of the village dedicated to Thomas Edison best and instructed those of us who cared to listen, about the man and his many inventions (1,000 patented in his lifetime). The one *she* liked best was the phonograph and we all listened enraptured to hear the first voice recording made by Edison himself. '*Mary had a little lamb*' were the first words to come over the ether by a compromised Edison who had been unable to persuade a friend to make the inaugural speech for posterity. Edison's dedication to making electricity available for the ordinary family man with the invention of the generator and then the light bulb, are the things most of us remember him for. But did you know that it cost more than the average working man's weekly wage at that time to run one light bulb? And did you also know that Ford and Edison were such close friends that they even had their holiday homes next to each other in Florida? Ah well, you do now!! One other highlight at this outstanding park was when Agnes and *she* rode on an old carousel complete with flashing lights and mechanical organ. Chuck and *him* were content to watch their women-folk sit astride the highest horses, even see them standing up in the stirrups from time to time, showing off their long unused expertise from when they rode bareback on them bucking broncos! Well, imagination is a wonderful thing!

Our time with Agnes and Chuck passed all too quickly and before we knew it Saturday afternoon arrived and once more we had to say farewell to folk we think of as close family. That afternoon and evening were spent in the small town of Brighton,[84] with MaryCarol's sister Julie and her family of husband Dave and daughters Cory and Brooke. We ate ice-creams in the town center park by the river; the adult ice-creams nothing like as horrendously colourful as those chosen by Cory and Brooke. We felt very privileged to be invited to their church for an informal evening service over coffee. It was a

---

[84] *Brighton–5,700*

lovely relaxed service and we sang to the accompaniment of Dave on drums, Cory on trumpet and Brooke on keyboards and percussion – wonderful. Afterwards we had so much fun over a delicious American dinner of homemade burgers with corn cobs. We laughed a lot. Cory and Brooke were somewhat freaked out by our fondness for Ed, Dolly and Geo and the way we talked about them as real friends. Wonder why? Thanks to all in that part of Michigan for a great welcome and an awfully good time.

Ohio and Pennsylvania

Sunday 16 May through Saturday 22 May

Ohio will be remembered by us as the State where we camped by Lake Erie and the one which made our number of States visited as twenty-seven. Many times on this journey of ours we would have liked to stay put in a given place for longer than schedules allowed and we had decided that we were going to relax for a few days in Pennsylvania – the first State we got to know almost nine years ago and the one which made us want to make this trip. We had made another decision – *not* to be in any of America's recreation parks for the coming American holiday – Memorial Weekend. This particular weekend was the one when many Americans camped out as we had discovered when we were completing the registration procedure in various Park offices during the past few weeks. Some camp grounds took advance bookings; others did not (see Appendix 6). It didn't really matter as the buzz was that *all* Parks were going to be filled to maximum capacity for this national holiday. Fortunately for us senior travellers who preferred camping experiences to be quiet affairs, Connie and Leon had invited us to spend this weekend with them. We were expected in Columbia on Friday 28 May.

So, we were now in our last ten days on the road with Ed, Dolly and Geo and wanted to spend them happily. Thus it was that we sped through the Ohio countryside, which is much like that of Michigan, camping in that State for only one night at Geneva State Park by the holiday resort of Geneva on the Lake.[85] This small tourist haven was extremely busy on Sunday, as hundreds of people milled around its many attractions, all of which were endeavouring to part the holiday-makers from their dollars – and succeeding. It was pretty well shut down, however, when we passed through it again on Monday morning *en route* south to cross the border into Pennsylvania to a bonnie quiet State Park called Parker Dam. This dam is in the hills, ten miles north of the I-80 and close to the 'Highest point east of the Mississippi' on that interstate. So we were at a mini-continental divide. Behind us the rivers all found their way

---

[85] *Geneva on the Lake–1,600*

187

to the Mississippi; in front of us they went to the Atlantic coast. *Some* geographical tit-bits are fascinating. We might have remained there in the hot sunshine with the birds and ground squirrels a bit longer, but we were keen to get as close as possible to State College[86] where we could nostalgically reminisce of days gone by.

The park we had chosen to relax in was Bald Eagle State Park, about twenty-five miles north-west of the university town Mark and MaryCarol once called home, and was in the midst of green hills on a lake made by two dams. We had forgotten just how beautiful Pennsylvania is, and were delighted to be back in its lush hilly environs, especially as our two previous visits, eight and nine years earlier, were in fall and early spring. That first visit had memories of riotous fall colour and the second, memories of a sprinkling of snow on the morning of the day Mark and MaryCarol got married. This time, in late May, the dales and hills were full of summer colour and heady perfume. Honeysuckle is profuse here and was entwined around hedgerows of brilliant white bridal wreath viburnums. Azaleas and rhododendrons, in every conceivable hue, bloomed in gardens and parks, while along the edges of highways and in the medians of interstates, beds of wild flowers thick with multi-coloured poppies turned endless grey concrete into a fabulous natural picture.

Many of the small towns are built on hillsides and are all the more engaging because of it. Towns which we walked through again were just as pretty as we had remembered them and our favourite-ever shop in picturesque Lemont,[87] called *Cats Miaow* welcomed us with a bouquet of perfumes and dainty displays of *very* collectable mostly cat-oriented *objets d'art*. *She* would have taken half the shop home if only *he* had been more reasonable. We did take a little of it! And we bought two pairs of shoes when we revisited another favourite store, the Amish shoe and saddle shop in Madisonburg.[88] The gentleman who helped us make our shoe choices was the same gentleman who had helped us with them last visit and he consulted his records, where he found our names with shoe sizes and Scottish address. Their records are kept for ten years and if the customer does not return to make another purchase within that decade, their details are removed. Luckily for us, then, that we didn't leave our Madisonburg shopping until the new millennium! Also lucky

---

[86] *State College–39,000*
[87] *Lemont–2,600*
[88] *Madisonburg–too small to count*

for *one* of us that the owner of the store had the exact same shoes in stock which *he* had previously purchased and found *the* most comfortable footwear ever. He had sadly declared them worn out about six months earlier. *Her* favoured shoe-style was no longer in production (but still intact at home). However *she* dutifully searched the racks until she found great shoes, determined that *he* would not be the only Carrie on the records for the next ten years! As we drove away with promises to return we spoke with another gentleman from this community who remembered us Scots. He invited us to buy shoes from them any time by mail order. We explained that we'd rather call back in person within ten years. The word gentleman when split into its two parts would best describe the gentle men we met each time we came to Madisonburg. We saw the Amish women-folk working in the fields or driving in their buggies as they went about their daily lives. You can't capture this gentle life by mail order. We have a great respect for this Amish community whose lifestyle is very different to most of the other people we know whose lives, like ours, are more complex and more competitive.

The wild-life around our park was varied, prolific *and* competitive – especially the birds. As we settled in on night one, a skunk sniffed round our site; amazingly we couldn't smell him! Despite the ever-ready odour sacs skunks carry everywhere with them they are very pretty creatures and vary in size, but all species have black and white coloring. The striped, or common, skunk is found everywhere in the United States and was our nocturnal visitor. It had long black fur and a narrow white stripe on its forehead and a white stripe running from its head down its back and on to its tail. On the second night *one* of us met Mr Skunk as *he* came out of the showers – don't know which got the biggest surprise, and neither smelled a bit (allegedly). We saw several live ones at this park which made a pleasant change from the dead ones we saw too often by the roadsides. Roadkills are only too plentiful in this large country which has so many birds and animals. There are also many flower-decorated and named crosses by the roadsides States-wide (like the ones mentioned which caught *her* eye on the too twisty, too high road in New Mexico) where people have fallen victim to automobile accidents. It has become commonplace in the UK to leave bunches of flowers at the scene of a more violent death. They generally last a few days. The more permanent roadside memorials in the USA take a bit of getting used to.

But back to pleasant thoughts and a bit of bird-name-dropping. We saw our first Baltimore orioles wearing their yellow/orange and black outfits as they flew and sat on beautifully constucted nests. We saw our first scarlet tanagers and yellow warblers. We saw cowbirds, catbirds and goldfinches. We saw bluebirds, red-winged blackbirds, wrens and robins. We saw swallows and different sparrow-species, unidentifiable in their striped and spotted browns and beiges. We saw woodpeckers, wild turkeys and hawks – and we loved them all. We did not see bald eagles in this birding paradise at Bald Eagle State Park which is also a paradise for butterfly enthusiasts where butterflies abound in many colours and sizes, some larger than humming-birds. The one *she* liked best was a tiny little forget-me-not blue one which flitted low amongst the ground hugging plants. Work is in progress at this Park to increase the numbers of bluebirds which have seen a bit of a decline in this area in recent years, so numbered nesting boxes have been set up at strategic points throughout its vast acreage. One of our funniest sightings was of a swallow keeking out from a bluebird nesting box unaware that, not only was he the wrong species, but that, according to the house-numbering system, he was number one hundred and six. And the sun shone warmly every day we were in pretty Pennsylvania and we did not want to leave. We said this to Jack and Heidi, old friends and colleagues of Mark and MaryCarol, and friends of ours since Jack, who was responsible for first inviting Mark to this country, visited us in Scotland. Jack and Heidi, with their four-year old daughter KatArina, live in a wonderful old ranch-style home set in several acres of typical Pennsylvanian countryside – the kind we just love. We had dinner with them one evening and the wine bottles gradually emptied as we talked and talked of things past and things to come. We didn't think in the late eighties that we would ever thank Jack for enticing Mark from his home country and us, but we do now most sincerely, because we got MaryCarol for a daughter-in-law and the excuse to visit this marvellous country again and again.

We repeated our sentiment of not wanting to leave Pennsylvania, tearfully to each other as we took the high road out of State College towards the next interstate and West Virginia via Maryland. 'Imagine,' *he* remarked as we left this special State, 'how we might feel if we knew that we could never come back to either Pennsylvania or any part of this continent.' For once words failed *her* but '*devastated*' was the one screaming in her head.

Maryland, West Virginia; Kentucky and Virginia

Perhaps the weather angel understood our misery as by the time we reached Grantsville,[89] Maryland, the heavens had opened and the rain was lashing down to the loud accompaniment of thunderclaps and Ed's reluctant windscreen wipers making a sad keening noise. So what we saw of Maryland can best be described as a watery blink, although the drive into it from Pennsylvania was quite wonderful with the road continuing to climb up and up to reach the breathless heights of West Virginia. Talking of heights (*again*) . . . the first State Park we attempted to stay in during the storm was 2,800 ft up, along twenty-six miles of (*another*) narrow twisty minor road. What we did not realise, and the *RV Guide Book* forgot to mention, was that 1,000 ft of this was in the last four miles. Pretty well straight up and an impossible task for *him* and Ed in the deluge, especially with *her* screaming blue murder at every bend – and there were a few! So back we-all went down the long wet twenty-two miles of tortuous minor-road to the main road and then along yet another twisty very narrow, but not-so-high US Route for sixteen miles to Audra State Park. This was a primitive park with no electricity or water on tap at individual sites. It did, however, have water over and around each site, and in copious abundance on the even narrower road into the park. This water carried the red mud from the river banks over and around the roadsides in torrents. How the wonderfully clever driving duo did not skid us all into the over-full muddy river that ran along one side of the dangerously overflowing park, the rest of us weary, grateful travellers will never know. As we drove ever-so slowly through the camp ground in the pitch black looking through the downpour for an unoccupied site, wet vans and wetter tents loomed at us through the water-drenched windscreen and we could not but feel sorrier for those in recreation under sodden canvas. This dripping wet park-road was so narrow that trees brushed against the rig on both sides as *he* skilfully manoeuvred us to an empty space almost at the end of the small dark dismal park – a park that was destined

[89] *Grantsville–500*

191

to be dark and dismal in non-wet daylight with its thick canopy of large trees. It was with considerable relief that we sat with the comforting sound of Ed's generator giving us light enough to eat our soup and bagels, appreciating that our twilight adventure was over and that we were safe. And how marvellous it was for *him* that there was a generator starter switch on Ed's dashboard, so there was no need to get wet to get electricity!

Sunday 23 May through Tuesday 25 May

We slept reasonably well despite the thundering of rain on the roof all night, waking occasionally to wonder if Noah's flood was having a revival in West Virginia, and if Ed would have developed flippers by the morning. The drip, drip, drip of wet leaves shedding their heavy watery weight woke us and, realising that the rain had eased, we made a quick getaway from damp dismal Audra State Park, driving along a road running with water which was seeking out the already overloaded ditches. We reached the welcome main road and the gas station where we ate our breakfast of danish and coffee-to-go at 8.00 am. The day was ours, and we would enjoy it more than yesterday, that's for sure!

We made a sudden decision to join the young men going west again, in an attempt to avoid the storms still hitting West Virginia and the gloomy weather forecast for the eastern parts of Virginia. The State Park we chose was close to the border town of Huntington which, although still in West Virginia, is very close to the States of Kentucky and Ohio. The sun was certainly shining brightly there and hundreds of happy campers did not seem to mind that there was no shade to keep the pre-storm heat from assaulting their bodies. We had only driven a distance of 120 miles and yet we had left a park which was so enclosed with its dense canopy of dripping trees as to be claustrophobic, into a dry plain where there was no remittance from the hot hot sun. We ate lunch in this park, with Ed's air conditioner going full blast, surveying the walkers, joggers and runners pass by dripping with perspiration. The decision to find somewhere more conducive to our needs was an easy one and we found ourselves unexpectedly in Kentucky around 4.00 pm; in Grayson Lake State Park which offered sun, shade and near-solitude, but no lake – it was a mile or six away! However the Kentucky-Fried Chicken dinner was finger-lickin' good!

The storm began to hint its intention to move into our resort by morning with some spots of heavy rain and a strengthening wind. We did not intend to hang around and indulge its Carrie-clinging proclivity. Our well-proven weather guide in *USA Today* told us that we were acting in a sensible manner and to get as far into southern Virginia as possible. But first we paid a very quick visit to Ohio to buy a couple of postcards to say that we had stayed there earlier. As we had travelled east to west and back again, we had bought extra postcards to decorate our already extremely handsome Ed and to give us pictorial reminders to take home of places seen. We had managed to forget our compulsion for postcard purchasing in Maryland, Florida and Ohio. The former two States were going to remain unrepresented on Ed's many surfaces, but we could get a view or two of Ohio by crossing the Ohio River from Kentucky and recrossing it a few miles to the east back into West Virginia. *One* of us was pleased with this travel arrangement as *he* got to cross a river twice inside an hour. *She* didn't mind too much as it was a fairly narrow river at this point, and she even managed to appreciate some of the inevitable geography lecture which accompanied each crossing – something to do with river-flow direction etc etc etc . . . and even . . . *etc!* Thus we paid a second quick visit to Ohio and have the postcards to prove it! Our route through West Virginia into Virginia and Clayton Lake State Park was through *the* most beautiful scenery, so many spectacular green valleys and hills to enjoy and this on an interstate which was pretty busy most of the way. The rain threatened a few times but did not become a serious component of the journey. Only two things marred the day and they were both tunnels – carved out of the hillside rocks. They came upon us unannounced on either map or road sign which for *her* is definitely the way tunnels should happen if they *must* happen at all. One of these tunnels was very loo—ong and *she* thought that light at its end would never appear. *He* reminded her of the sign seen in the South Carolina's Old Friend of Charleston Railway Museum: 'Don't get too optimistic. The light at the end of the tunnel might be a train coming the other way.' Hmmm!

Clayton Lake State Park was also not on a lake, and it was slowly dawning on us that lake being in the title of east coast State Parks did not necessarily mean that the park was actually on one, or that one was even in close proximity. We didn't bother to try to find the lake, preferring to shop and stuff laundry into a machine in the nearby college town of Radford.[90] This choice of evening

---

[90] *Radford–16,000*

entertainment was in preference to watching and listening to a man and his digger trundling past our little bit of Virginia very slowly every fifteen minutes, as he moved red clay from one part of the park to some other more appropriate location. Why? Goodness knows, unless he was leisurely constructing a one-man-made Clayton Lake. Our hopes of finding a really great State Park in which to spend our last few days with Ed, Dolly and Geo before that penultimate ride together, were dashed. This most certainly was not it, and so we would leave it and the red-clay shifting programme tomorrow. It rained only a little with a distant rumble of thunder and we felt that, even if our dream site was not in this part of the country, then at least we had outrun the storms.

Tuesday dawned brightly and with the bird-song of the Carolina wren to brighten up our day even more. We left Clayton (no-lake) State Park without a backward glance, skilfully avoiding the man and his digger. So it was that we journeyed through North Carolina and into South Carolina and our last hope of a good place to stay for our last three nights with the trio. Kings Mountain State Park was OK but not great, being overly wooded to keep its visitors cool in the increasingly sultry weather, now 75°F in the shade. We were fortunate to get a reasonably isolated site before the park got busy, which it did later that evening.

South Carolina

Wednesday 27 May through Thursday 28 May

We tried very hard to enjoy our last two full days 'on the road' in Kings Mountain Park but it was a lot less appealing than most of the other State Parks we had enjoyed *en route*. We eventually found a small open clearing where we could top up the sun tans, watch the wild life and feel a little less encaged. We also found the lakes not mentioned in the title this time but flagged up in Good Sam (not our most trusty Guide) as being the park's recreational areas. The larger was a mile drive away, and closed to all but people hiring fishing boats and clutching the requisite permits, or to group campers. The small one, within half a mile and used for swimming and pedallo boating, was also closed until Memorial Weekend two days away! We were saddened that we could not eat our lunch and observe the water fowl highlighted in 'the things to see in this park' beside their designated habitat. We began to long for our days in the west and mid-west when State Parks advertising lake or river recreation kept to their promises and welcomed us to their waters. We also began to long for the elbow room we had enjoyed in the west and mid-west. Granted we had travelled there in the winter/early spring months and the USA population is far greater on the east coast than the west, but even so, many parks in the south-west had been busy and the water featured as an attraction was accessible to everyone all year round. York[91] and Clover[92] were two attractive towns we spent a little time in. Clover had a great library for such a small town; York had a great Goodwill Store!

By Wednesday evening the camping area of the park was really filling up. There is no advance booking system in South Carolina's State Parks so many people were arriving early for the coming weekend holiday, preferring to make a longer daily journey to work until Friday evening in order to secure a place at Kings Mountain State Park. By Thursday afternoon there was a FULL sign up at the entrance gates and, according to one of the rangers, *all* of South

---

[91] *York–6,700*
[92] *Clover–3,400*

Carolina's State Parks were full. As we took our evening stroll past overcrowded camp sites with little or no elbow room, we realised two things: one, that we considered ourselves travellers rather than campers, pleased to pay for and enjoy the facilities of the many camp grounds we had stayed on; two, that we had been so lucky to have had the real pleasure of quieter more attractive State Parks before reaching the busier east coast at the start of the summer season. *She* wept a bit as she sat at this lap-top trying to be less downhearted as she wrote, but failing miserably. *He* was pretty fed up too and we both let silent tears fall as we settled into Ed's soft comfortable mattress for the last time. We had *so* wanted to spend this last night with our trio of travel companions in a pretty place with a pretty view to greet us on the last morning. It was hard not to think about the perfect places we had slept on and woken in, and ironic that this last one was *soooo* different. This country had been so marvellous to travel across and its people so welcoming to their Scottish cousins. Why, oh *why* did it let us down so badly at the end? Well, perhaps so that the end would not be too traumatic. Would we rather have ended the tour bereft at leaving beautiful Lake Ouachita? Well, *yes!* But it did not take great mental acuity to figure out that beautiful Lake Ouachita would also be seething with visitors right now. Much better to have enjoyed it by ourselves. Much better to end the journey – not looking back!

Friday 28 May through Tuesday 1 June

. . . and we did not look back as we pulled out of our last RV site. The morning had arrived early, as camping commuters revved up their engines in readiness for their daily grind. The camp site was ours until 2.00 pm but we had little appetite for staying on. We had little appetitite for breakfast either, preferring to do the packing-up chores so ingrained in our thirty-eight week travel rites. Within twenty minutes we were pulling off the site and checking out at the Park Office. Within twenty seconds our vacated site was under new ownership from one of the many hopefuls queuing for this or *any* vacated desirable property! Mmmmm!

Our second last journey in Ed was as delightful as always and by the time we reached the home of Connie and Leon in Columbia some of our dejection had been overtaken by the lovely day and the *en route* Carrie reminiscences. Our mood heightened as we sat pool-side with our favourite lunch of bagels and cream cheese. By the time Leon and Connie got in from work we were in more optimistic mood, having reorganised (on paper) part of the garden back home which had got blasted in the unusually severe December gales. Friends are such an important part of life and friends like Connie and Leon, who gave us so much love and consideration during our long weekend with them, are truly precious gifts. They knew without being told just how sad we were at the ending of our American adventure and knew exactly how to handle two woebegone Scots. We watched the wonderful film of *Mrs Brown* set in our ain wee homeland, and boy, isn't Scotland just a marvellous country!

We shopped, we ate in, we ate out, enjoying the company of the variety of birds who came to their feeders to eat too. We sat around the pool in glorious sunshine with or without shade as we felt inclined. *One* of us swam, the other contented herself by dangling her hot feet in the cool water. We met some delightful friends of our hosts and we went to a Memorial Day concert given by the University Concert Band and listened enthralled to American music with a bit of Gilbert and Sullivan thrown in for good measure. Mostly, we talked and listened and learned that special friends are very special indeed. Our thanks to two of the world's most attractive and thoughtful people. To Connie and Leon – for being there just for us as we approached our last two weeks in the US with all the awful stuff that this entailed.

Our South Carolina home-from-home, courtesy of Leon and Connie in Columbia

The Final Weeks

Wednesday 2 June through Friday 11 June

On our previous visits to Georgia we had thought it a lovely State and now we were seeing it for the first time wearing summer clothing. Our drive to Athens was good and bad. Good for the scenery and the pleasure that being with Mark and MaryCarol once again would bring; bad because it was the final journey for both of us with the trio who had made it all possible. Somewhere around Lexington it all became just about OK. OK, we had the selling of special vehicles to do, the worry of our depleted finances to deal with, and the dreaded *packing!* But we could deal with all this stuff *and* enjoy our days in Athens, making the most of them. The welcome home from our American family was warm and tinged with relief that *the old folks* had done so well with nary a scrape to them or vehicles since the grey water tank episode, which seemed such a long time ago. Mark and MaryCarol admired our wonderful tans which pleased us no end.

To recap then, as we did with good old G&Ts as we recounted some of our coast-to-coast adventure to Mark and MaryCarol: we had travelled 13,500 miles in Ed with another 4,500 either in Geo or transported by friends. We got in to 32 States and one Canadian Province. The variable weather factor stopped us from visiting some National Parks, and we stopped ourselves visiting too many American cities, preferring to visit many American small towns.

And so we settled into our home from home, taking our time to adjust to living permanently in a house again. There were many plusses to this, like having great cooks prepare most of our meals, watching television and videos when we felt like it, doing the laundry in-home, having a proper bath or high-speed shower, and having more privacy in a lovely garden than we had on the most recent camp grounds. The minuses all ranged round the trio. Having to sell them; having to wait anxiously for people to respond to the ads; showing off Ed, Dolly and Geo, striking the right bargaining tones with hearts in mouths; letting them go to their new owners; then the agonising realisation that these true friends were no longer ours. We should have been relieved that it all went so well, but even banking and transferring the money home did not lighten our mood. So, by Wednesday 9 June, we had sold our travel companions, and on Friday 11 June we said goodbye to Ed and Dolly who would stay together, which was good considering how long they had been attached to each other. They went home with a most delightful couple, a little younger than us, who fell for Ed the minute they saw him and did not argue his most reasonable price. We do wish them as much travel joy as we had in his capacious care and know that Dolly will trail along happily behind Ed carrying whatever vehicle she is asked to tow. It will not be Geo. He went home with an equally delightful, but very young couple, who bargained hard but courteously and made an offer we were happy to accept. For anyone interested in these financial exchanges, we were down only $1000 (£700 sterling) on our beloved purchases. $1000 seems so little, given the pleasure of owning the trio of Ed, Dolly and Geo for five months, travelling with them coast to coast and enjoying so many good times together.

Marvellous country. Marvellous companions.

Friday afternoon 11 June through Thursday 17 June

As that last chapter was being written *she* could hardly see the lap-top keys through misted spectacles and *he* was doing a lot of noisy nose-blowing. It did not get any easier. On Saturday the yard in front of the Athens home was empty of the trio and an unknown unloved hire-car was sitting in their place. Our bedroom was filled with our travel things, including the postcards taken carefully down from Ed's insides. We viewed it all with some dismay as they were the remnants of *our* American Dream. Much as we loved our family here and appreciated the home comforts, we would both have preferred drinking our morning tea in Ed's big bed with Dolly and Geo close by and grackles or jays encouraging us to rise and join them beside some lake or country park. A short morning visit to the small town of Commerce about twenty-three miles north of Athens was intended to help us cope with our sadness. But even the atmosphere of this small town, made famous by the novel *Cold Sassy Tree*, didn't lighten our mood.

With MaryCarol and Mark visiting the family in Michigan, this was the ideal time to start the dreaded *packing*! Suitcases came out of the attic and unfortunately they had not grown any larger despite the intense heat and humidity in Georgian lofts. Packing was definitely going to be even trickier than anticipated, we realised, as we surveyed the stuff to be packed versus the packable area of our suitcases. This needed some careful planning and a shoe horn. Later that afternoon, we acquired more luggage space in the shape of two extra suitcases by searching the Goodwill Stores (which sound much friendlier than Charity Shops?) and a neighbour's attic. We decided to defer the actual packing till the morrow. We had had quite enough trauma for one day, so we added less ice and tonic to the gin than usual and zonked out in front of a video we had long wanted to watch, *Driving Miss Daisy* . . . good movie . . . good gins! Shshimply marvelloush country.

Sunday was the day we packed and it became a nightmare scenario when things put in one suitcase were then exchanged to another more suitable one and exchanged back again with unsuitable words exchanged between *him* and *her*. *One* of us was less happy than the *other* to part with *anything* brought *to* this side of the ocean or *anything* bought *on* this side of the ocean, and *she* said so several times on several occasions throughout fraught Sunday. By suppertime we had just about agreed on what went into which of the six cases and had in fact got just about all of it in. *He* had an amazingly worrying experience when he took the heaviest case to be weighed on the local supermarket scales, as we needed to give a rough idea of our excess baggage to the airline prior to the flight. A weighing machine ticket announced that it weighed 210 pounds and added some helpful hints for weight reduction. None of them included shedding clothes or acquired touristy things. It transpired that the ticket was left by a red-faced man seen slipping away from the scales by *him* as *he* approached, with suitcase dragging behind! Packing had been the expected exhausting process and called for even less tonic and ice in the evening gins, sipped as we tackled the mound of paper collected across America. The late evening video movie was *Pretty Woman* . . . pretty neat.

Monday we had an easier day, congratulating ourselves on our packing skills every time we passed the mound of suitcases. Mark and MaryCarol had returned home at 2.00 am, very late because of flight delay due to severe storms in Michigan and the surrounding States. They were sleepily impressed that just about all of the mess in their guest bedroom had been accommodated inside plastic or leather (the latter the suitcase from the neighbour!). The temperature reached a muggy 87°F by mid afternoon, not a day for any exertion, we agreed as we watched the acrobatic squirrels pinch the bird food from the squirrel-proof bird feeders. The G&Ts were back to normal strength that evening as we were more relaxed and also not to unduly worry the offspring! The storms which were hitting the north were due to make an appearance in the south by Tuesday, and they did by Monday evening but had lost a good deal of their venom *en route*.

The last three days with Mark and MaryCarol were good ones when we could comfortably come together for a while and separate for a while as work and final travel arrangements decreed for the four of us. Our relationship with these two much loved ones has always been a comfortable and happy affair built on affection and respect, whichever of our two countries we meet up in. This visit, Mark and MaryCarol had helped us cope with a lot of extra stuff as we planned our travel in December and ended our travel in June. Oh boy, those tears are gathering again as she writes and it's only mid-day on this Tuesday before the Wednesday before the Thursday we say goodbye to them and goodbye to Uncle Sam. Too early for even a weak G&T? Yep . . . water with ice will do it for now! The temperature was around 90°F in the shade but not too hot to leave the air-conditioned house and drive the air-conditioned car to our favourite bagel bakery and restaurant – also air-conditioned. And then a final drive through Athens with its lovely college buildings and fraternity houses with rocking chairs on their decks. To its square with its City Hall and old unique double-barrelled cannon, an unused relic of the civil war. Perhaps not the prettiest small town of our travels, but it feels like home, for home is where the heart is and ours are often here.

It's Wednesday evening; *she* is writing the last words in this journal for now, having been out for lunch with Mark while *he* had lunch out with MaryCarol. Our thoughtful daughter-in-law just knew that mum and son needed a last wee blether together. Tomorrow we leave and, amidst the sorrow of parting, the disbelief of the adventure concluded, and the angst of air-line travel to come, there is a certain excitement in *going home*! It will be good to see our Scottish land again, to say nothing of our other families and friends. East Lothian will do us Scottish seniors quite nicely – at least for a year or three – then who knows? We don't, and that's part of life's rich tapestry – the unknown. We feel we dealt pretty well with the unknown America we journeyed across over the last months; we will deal with the unknown ahead in Scotland with the equanimity which comes with our senior years. And, as we recall the magic moments of our US trip and recount our adventures to all who will listen, we do count ourselves most fortunate indeed to have had the time, money, and health to travel in another country, to see some of its unforgettable sights, and to meet its most hospitable citizens. Goodbye – for now! Marvellous country!

Postscripts from Scotland – December 1999

Postscript from Martin

Sometimes I wonder if it was all a dream; did we really make that trip?

One of our sons gave us an enormous Michelin roadmap of the USA for Christmas 1998 so that we could plan our journey round the States. Ed was big, but not big enough to display that map, but now it is pinned up above my desk with our route marked on it. So whenever I do wonder if it was all a dream I look up at that map – and remember . . . so many different places, so many different people . . . that, yes, I know we really did it.

It's good that we had enough time to see so much, and sad that we had so little time that we missed so much more. Another son, when told of our creditable visitations to thirty-two American States, asked, tongue-in-cheek, if we realised that there were twenty more! Perhaps we should have made more of an effort to get to more of the truly great scenic marvels of the USA, but for me the greatest enjoyment came from doing simple things in the faraway places that we visited: chatting with people and getting on so well that it all seemed unremarkable – until I remembered that I had never met these people before and that I was 6,000 miles from home; coming across so many beautiful sights; feeling at ease in so many different states. I enjoyed the feeling of visiting with friendly people rather than being on a tourist trail.

Driving big Ed was a dream – a dream come true! It was a delight. Driving little Geo up the narrow ramps on to Dolly was a nightmare! The driver can't see the ramps, and Geo must go up straight – and fast enough to reach the top! But we managed OK every time bar one!

Other high spots: it was awesome to stand beside the Grand Canyon, but the unexpected vista of the beautiful Arizona bluffs as we came out of the doors of the Cottonwood supermarket was just as breathtaking; the sunset on Lake Ponchartrain; the country and western entertainment in Nashville; the view of the Rockies as we ate supper in Estes Park; the birthday breakfast at the Hoito – and being given a copy of *Breakfast at the Hoito;* the rough seas of Lake Superior in Minnesota and the tranquility of the same lake at Pancake Bay; the bald eagle at Lake Ouachita; the great blue heron fishing beside us in Nebraska.

Big worries as we set off? That Ed would let us down – no way! That we would find RV living claustrophobic – not a problem. That we would find the business of travel wearing – not a problem either. That we would be caught by a tornado. This worry stuck, but most of the time it was out of mind because it is statistically most unlikely, and there would be nothing we could do about it anyway.

Any real disappointments? Only one: my arthritic hip let me down more than expected, preventing me from exploring too far afield on foot. Driving Ed was not a problem at all; in fact I really miss his comfortable seat and automatic transmission.

Anything that I *really* miss now that I am back in Scotland? Paying for my gas 'at the pump'! Why do we not have this facility back home? It is so quick and easy to swipe the credit card through the slot on the pump and saves so much time spent queuing at the gas station checkout. Pressing the button on the remote control which opened the Athens garage door as we turned into the drive – some day we might pamper ourselves with similar automation.

Anything that I expected to miss? Corn-on-the-cob, which was delicious in USA. But it is now more plentiful in our Scottish supermarkets, and we indulge ourselves at least twice a week – marvellous!

Travelling by elderly RV is a great way to tour a country: you can see so much as you go, you meet so many friendly people, and you don't have to pack and unpack the suitcases every day.

Feel tempted? Go for it! *We* long to do it again.

Martin (him)

PPS A new supermarket has opened near us. It has a filling station and – guess what – it has 'pay at the pump'!

Postscript from Margaret

One whole year has gone by since we were preparing for the trip of a lifetime, madly cramming stuff in to attic space so that our house guests could have some house-space, and madly cramming suitcases with suitable clothing for a six-month, all-weather adventure in America. Looking back from a more relaxed point of view, it was a very exciting time and an extremely frantic one.

Half a year has gone by since we arrived back home, tired, happy, and ready to bore the pants off family and friends with travellers' tales accompanied by endless pictorial back-up. The few friends and family members who are still speaking to us felt that we should enlarge on the journal which had been kept 'on the road' for them to read and for us to indulge in as the months pass by. Perhaps they thought that might keep us quiet! This did seem like a reasonable idea, but it was several weeks before I had the heart to begin the unnerving task of reading and editing the diary, written in many marvellous places as we journeyed across North America. For a long time I much preferred to imagine that the Senior Carries' adventure was yet to come and even now, on some real nostalgic days, I make believe that it is still December 1998 with it all still ahead of us. And some mornings, as wakeful reality nudges slumber aside, I pretend that it is Ed's bed which helps me gently out of sleep and I can almost believe that I am back at Lake Kanopolis in Kansas with the **pelicans**, cranes and jays.

It is always Lake Kanopolis that first enters my mind. Why there, out of all the wonderful places we visited? I do not know. And it is always a small road between the Oregon Coast and Corvallis that I visualise as I dreamily relive the days spent sitting in my high chair in Ed, being driven so skilfully and happily by Martin, with Dolly and Geo following jauntily along. Why that road of all the roads we travelled? I do not know; perhaps because it was not a high twisty one! Why is my instant recall not of standing by the edge of the spellbinding Grand Canyon, or driving up the Thompson Gorge to the Rockies? Both are more scenically memorable than Lake Kanopolis or US 20. Oh, make no mistake, the national wonders of America come regularly to mind, when I daydream about that other much loved country. Before this sojourn in the USA, I imagined that the most lingering memory of this vast country would be of its wide open spaces – and it is. Wide open spaces, diverse and beautiful from desert to plain; from lake to mountain.

I am often asked which are my favourite States. Now this *is* hard, but if I have to name them, then Oregon, Arizona and Pennsylvania would come out top and not necessarily in that order, but it is in that order that they spell out **O**ld **A**ge **P**ensioner which is the depressing name given to older Scots in this country to remind us of our years. *Him* and *her* prefer to be thought of as seniors who might still have some get-up and *go!*

While enjoying our new trophies like the Kansas crow swinging in the garden room; the red-wood **pelican** nestling near the moose with Montana on his rear; and the Oregon covered bridge brightening up the hall, I still would rather be setting off for Edinburgh Airport, with it all still to come. And I was seized with such irrational anger recently when the last possible drop of the Cracker Barrel Country Store Mountain Wild-Flower hand-cream was sqeezed out of the bottle.

E-mails between us and our American friends, both old and new, keep me sane, and us-all up to date with our separate lives, lives separated by an ocean but lives close in spirit. Jack and Lorry, from North Carolina, spent a few days with us in September and that was lovely. Jan and Rich from California, with Judy and Ron from Wisconsin, are giving some thought to coming over in September 2000 and that will be lovely too. But what would be really, *really* lovely? To be able to pop *over there* every few months, instead of wondering when our next Trans-Atlantic flight to family and friends will happen.

Things missed, although not as much as people, are going out for breakfast and eating a stack of blueberry pancakes with maple syrup, or maybe ordering eggs, over-easy, with hash browns and biscuits on the side. However, some food stuffs are so much better here – like bacon and sausages, fish suppers and most fruit and vegetables. But then we remember bagels, muffins, doughnuts and *coffee-to-go* and would swop the bacon and sausages for them in a second! Well *she* would. Mind you they don't have bannocks, although quite a number of American people and Canadian Immigation Officers now have that recipe!

But the birds. Oh, I do so miss the jays, the cardinals and that Carolina wren. The whip-oor-will, we only heard the once and never saw, but his night-call haunts me. So I listen to him on my Encarta CD from time to time – it may not be authentic, you need the background of dark woods for that, but it sounds so wistful and touches a spot deep inside me. I need to hear him properly again. During this last summer our Scottish birds sang to us morning and

208

evening as sweetly as any American birds, especially the song-thrush whose numbers are declining. Bird disappointment? Owls. We had expected to see many of the species over there and in greater numbers. We saw only two and they were great! Perhaps that was down to our lack of birding experience in knowing where to find them; or our disinclination to search unknown woods at night! We had assumed that like the bald eagles, *they* would find us!

Most folks over here don't understand our love-affair with America and why it has such a special place in our hearts. Well, I can't speak for *him,* Martin has done that for himself. But for me, apart from the more obvious ones like America's vastness, its diverse and colourful wild-life and awesome National Monuments, it is being in a young country. Whenever I get ready to unbuckle the airline seat belt on American soil, I find myself humming the popular tune from the slow movement of Dvořák's symphony *From the New World.* For America is still a very young country, full of ebullience and hope. Its multi-racial peoples are sure they live in the greatest country on earth. I can absolutely appreciate that sentiment, but would add that my ain wee country still has the first place in my heart. Scotland is marvellous: America is marvellous. In fact being alive in either land is just *marvellous.*

Margaret (her)

Appendices

(Written by Ed's driver, number 1 navigator, head cook, chief bottle washer and erstwhile plumber, mechanic and odd-job man. While she, of course, did some serious writing, drove Geo occasionally and learned the rudiments of map-reading, becoming an expert by South Carolina – the second visit!)

Number 1: For the Mechanically Minded

a) All about motor-homes

We knew, from our previous visits to the USA, that there are several different types of RV commonly seen on US roads. The Class A Motor-home is one based on a bus chassis. Some are very big. Purchased new, or nearly new, they cost really serious dollars. Most of these big fellows that you see on the road are towing a car behind so that the travellers can shop or visit the laundromat without taking their mobile mansion with them. The Class C type are smaller motor-homes, based on a van body, and often with a sleeping area above the driving seats. A few of these have tow-cars but more often they don't, because they are generally not so big that parking becomes a problem. There are also travel trailers (caravans), often enormous by British standards, requiring a heavy-duty truck to tow them. Fifth-wheelers are travel-trailers with a raised goose-necked front which attaches to a hitching point on the back of a pick-up truck. Once on site, the front of the trailer is supported on legs leaving the pick-up free for regular use. Finally, there are campervan bodies that can be fixed to the back of any large pick-up truck.

What sort should *we* try for? Fifth-wheelers were out because there are not any old enough to be cheap enough to fit our budget. Some friends advised us that it would be easier to tow a trailer but we found that a good enough, big enough, truck was going to cost lots of dollars. And, although there are masses of such trucks on the market, they often have a hard life and might no longer be sufficiently reliable to travel the many thousands of miles that we had in mind. We needed space, comfort and reliability, and that pointed us to the

211

Class A or larger Class C vehicles. The Class A gave more space and comfort, and, we hoped, would be mechanically reliable because these bus chassis and engines are designed to run for tens of thousands of miles each year. The one we eventually chose had covered only 52,000 miles in sixteen years. Mechanically it was still in great condition despite the bodywork looking a little old. Some of its joints needed new sealant. Not a problem. It was one we could afford, and that made the difference!

Two other plus points for the big motor-home. It felt safer to tow something small with something big than the other way round. Secondly we wanted to see the countryside as we travelled. The visibility from the motor-home we would call Ed was fantastic, and made the business of travelling a joy.

b) *All about Ed*

28 ft long, 8 ft 6 in wide, 10 ft 8 in high. None of it a problem except the driver had to learn the hard way that the back end overhangs the back wheels by at least 10 ft. This means that the back swings out much wider than the

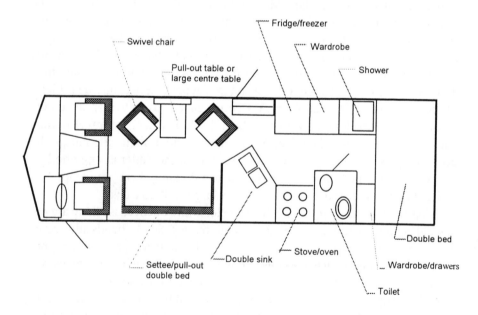

Ed's floor plan

wheels. Need to keep eye on mirrors when leaving gas stations! The hard way involved an Athens mailbox. US mailboxes are placed on the street so that the mail van driver can deliver from his cab. Picture this: proud but novice driver having successfully reversed Ed into the limited driveway space in Athens decided for a now obscure reason that Ed should come in frontwards. Drive out, back down road, drive in. Success. Later: reverse out. 'No, fine – don't need help.' Concentrate on making sure nothing is moving up or down the road, difficult when you are 25 ft down the driveway when the back end enters the road. Watch the mirrors; watch where the opposite kerb is; swing wheel as soon as front wheels, right under your seat, leave the driveway; watch that mirror again, plenty of room to the kerb, crunch. What the blazes was that? Stop. Jump out. Mailbox off its wooden stake, wooden stake pushed over. What has *he* done? Fortunately US mail boxes are all on the same side of the street so that the mail van doesn't have to weave from side to side as he comes up the road. It was Mark and MaryCarol's mailbox that had been demolished, not the neighbour's!

Lesson: there is a mighty big blindspot behind this bus. Never reverse without assistance. And make sure that you don't keep backing while your assistant traverses from one side to the other of your blind spot.

c) *On towing Dolly + Geo*

Again few problems when moving forwards. Dolly and Geo follow sweetly behind and if Ed gets round cleanly then so will they. Except Dolly's wheelbase is wide and that coupled with Ed's long rear overhang can mean that when parking on a slight curve Ed can arrive with aplomb while poor Dolly is dragged up on to the kerb!

Reversing is quite another story. Having learned to reverse a simple trailer or caravan back home the driver was prepared to have a go reversing Ed plus Dolly plus Geo. Can't be done! There is an extra swivel point built into Dolly and with two hinge points, plus that long overhang, reversing is not an option. Lesson: think long and carefully before entering gas stations, parking lots etc. Will we get out again?

d) *Black water and other plumbing niceties*

Ed has three large tanks about his person. A large freshwater tank hidden beneath the bed-settee in the living area and two waste water tanks hanging from his chassis. The grey water tank takes the waste water from the kitchen sink, washhand basin and the shower and the black water tank holds the toilet waste. Both need emptied from time to time. A set of indicator lights in Ed's kitchen were intended to alert us to the level of water in the tanks but, being a fairly elderly chap, his electronics were not as reliable as those on his modern brothers. In fact they did not work at all. We learned to visit the dump station every two or three days, generally as we left a campground. Three inch flexible sewer hose made the job easy and not at all unpleasant.

The water supply system was very clever and gave us hot and cold running water in kitchen, bathroom and shower. If we were hooked up to mains water the system worked on that. If we had no external supply a pump took over and delivered water from the freshwater tank whenever we turned on a tap (faucet). Apart from the low hum of the pump while the water flowed we could not tell the difference and the pump delivered plenty water for the shower. The hot water came from a rapid response propane boiler. It was very hot and could provide as much as we needed, even for a shower.

e) *Gas etc*

Ed, with his 7.4 litre V8 engine drank the stuff. We seemed to get about 7½ miles per US gallon (when towing, that is). Gas prices varied from state to state, the lowest price being about 95 cents per gallon, highest about $1.15 till OPEC production cuts, coupled with two refinery fires in California, put the price up to $1.60 in remoter parts of Oregon. Still very cheap compared with UK prices, even allowing for the fact that the US gallon is only 0.83 of the UK gallon. We discovered that in Oregon it is illegal for the customer to operate the gas pump. It was sometimes frustrating to have to wait for the attendant, but rather nice to be able to remain aboard if it was cold and wet.

Number 2: Driving in USA

a) *The difficult bits*

We have always found it easy to drive on the 'wrong' side of the road and it seems to come naturally after a day or so. But beware in parking lots and when leaving roadworks. It is very easy to have no wrong, or right, side in these situations.

Navigating in USA does take some getting used to. First, many of the road signs are rather small and may be positioned very close to the junction. So, approaching I-40 on a US highway and wanting to travel east, we look out for the little green sign *JCT I-40 ½ mile ahead* and find it. What we don't find until we are right on the junction is whether we have to turn right or left to get I-40 East. And knowing north, south, east and west is not necessarily an advantage. In many cases to turn right there is a straightforward right turn on to the approach road, but every now and again they throw a left turn at you and send you round a tight clover leaf. To turn left you will cross the interstate and then ???? Well, it could be a left turn with or without traffic lights, or it could be a right turn round a sharp clover leaf. The one common attribute of all such junctions is that they will keep you guessing until the last possible moment.

US Interstates are numbered in a very logical fashion. For two digit numbers, if even, they are basically east-west routes, for example, I-10 in the far south from Florida to California; I-40 around the middle; I-80 in the north. If odd, they are basically north-south routes. But I-40 East does not mean that the road will be going east at that particular point, it could be going north. All it means is that if you get on to it you will eventually end up nearer the Atlantic and further from the Pacific. Three digit interstates are either ring roads (loops) by-passing a town, or link roads into the town, and the evenness or oddity of the initial digit signifies which of these categories you are on. But, anyway, by the time you discover you are on the wrong road – it's too late – you have to go on to the next intersection. Follow it so far? Then you have done better than we did. And, confusing for us foreigners, the same piece of road can have multiple numbers. Thus I-40 crosses I-85 somewhere in North Carolina. (You will remember this was fairly early on in our travels.) For several miles they share the highway and we were on I-40 East and I-85 North at the same time. As we were wanting to head in a south-easterly direction on the I-40 the signs were just a little muddling. The most road numbers we found for a single road was somewhere in Nebraska where we had four; one interstate, two US highways plus one state route.

Proudest navigational achievement? Recovering from an error in Memphis, in Geo, in heavy rain, on the way to Gracelands. I-55 crossed the Mississippi and according to the map swung south. It did, but at an intersection, not a curve, and we missed it. Knew at once, but could not get across the traffic to the exit. Quick! Exit next right, round clover leaf to head north under the bridge we had just crossed. Exit immediate right on to another clover leaf to send us back towards the Mississippi. Exit immediate right again on to a third clover leaf to get us under that bridge again and back on to that I-55 heading south for Gracelands. Wow! Glad we were in Geo and not Ed.

Many states number the intersections in terms of the miles from the west, or south, boundary of the state. This is a great system becuse if you know you have to leave at exit 183 and you are passing milepost 51 you know that you have 122 miles still to go. Of the States we travelled through, only Georgia and California do not use this system. Georgia number their junctions in sequence as on UK motorways. California seems to do without numbers altogether. In both cases it made for magnifying-glass peering at the tiny mileage figures on the *Rand McNally Road Atlas* and much mental arithmetic to estimate the distance to be travelled on the morrow, and where, if at all, we might find a convenient rest area to pause for lunch.

b) *Other quirks of US road signs.*

We never got used to the contrast between the huge bill boards that informed us that in 25 miles we should make a right two blocks on the US XY for Cracker Barrel, or the next Dennys, or Amoco Gas Station, and the tiny little, discreet almost to the point of invisibility, signs at the crossroads on the XY where we had to turn for whichever of these establishments we were looking for. We could see their huge overhead signs, but not necessarily the way to get to them.

. . . And finally, three intriguing billboards:

1) Harmony Avenue Gun Store

2) Somewhere in the South, a shared sign announcing:

> 'Jesus will solve your problems'

and

> 'Abe Smith for all your plumbing needs'

3) Life is full of surprises, but do you want them all in your motel room? (An ad for a motel chain!)

Number 3: For the Geographically Inclined

a) *... it's a big place ...*

We knew before we started that the USA is a vast country; but how vast? Well, if there had been bridges between Canada, Greenland, Iceland and Scotland we could have brought Ed home without adding very much to our over-all mileage. We also knew that it is a diverse country and we saw, and loved, the coasts, the mountains, the deserts, the huge navigable rivers, the forests, the agricultural plains. We knew that we would be high up and that we might pass through places lower than sea level. We knew that we would be hot, very hot by Scottish standards, and cold, very cold by Scottish standards, and we were. We knew that there are huge cities, small towns and villages (all called cities), and vast areas with very few people. Wyoming, for instance, has three times the area of Scotland but only one tenth of the population. What we didn't expect was that wherever we went we would find things we really liked, except perhaps in the big cities; neither of us are city folk.

The mountains and the river systems are the natural features that divide up the landscape. They are huge, but because everything is on a big scale they don't necessarily appear to be so large. For example the beautiful crystal clear view of Mount Hood that we had as we left Maryhill State Park in Washington looked very like the sort of picture we sometimes see of a Scottish snow-capped mountain. But Mount Hood is over 11,000 ft high and our highest mountain in Scotland is only 4,400 ft; and the bridge over the Columbia, which was in the foreground of our view, didn't seem out of the ordinary, yet it is more than half a mile long. Similarly, the bridge over the Golden Gate at San Francisco looked smaller than our Forth Road Bridge even though it is longer and much higher than the Scottish bridge. Maybe it looked smaller because we were looking down at it from high above the roadway. We can't do that at the Forth Bridge.

We drove along a long straight stretch of the I-10 in west Texas across miles of desert with mountains in the distance before us. We drove for fifty minutes with scarcely any perceptible change in the scenery save that those mountains ever-so-slowly grew larger as we moved closer. It was as if we were looking through a camera set to make a very slow zoom. Eventually the mountains were on either side of us – we had at last reached the end of that long straight road.

b) *Towns*

The approach roads to many towns are lined with a profusion of fast food eateries, shopping centres, gas stations, motels, car lots, and video stores. These 'strips' can be long and grim and can make any town look like every other town. But keep going: the town centres are quite different and often delightful. Some small towns are very pretty, others are marred by an enormous yard of scrap cars right next door to quality housing. It seems that the selfish attitude of 'this is my land, I can do what I want on it' can militate against the development of a community attitude proclaiming, 'This is our town, let's make it look great.'

c) *Continental Divide*

In principle this is easy to understand: it is the line of highest points between the Atlantic and Pacific oceans. So east of this line all rivers end up in the Atlantic, west of it and they flow to the Pacific. When we crossed through New Mexico we passed a sign telling us that we were crossing the Continental Divide. The ground was fairly flat and we weren't very high up so it was interesting to know we had crossed the divide. But in Wyoming, where we crossed the Rockies, it was more confusing. Again the route was on flattish terrain, high up at 8,000 ft, but with no sudden steep climbs or declines. The map showed the dotted line running pretty close to the I-80 for thirty miles or so and we twice passed road signs telling us that we were on the Continental

Divide. Neither of these points were at the highest point on our route and presumably we must have crossed the divide an odd number of times to get from the west coast to the east. Maybe the one at the summit had blown away. But probably they are a bit more casual about these things in the mountains and reckon that drivers will notice when they reach the top.

There is another 'divide', to the east of the Mississippi, in the Appalachian Mountains. We crossed this divide in Georgia, West Virginia, and Pennsylvania. This is not nearly so high, we were rarely above 2000 ft, and the mountains, being tree-covered, did not look like mountains to us Scots, and yet the roads were steeper, the climbs and declines were longer, and more worrying to *one of us*, than the crossing of the Rockies. The *other of us* was convinced that the Carolinas had mysteriously dropped a few thousand feet between our January visit and our return in May. *He* had no doubt that we had descended much further between West Virginia, through Virginia to North Carolina than we had ever climbed up from Lake Erie! *He* much preferred driving uphill to going down, *she* felt otherwise.

d) *A north-south divide?*

A neat sign that we saw twice in Oregon alerted us to where we crossed the 45° latitude. We were then equidistant from the North Pole and the Equator. We crossed it again in Wisconsin and Michigan, but they did not have signs up.

e) *Rivers and lakes*

From our schooldays we had known that the Mississippi and the Missouri are very long rivers. But we had never realised until now how vast an area of the USA drains into the Mississippi. Very little of the country between the Rockies and the Appalachians slopes towards the Great Lakes so, for example, the river that we saw in Waukesha, less than twenty miles from Lake Michigan, flows south and west towards the Mississippi and the Gulf of Mexico one thousand miles away at New Orleans. There is even some water from Canada contributing to that great Old Man River.

The enormous size of the Great Lakes is another indicator of the vastness of the North American continent. Thunder Bay is one of Canada's largest ports; and yet a 'Salty' grain ship (sea-going) setting out for Europe has about two thousand miles of sailing before reaching the Atlantic Ocean. Forty per cent of its journey is within Canadian waters.

Lake Superior, our ship's starting point, is 600 ft above sea level. The Soo Locks at Sault Ste Marie connect Lake Superior to Lake Huron at 579 ft. Had our ship been a 'Laker' (staying within the Great Lakes) bound for Chicago or Milwaukee it would have made a right in north Lake Huron to head west through the Mackinaw Straits to Lake Michigan. No locks here because Lakes Michigan and Huron are at the same level. Our Salty sails south to Port Huron, down the St Clair River to Lake St Clair (not a 'Great' lake, it's only about 25 miles across), past Detroit and into Lake Erie, a little lower at 570 ft. North-east now towards Niagara, where our ship by-passes the falls by taking the Welland Canal which descends more than 300 ft in the 25 miles to Lake Ontario. Kingston, at the east end of Lake Ontario, is where she leaves the Lakes for the St Lawrence River; downstream lies Montreal, Quebec and the Atlantic. At Kingston our Salty is about halfway to the open ocean at Newfoundland.

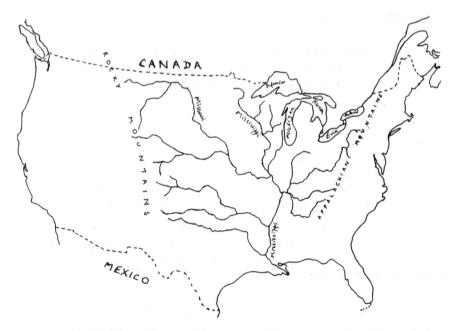

The Mississippi-Missouri river system drains a vast area of the USA

Most of the lakes in the USA are man-made by damming the rivers for flood control and/or irrigation projects. Hydro-electric power is a useful by-product from the dams but was not the prime reason for the formation of these lakes. All the big rivers in the south-west have irrigation projects along their lengths. The Rio Grande supplies water to New Mexico, Texas and Mexico, and Lake Havasu on the Colorado feeds more than 1 billion gallons a day into the Colorado Aqueduct that carries water as far as the Pacific coast for the towns, cities and agriculture of southern California. The lake also provides water for the central Arizona irrigation project. This involves pumping another billion gallons a day to 800 ft above the lake's surface from where it flows through a tunnel in Buckskin Mountain to an extensive aqueduct system that runs east and south towards central and southern Arizona. Further pumping plants along the aqueduct system raise the water to about 2,900 ft above the lake.

Number 4: Communications

We did not know how well our communications systems would work once we left our fixed address in Athens. The prepaid telephone card is a marvellous development. We bought one before leaving the UK and topped it up from the credit card whenever it ran low. We could phone from any public phone box without cash, and from any of the friends we visited without embarrassment on either side. Telephone banking is another modern facility we appreciated as we kept in touch with money matters back home, and arranged payment of our credit card bills.

E-mail from our lap-top was also an excellent way of sending progress reports to friends and family at home and of getting news back from them. Our service provider had a system of local (free) phone numbers and also a 1-800 free number so there was never a phone charge for sending and receiving mail, although finding a place to 'hook up' was a bit hit or miss. Some of the RV parks advertised facilities for e-mail connection although most have not yet got this organised. In some parks we were the first customers to try the hook-up procedures and it was a learning curve for the staff and us as we searched out suitable jack plugs on their phone or fax system. The small town libraries were usually helpful and the librarians in the remote mid and far west were often thrilled at the thought that messages from their little library were flashing across the waves to Scotland. The transmission time was always fast; the courtesies of making the arrangements could not be hastened, but always added to our enjoyment of the visit to their town.

And of course postcards. We sent a load of those. Just one word of warning: don't buy your stamps in Chapel Hill Post Office, North Carolina at 11.00 am on a Saturday. When I eventually reached the head of the queue the clerk explained that everybody in Chapel Hill (a University town) gets up late on Saturday, has a leisurely breakfast, and then decides to go to the post office before it shuts at noon.

Number 5: The Weather Page

The only reason we occasionally missed having a TV was that we have always enjoyed watching the USA Weather Channel and knew that it would have kept us up to date on the weather conditions across the whole of USA. The Weather Page of *USA Today* did that for us as we travelled. We discovered that conditions can change very abruptly which is why we tried, successfully, to keep ahead of the stormy weather on our way to the Rocky Mountains, but, unfortunately, not successfully on the following two days when it blasted us across Nebraska. The Weather Page also printed little illustrations of the meteorology responsible for some predominant weather feature of the day. This could be interesting, though we could have done without the heading 'Spring can create killer tornados'.

Number 6: Good Sam and the *Trailer Life Campground Guide*

Good Sam is a club for RV'ers, offering information to travellers, insurance deals, emergency roadside assistance, discounts at some camp grounds and other perks. We joined because of the comfort of knowing that we would be able get help if we needed it. As it turned out we never needed their assistance.

A Guide to the campgrounds is an essential. We chose the *Trailer Life* publication. It is printed in small type on very thin paper but still stands 2½ inches thick and weighs a ton. It gives a lot of information about the sites (and also about RV Sales and Service facilities). The campgrounds have been graded on three separate 10-point scales for the range of their facilities, the cleanliness of their facilities and their environment. We discovered early on that we were not necessarily looking for high scores on all three counts.

It is a sweeping generalisation but in the main the good private establishments scored highly on scales one and two but not so well on the third scale. Typically they might offer laundries, showers, games rooms, phones, LP gas supplies, on site shop and TV hookups along with the water, electricity and sewer connections. But they might be no more than 200 yards from the interstate, and, being private, they would cram as many RV sites as possible into their camp.

We much preferred the State Parks, the National Parks and the Corps of Engineers Parks (the Corps of Engineers built the dams that made the lakes). These parks are generally near some feature of geographical, historical or ecological interest. In other words there is a reason to go there, they are not just an overnight stopping place for the travellers hurrying along the interstate, and they tend to have much more spacious sites for each RV than private parks. Many have water and electricity hook-ups, but in some it is a case of 'dry camping': not a big problem for Ed with his water tanks and generator. So we generally looked for a high score on that third scale and did not worry much about the first one. As we said this is a generalisation. Some private sites are great. We spent several nights at the Country View Campground near Mukwonago in Wisconsin. It was really good.

Advance booking of sites in State Parks was sometimes possible but others stuck firmly to a no-booking – first come, first served basis. The conflicting needs of travellers who enjoy taking each day as it comes and those who have to plan vacations in advance are hard to reconcile. Some states in the east believed that a centralised and computerised booking system would achieve this reconciliation. Not so, as we and harassed Rangers in the Parks found out as they tried to cope with the new software installed from a centre hundreds of miles away by computer experts who had no notion of what camping was about.

Number 7: The Oregon Trail

The evening spent with our new-found friends, Art and Diana, at Buckskin Mountain in Arizona was the first time we had heard of the Oregon Trail. How could we have been so ignorant? This trail was the route followed by

223

perhaps as many as 500,000 people in the 1840s as they moved house on a grand scale from Missouri and Kansas to the fertile lands of the Pacific Coast. It was almost two thousand miles long and most of the people walked the route because their unsprung covered wagons were heavily laden with their possessions and provisions and gave an exceedingly uncomfortable ride. What faith these settlers must have had to uproot their families and travel so far through unknown and often difficult territory to their promised land. Art is sure that he would have been one of them had he been born a hundred years earlier than his true birth date. In fact he did live in Kansas, and moved from there to Oregon. He loves the rain, the trees, the gentle climate and the fertile soil of Oregon. So yes, he would have walked that trail. We doubt if we would have had enough 'get up and go' to follow him, though if there had been an Ed to buy in Kansas City we might have done just that.

We saw the end of the trail first. Oregon City, a little south of Portland, was the terminus of the settlers' journey. The trail is commemorated there by a marvellous walk-through Interpretive Center which offers hands-on experiences. The staff are in period costume and, apart from the twentieth century prices in the souvenir gift shop, it is hard to trick them out of the 1840s. The Missouri shopping lists of essential provisions along with the diary entries, written at the end of a difficult day on the road or as the travellers faced up to their choice between floating their wagons down the Columbia River on rafts from the Dalles or the hazardous high route round the south of Mount Hood, all brought the trail to life for *him* when he and Art had their day out. There is another fantastic Interpretative Center at Flagstaff Hill near Baker on the I-84 in Oregon. Sadly, we had no time to stop off there.

Much of our journey back east followed the path of the trail, in reverse. Our campsites by the Columbia River, at Farewell Bend, Glenn's Ferry and Fort Kearney were all in State Parks sited on the trail. We found the imagery at Farewell Bend particularly vivid because there we saw some of the original wagons and the ruts made by the wheels of hundreds of such wagons. For modern day campers who want to try out the spacious ten by four living quarters three replica wagons are available to rent by the week. Mind you, they're fixed in place, no horses, mules or oxen to be fed, and they do have modern-day hook-ups to water and electricity. Not quite the lifestyle of the early travellers. At Glenn's Ferry we were told to return in late summer when the locals re-enact the river crossing at the Three Islands. Sadly we would be home in Scotland by then.

The Oregon, California, and Santa Fe Trails all start in Independence, Missouri, and set off west along the Kansas River. The Santa Fe Trail, an established trading route from about 1820 until 1880 when the railroad came to Santa Fe, goes south-west after about forty miles. The others continue west through Topeka then turn north-west up into Nebraska and along the Platte River to cross the Rocky Mountains in Wyoming not far from our eastward route along the I-80. The Mormon Trail to Salt Lake City (1846) follows the same general route through Nebraska and Wyoming but on the other side of the rivers. The Mormons did not want to rub shoulders with other travellers. From south-west Wyoming the Oregon and California trails continue north-west into Idaho and along the Snake River. The California trail branches south-west near American Falls, the Oregon travellers continuing along the Snake to Three Island Crossing. There they either crossed the river by swimming their animals and floating their wagons, not possible if the river was full, or they gave up on the crossing and took a more difficult route that kept to the south of the Snake. Mr Glenn established his ferry in 1869, easing matters for the settlers and giving his name to the town. The two routes rejoin near the Oregon border and the trail leaves the Snake for the last time at Farewell Bend to cross the high ground to the Columbia River. The journey took five to six months and the timetable was tight. They left Independence, Missouri, in the spring, not too early or the Rockies would be snowbound, not too late or the Oregon mountains would be impassable.

As we journeyed along modern American roads built for more modern wagons close to parts of the Oregon Trail, we admired the fortitude and optimism of the early travellers. We will long remember their story.